ILLUMINED BY
WISDOM AND LOVE

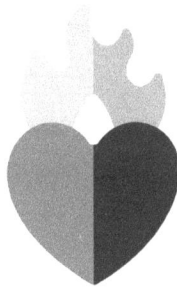

ILLUMINED BY
WISDOM AND LOVE

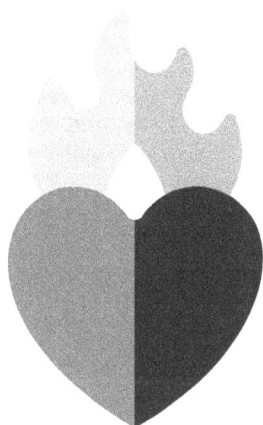

ESSAYS ON A SOPHIO-AGAPIC CONSTRUCTIVE

POSTMODERN POLITICAL PHILOSOPHY

G. CHRISTOPHER SCRUGGS

Quansus

QUANSUS PRESS
1324 FM 1340, Hunt, Texas 78024

Illumined by Wisdom and Love: Essays on a Sophio-Agapic Constructive Postmodern Political Philosophy, by G. Christopher Scruggs.

Published 2025 by Virtualbookworm.com Publishing, P.O. Box 9949, College Station, TX 77842, US. Copyright ©2025, G. Christopher Scruggs. All rights reserved. No part of this publication may be reproduced, stored in a retrieval system, or transmitted in any form or by any means, electronic, mechanical, recording or otherwise without the prior written permission of the author.

For information regarding permission to reprint material from this book, please mail your request to:
Quansus Press
1324 FM 1340, Hunt, Texas 78024

Library of Congress in Publication Data
G. Christopher Scruggs 1951-
Illumined by Love: Essays on a Sophio-Agapic Constructive Post- Ideological Political Philosophy
Includes bibliographical references
ISBN No. 978-1-63868-190-8 (softcover);
ISBN No. 978-1-63868-189-2 (eBook)

Library of Congress
No.: 2013524921
Cover Design: Frank Gutbrod

To my children and grandchildren, with hope they will enjoy the freedom and advantages I have enjoyed because of the sacrifices my parents and our family has made for our family and for the communities they served.

I particularly dedicate this to my father, who in World War II served in the United States Navy; after the war, until retirement, in the Federal Bureau of Investigation; and as a city council member and as Mayor of Springfield, Missouri. His entire life was one of service to God, Family, and Country.

I also dedicate this to my mother, who supported and loved him, raised two rambunctious boys, and carved out her own areas of public service in Springfield.

LIST OF ABBREVIATIONS

AI: A. N. Whitehead, *Adventure of Ideas* (New York, NY: Free Press, 1933)

ECSP: Peirce, Charles S, *The Essential Writings* Edward C. Moore, ed. (New York, NY: Harper & Row, 1972)

EDB: *The Essential David Bohm* Lee Nichol ed. (New York, NY: Routledge, 2003)

PK: Michael Polanyi, *Personal Knowledge: Towards a Post-Critical Philosophy* (Chicago, IL: University of Chicago Press, 1958)

MT: A. N. Whitehead, *Modes of Thought* (New York, NY: Free Press, 1938, 1968).

OD: David Bohm, *On Dialogue* (New York, NY: Routledge, 1996, 2004)

PC: Josiah Royce, *The Problem of Christianity*, *The Problem of Christianity* (Washington, D.C.: Catholic University Press, 2001)

PL: Josiah Royce, *Loyalty* (Long Island, NY: Sophia/Omni Press, 1908 [2017])

PR: Alfred North Whitehead, *Process and Reality* (New York, NY: Free Press, 1929, 1957)

RM: Alfred North Whitehead, *Religion in the Making* (New York, NY: The McMillian Company, 1936)

SFS: Michael Polanyi, *Science Faith and Society: A Searching Examination of the Meaning and Nature of Scientific Inquiry* (Chicago, IL: University of Chicago Press, 1946)

SM: Alfred North Whitehead, *Science and the Modern World* (New York, NY: Free Press, 1925, 1967)

TEP: *Collected Papers of Charles Sanders Peirce* Vols. 1 and 2. Charles Hartshorne and Paul Weiss eds. (Cambridge, MA: Harvard University Press, 1965)

TTI: John Dewey, *Logic: The Theory of Inquiry* (New York, NY: Henry Holt and Company, 1938)

WIO: *David Bohm, Wholeness and the Implicate Order* (London ENG: Routledge, 1980)

TABLE OF CONTENTS

PREFACE

This work emerged from a concern for the condition of political thought and practice in contemporary society. As intellectual circles have increasingly come to be dominated by postmodern thinking, in which all truth claims become bids for power, practical politicians have increasingly engaged in ideologically driven politics. The result is a view of politics as a never-ending war the sole purpose of which is the acquisition and use of power. This is the precise definition of politics given to me many years ago by a professor of political science. At the time, I agreed. Today, I am not so sure.

The style of negative, attack-oriented, ideologically driven politics we see in America undermines our democracy and fractures our society in very unhealthy and unproductive ways. While politics is about the acquisition and use of power, it is also about the wise application of that power in the search for social harmony and justice. Where there is not a wise and devoted search for justice, there is frequently some kind of totalitarian state ("soft" or "hard") in which those with power are not constrained in their exercise of power except by others with power. I think this has led to the sorry state of our politics.

The following work flows from an engagement with the philosophical ideas of Charles S. Peirce, Josiah Royce, Alfred North Whitehead, John Dewey, Herbert Mead, Michael Polanyi, David Bohm, and others. It outlines the contours of a *"sophio-agapic"* approach to political philosophy. This approach emphasizes the importance of a commitment to the rational acquisition of political truth, the noetic reality of ideals such as justice, the importance of traditions of inquiry, the centrality of communally validated values, and the role of reasonable dialogue in achieving a just society. The approach embraces a process understanding of reality, a pragmatically inspired epistemology for conducting political life, and the importance of conversation and dialogue as practical aspects of instituting and maintaining the suggested *sophio-agapic* approach. Thus, the argument moves from theory *(Theoria)* to wisdom *(Sophia)* and then to practice *(Phronesis)* in arriving at its conclusions.

Peirce and Royce wrote before the impact of relativity and quantum theory on philosophy. Dewey and Mead wrote after the effects of postmodern science were felt, Whitehead, Polanyi, and Bohm were trained in physics and contributed practically and theoretically to its development. In addition, all participated in developing a conceptual foundation for a positive form of postmodern thinking and reviving the ideal of justice in political theory. In the sphere of epistemology, Peirce and Royce emphasized the reality of universals and the importance of communities of interpretation in advancing knowledge in all areas of inquiry. Polanyi and Bohm defended freedom of thought and were anxious to create a more rational political process in which a pragmatic and communal approach replaces ideological approaches. Polanyi had experienced the dangers posed by a totalitarian ideology for freedom, democracy, and social progress. He was determined to set out an intellectual program to overcome the kind of ideologically driven science the Soviet Union produced.

The argument concludes that justice is a "noetic ideal" under continuing development as part of an unfolding social reality that best arises from a continuing conversation within a community of seekers dedicated to *a sophio-agapic* approach to political life. The argument for the reality of justice begins with Peirce's defense of the reality of universals and its extension by Royce. Both Royce and Peirce defended the importance of communities of inquiry and dialogue in seeking truth. Polanyi further developed the notion that communities of inquiry require faith in their ideals and observes that, by the 20th Century, Western civilization had applied a reductionist and critical reason to all areas of human life, ultimately exhausting and dissolving its intellectual heritage. A newer, post-critical approach is needed.

In every discipline, human reasoning is always and everywhere a rational attempt to understand some feature of reality. The universe gives us reason to believe that it is both comprehensible and ultimately reasonable. The progress of science supports this conclusion. The progress of human society is not merely scientific; humanity's progress includes every area of inquiry, including politics, in which human civilization has made reasonable advances throughout human history. This progress is possible in every human endeavor, including political institutions. This gives reason to believe that not only science but all areas of human inquiry can be conducted reasonably with a view toward the prudent solving of problems. This is the "*sophio*" side of this inquiry.

On the "*agapic*" side of the inquiry, the paper begins with Peirce's notion that chance, law, and "agapistic" or "cherishing love" are operative in the unfolding process of the world, particularly in the unfolding development of human societies. The concept of "*agapic* causality" is a notion that can be extended to political philosophy. Royce broadens the idea of love as a causal reality in his work by developing a "Beloved Community" founded on his ethical ideal of loyalty. Polanyi refines the argument with his notion of traditions of inquiry and the importance of universally held values to a truth-seeking community.

Whitehead gives an explicit processual account of the creative development of societies of all types, emphasizing the *agapistic* "lure" of ideals such as justice in social development. Bohm emphasizes that the underlying relationality of the universe perceived through relativity and quantum theory gives reason for developing the notion of dialogue as an underdeveloped aspect of modern political thought and practice. Through his analysis, Bohm extends the idea of community by highlighting the importance of reasonable dialogue in forming and maintaining community and overcoming the divisions in modern society.

Dewey's notion of instrumental logic provides a conceptual foundation for the conduct of a kind of dialogue that involves not merely stating opinions, but rather constitutes a socially embodied conversation and exploration of pragmatic solutions to social problems through exploration, testing, analysis, and further exploration. In this, Dewey advanced the logic of abduction that Peirce developed in his scientific work.

The study ends with the author's reflections on a *sophio-agapic* approach to political thought. This work was motivated by a deep concern for the condition of our society and the problems we face, which our children and grandchildren will probably face in more dramatic and tragic ways unless adjustments are made to our social, political, and legal communal life. It seeks to make some small contribution to the restoration of our local, national, and international communities, which must work together to solve the problems our society faces and will continue to face for some time to come.

This work did not arise from a disinterested desire to write on political philosophy. For some time, I have been alarmed by the state of American political life and concerned enough to research a series of shorter essays beginning in 2020. The initial essays were a "research project" designed to increase my understanding of political theory in search of some way out of the excessive hostility evident in much of our politics.

It seems to me that revitalizing our political life requires a pragmatic post-ideological application of the insights of postmodern science, with its emphasis on relationships and community. In this vein, learning to dialogue with others about differing insights seems essential to overcoming the current polarization. I hope these essays help outline one theoretical approach that might undergird a way forward.

I am not a professional philosopher. I have been a practicing attorney and local church pastor for my entire professional career. My interest in political philosophy began during my undergraduate years at Trinity University in San Antonio, Texas. Without the education I received there, this project would have been impossible.

I appreciate every reader and wish all readers well— including those who disagree with my ideas.

Chris Scruggs
Ephiphany, 2025

CHAPTER 1

GROUNDWORK FOR SOPHIO-AGAPISM

P hilosophy means "the love of wisdom" (*philo/sophia*). The first part of the term comes from the Greek word *phileo*, which means "love." *Phileo* is a specific kind of love. It is the love of kinship, and refers to the love one feels for parents, children, employees, household servants, friends, and even gods.[1] This is important for understanding philosophy, for the word indicates that there is a kind of kinship between the world and human beings such that humans naturally enjoy coming to an understanding of the world, and the world, in turn, has a sort of kinship to the human mind that allows it to be understood. One might even say the universe enjoys the experience of being known by human beings: as we come to understand the nature of reality, as far as the universe is concerned, it is like a child learning about a parent. Perhaps even more deeply, it is like someone coming to know themselves. The universe is becoming aware, known, and understood as humans learn, know, and become wise. The love of wisdom grows as we cherish and indwell the kinship between the world and the human race.

Sophia, Theoria, and Phronesis

The second word that makes up "philosophy" is the Greek word *Sophia*, meaning "wisdom."[2] In its most basic meaning, *Sophia* refers to the quality of mastering some aspect of human life, intellectual or practical. In the beginning, the sages of the ancient world were known for their practical wisdom and learning. Often, the wise person proved their wisdom through practical achievements in politics, commerce, agriculture, and the like.

The notion of wisdom as essentially practical is an element of wisdom in almost all early civilizations. For example, for the ancient Hebrews, wisdom and understanding were crucial to a wise and successful life. Proverbs teaches:

> Happy are those who find wisdom and those who get understanding, for her income is better than silver and her revenue better than gold. She is more precious than jewels, and nothing you desire can compare with her. Long life is in her right hand, in her left hand are riches and honor. Her ways are ways of pleasantness, and all her paths are peace. She is a tree of life to those who lay hold of her; those who hold her fast are called happy (Proverbs 3:13-18 (RSV).

The wise life involves study, instruction, seeking knowledge, being taught, discernment, and understanding (see Proverbs 1:1-7). However, this intellectual feature (*sophia*) cannot be separated from practical insight and prudence in action, which is the living out of wisdom in everyday life (*phronesis*). While the practical and the abstract can be distinguished, they can never be entirely separated in one unified life.

Theoretical knowledge emerges from a desire to understand the world theoretically. Actual theoretical knowledge emerges from the pragmatic desire to understand some feature of reality so that human life can be enhanced, even if that enhancement is theoretical in nature. The term "theoretical" derives from the Greek word *theoria*, which means "to contemplate, view, look at, consider, or speculate." From the change in the understanding of the words, one can see a move from a superficial understanding of appearances to a more speculative kind of wisdom one gains from observing and theorizing about phenomena. A lover of wisdom learns to look beneath the surface of reality into its genuine but sometimes hidden structure and meaning.

In his *Nichomachean Ethics*, Aristotle distinguishes between *sophia* and *phronesis*. *Sophia* involves reasoning concerning universal truths. *Sophia* is a kind of "transcendental" wisdom, the kind of wisdom that Plato seeks in his proposal concerning the forms.[3] *Phronesis*, on the other hand, is practical wisdom. In the down-to-earth sense, a wise person reaches sound conclusions and acts after considering concrete circumstances.[4] *Phronesis* involves the kind of prudence that one achieves by incorporating both learning and practical experience. In this sense, *phronesis* is synonymous with the Hebrew, practical notion of wisdom. Theoretical and practical wisdom are not unrelated, for the development of theoretical wisdom is integral to *phronesis*. *Phronesis* is inevitably connected to *praxis,* which involves the application of wisdom in concrete, practical affairs. For example, one cannot be a wise politician without both knowledge of political theory and also practical experience in the political sphere.

In this study, I advance a way of thinking and acting that embodies a traditional model based on a movement from practical wisdom to theoretical understanding and then back to more profound practical wisdom in action. The approach recovers the importance of community and shared values in any group's political process. According to this understanding of community, any society that promotes human flourishing is necessarily based on a politics of love, human solidarity, and self-giving for the group's welfare.

Pragmaticism

The origin of philosophy in practical wisdom implies a connection between philosophy and action, a relationship explicitly recognized by American pragmatism, or what C. S. Peirce eventually called "Pragmaticism" to distinguish his ideas from other interpretations of the theory. The pragmatic theory of truth, as expressed by Peirce, begins with the "Pragmatic Maxim":

> *Consider what effects, which might conceivably have practical bearings, we conceive the object of our conception to have. Then, our conception of those effects is the whole of our conception of the object.*[5]

For pragmatists, all thinking leads, directly or indirectly, to the illumination of some course of action, physical, mental, spiritual, or otherwise. In other words, *theoria* leads in some way to a kind of *phronesis*, intellectual or physical. This is consistent with philosophy's original meaning and object, which concerns itself with developing the form of wisdom that enables human beings to flourish and achieve a whole and happy life.

Wisdom is not solely a matter of the mind or theoretical understanding. Those who promote philosophical inquiry should eventually provide ideas and systems to resolve intractable problems and promote human flourishing. For theoretical knowledge to have meaning, it must end by satisfying some human desire to know. Otherwise, it is mere speculation, and often the kind of speculation that Socrates despised—sophism, merely arguing for the sake of debate with no genuine desire to understand.

On the other hand, there are dangers in focusing narrowly on practical applications. Peirce warned of the dangers of conflating the search for truth with practical wisdom.[6] He follows the Greek philosophical distinction between *sophia* and *phronesis*, between the superior wisdom of pure thought and applying that thought in day-to-day affairs. His concern was the potential for corruption in the search for truth through practical or political pressures. Nevertheless, Peirce realized the importance of education in preparing leaders for practical action in the future.[7]

In advancing a *sophio-agapic* approach to political theory, advancing a philosophical, pragmaticist, communal path toward politics and political decision-making is helpful.[8] This study outlines a constructive postmodern method of looking at the problem of achieving a level of justice in society. The approach is referred to as "*sophio-agapism*" because it flows from a way of looking at the world as embedded with rationality (the "*sophia*") and characterized by relationally (the "*agape*"). Further underlying the study is the notion that generals, like the ideal of justice, are developed in and for a truth-seeking community to structure a sound, workable, and peaceable society.

Justice and Social Life

The movement from *sophia* to *phronesis* is significant in pursuing a just society. Most people instinctively believe in the importance of justice for human social and political life. Kathy (my wife) and I raised four children. Inevitably, there came a day when each child said to us, "It's not fair." The complaint could be about one child getting an extra helping of food at dinner or a gift given to one child that was more than what was given to another. It could be about any number of family decisions made by the parents. In each case, the child did not think they were saying, "I don't like what my parents have done" (though they were). Instead, the child thought they were saying, "What my parents said or did is unjust." That is to say, the child was complaining that an action taken by the parents was not equitable and fair to the child or children impacted. In so doing, the child is not merely expressing a personal preference. The child is appealing to a standard of fairness conceived to exist independently of what the parent or child may think.

Humans have an innate notion of fairness or justice, an innate capacity that (hopefully) develops as a child grows. The same thing is true of societies. Societies have, within their histories and traditions, notions of justice gradually evolved through the development of that particular society. When a community member says that a governmental decision is not fair or just, they are not just stating their opinion based on groundless feelings of self-interest. (Of course, that might be the case, and the claim that an action is just or unjust might be, and sometimes is, simply a personal opinion or a cover for personal advancement or preference.) Usually, however, citizens are making a claim about the nature of the reality of a course of action (or at least they think they are). They are saying that the course of action is incompatible with the evolving notions of justice within the existing social order. In other words, they make a claim based on an external reality, not just a personal feeling.

The Classical View of Justice

How can we understand what it means to claim something is just or unjust? The founders of the Western tradition felt that justice was important and rulers could be fairly examined from the universal perspective of justice. In one way or another, most of that tradition believed that justice is something real, existing independently of what you, I, or anyone else feels or thinks is just at some moment. In this way of thinking, justice was supposed to exist apart from any personal or social preference. If this is the case, governing is not simply a matter of getting and using power according to the ruler's or ruling group's preferences. Instead, the ideal of justice constrains the use of power. When justice is conceived as real, society aims to create a social order transcending individual preferences or the willful decisions of those in power.

Plato, often considered a naïve realist, thought of justice as having an independent, objective existence, irrespective of human ideation. For Plato, justice is an essence (or form in his language) existing independently of whatever you or I think is just or any particular just action. In fact, for Plato, individual instances of justice or injustice in human society are bound to be imperfect. The world of flux and change in which we live cannot be characterized by complete justice. Thus, the perfection of justice cannot be found in any concrete case of justice but in the "Form of Justice" as an ideal perfection: the essence of justice, independent of any particular instantiation thereof.[9]

Despite his views on the difference between the ideal form of justice and justice experienced by any concrete polity, Plato viewed justice as an essential characteristic of a well-ordered society. Plato felt that a just society is characterized by a functional degree of social peace because people of different groups receive what they are due. Thus, Plato rejects the view that justice is merely traditional, the result of power, or utilitarian. Justice is an independent reality adapted to the demands of human nature and the nature of human society. Only in such a society can the traditional view of justice and a social view of justice be combined so that all people receive their due.

Plato argued that justice can be discerned through reasoning by analogy with what constitutes a just person. A just person keeps the three constituents of the human person—mind, body, and soul—in a rational harmonious order. By analogy, a just society is one in which the significant groups of society co-exist harmoniously and according to their orderly arrangement characterized by social peace and harmony among classes and citizens. Plato divided Greek society into three classes whose characteristics mirror the human psyche: philosophers (mind), honor seekers (soul), and money lovers (body).[10] By analogy to the human person, a just society is a community where these classes co-exist harmoniously.

Rejecting Plato's formulation, Aristotle thought of universals, like justice, not as pre-existing ideal forms towards which societies move, but as purely noetic realities found in concrete actions in the political sphere.[11] He therefore distinguished between "complete justice," which requires the activity of altogether just people, and "partial justice," which is the practical application of the ideals of justice in political life. In applying his ideas to political life, Aristotle distinguished between corrective justice (enforcing rights) and distributive justice (righting wrongs).[12]

From the Classical to the Medieval View of Justice

The peace that the human race seeks is a kind of harmony where all parts of society are integrated justly. Augustine quotes the following musical analogy from Cicero:

In the case of music for strings or wind, and in vocal music, there is a certain harmony to be kept between the different parts, and if this is altered or disorganized the cultivated ear finds it intolerable; and the united efforts of dissimilar voices are blended into harmony by the exercise of restraint. In the same way, a community of different classes, high, low, and middle, unites, like the varying sounds of music, to form a harmony of the different parts through the exercise of rational restraint; and what is called harmony in music answers to concord in a community, and is the closest bond of security in a country. And this is not possible without justice.[13]

This notion of justice as harmony contains an important insight: Harmony is created by a rational and aesthetically pleasing relationship between the notes of a piece of music. A right proportion creates harmony, a rational relationship between the notes of a piece of music. In the same way, the harmonious unity of a human community is created by a just and fair relationship among its parts, that is, between the persons and institutions of which such society is composed. Where there is harmony, there is a kind of peace. On the other hand, there can be no peace where there is nothing but striving for power and position.

Augustine believed that no person or group can create a just society if the society is built merely by force (or what we might call "power politics"), his preeminent example being the Roman Empire. Such a society would be merely a "society of robbers."[14] This insight is at the center of his critique of the Roman system of government. The empire was created not by reason but by war and violence. Augustine bases his analysis on a distinction between peace (*shalom* in Hebrew) and justice.[15] Human beings, by nature, seek peace. All human striving, including wars, begin and continue in the search for peace. The kingdoms of this world, specifically the Roman Empire, cannot achieve this peace because they are inevitably implicated in an ongoing cycle of violence.

Building on Aristotle, Thomas Aquinas believed there is a kind of law, or an underly source of positive law, that has its roots in the basic nature of human life and human beings.[16] Thus, Aquinas distinguished between natural law and human law:

1. Natural law is implanted in human nature and guides humans in their day-to-day activities as they exercise their reason and conscience (ST I-II, Q 94, First Article).

2. Human law is very much like what we would call "positive law." It is a law promulgated by a lawful authority and varies with time, place, and circumstance. Aquinas defined this type of law as "an ordinance of reason for the common good" made and enforced by a ruler or government (ST I-II, Q 95, First Article).

In this analysis, justice exists when personal action and positive law are in concert with the natural law implanted in the human heart and reasonably act to create or sustain the common good. This emphasis on the heart and reason working together to develop and maintain a common good is central to the notion of justice. Human laws became just to the extent that they facilitate the common good and are consistent with human nature.

Nominalism and the Enlightenment

Like most premodern thinkers, Augustine and Aquinas were realists concerning universals, like justice. Opposed to the

Platonic or Aristotelian view that universal ideals are in some sense real is "nominalism." Historically, nominalism is associated with William of Occam, who rejected the idea that universals have a separate existence. To some degree, Occam's idea flows from his most famous maxim, "Entities are not to be multiplied without necessity."[17] To the nominalist, notions such as justice are mere "names" or "labels" we place on things. They are not "real" in the sense given the term by Plato, Aristotle, or their followers.

Since the Enlightenment, nominalism has ruled the day, and belief in the reality of justice and other values, which alone can sustain a free society, has come under increasing attack.[18] Increasingly, justice has been seen as what those in power desire and can force on those not in power. This is not a new idea. It is precisely what Thrasymachus argues for in Plato's *Republic*. For Thrasymachus, a prominent sophist, justice is what those in power say it is—a view likely to be familiar to modern people:

> This, then, is what I say justice is, the same in all cities, the advantage of the established rule. Since the established rule is certainly stronger, anyone who reasons correctly will conclude that the just is the same everywhere, namely the advantage of the stronger.[19]

No one better characterizes modernity's focus on power than Thomas Hobbes. Hobbes is an early example of the materialist tendency of modern thought. Hobbes was a student of optics and considered himself to be a scientist as well as a philosopher.[20] In *Leviathan* and other works, he attempted to produce what he would have termed a "scientific" philosophical account of reality, human perception, and human life and society. In his view, the world is made up of "one stuff" (matter), and the relationships between material particles can be explained on the basis of causal relationships between such material bodies (force). Even more complex phenomena, such as human society, can be explained on this basis. Human beings are simply extremely complex material phenomena, and human society is merely the more complicated combination of individuals.

Hobbes begins his analysis of the meaning of human freedom by defining freedom as follows: "Liberty, or Freedom, signifies the absence of opposition; by opposition I mean external impediments of motion; and may be applied no less to irrational and inanimate creatures than to rational."[21] There are two aspects of this definition that readers should bear in mind:

1. **Freedom is freedom from "opposition" or "impediments" of motion.** In the end, freedom for Hobbes is the freedom to do whatever we desire or intend to do without restraint.[22] Those desires and intentions, however, are determined by material forces. Human freedom is no different from the freedom of a rock to fall under the force of gravity.

2. **Lack of freedom is a matter of external restraint.** A rock falling is free to fall under the impact of gravity so long as no other force acts on it. Translated to human freedom, freedom is the freedom to act without external restraint. A free person is free to do whatever they desire to do without external hindrance.[23] Physical infirmity and external laws are natural and human-imposed restraints on freedom.

Thus, Hobbes's freedom is freedom "from" restraints on the human will, not freedom "for" human achievement and flourishing. In the classical view, freedom was not simply a freedom from restriction but a freedom of each individual to achieve the end for which human beings and each specific human being were made. In a classical view of freedom, while freedom from restraint is an aspect of freedom, freedom from restraint is freedom to achieve the good for which human beings were created. There is a "*telos*" (end or goal) to human freedom. In Hobbes's view, there is only "freedom from," for there is no goal to human existence.

For Hobbes, every action is caused (determined) by physical causes, which means all human behavior is necessary. Everything in the universe is determined by necessity, including human actions. This implies that human freedom is an illusion, a conclusion that flies in the face of ordinary human experience. The final cause, according to Hobbes, is God.[24] True existential freedom is not part of the universe. According to Hobbes, the fact that an action is caused and the cause is determinative does not make it less free.

In Hobbes's view, human society is instituted because of fear, the fear of chaos and violence. To achieve peace (an absence of violence and chaos, and freedom from the fear thereof), human beings give up their freedom, human society is formed, and human laws are enacted. These laws are "artificial chains".[25] The use of the term "artificial chains" is instructive. Laws are external rules imposed on citizens that constrict their freedom. Political liberty refers to those areas of life that are currently not the subject of some legal impediment to action.

Unlike in a classical or Christian view, in Hobbes's scheme free agents do not construct laws to seek the common good, social harmony, or the good of families or communities. Political society is not formed to provide a social structure within which human freedom can be exercised and human potential realized. There is no common good to which all human beings and their leaders should strive within human society. Political society is formed solely to eliminate chaos, violence, and fear, which Hobbes believes to be the natural state of the human agent. In Hobbes, an organic view of the origin and evolution of human society is lacking, as is the classic understanding of human nature and the organic importance of human society.

One result of Hobbes's vision is to discourage looking at law and justice as essential to human flourishing. For example, the laws against murder and assault are indeed partially enacted to prevent social chaos. Nevertheless, they are also a guide to healthy human life. Suppose we believe humans were formed to be rational, cherishing human life and human potential. In that case, the laws against murder and violence, as well as many other laws, are not merely restrictions on liberty but also guides to the achievement of human wholeness. Even as to such mundane matters as traffic laws, a Hobbesian view sees these laws as restrictions of human activity, like the laws on speeding that most of us occasionally chafe against. This view overlooks the common objective of such regulations: allowing people to travel safely and reach their destinations without accident so that they can profitably conduct their lives and businesses. This dimension of the law as essential to human freedom and flourishing is an aspect that Hobbes misses entirely.

Because Hobbes believes the sovereign has unlimited power (an unlimited capacity to restrict human freedom), he must defend his notion of freedom in a way consistent with the idea of absolute sovereign power. Hobbes begins by taking the position that nothing a sovereign can do constitutes an unjust deprivation of human freedom, even putting a subject to death.[26] This is a totalitarian position granting sovereigns unchecked power, and is the position Thrasymachus proposes and Socrates opposes in the *Republic*.

In fact, only a sovereign is politically free under Hobbes's doctrine. Therefore, the state and its rulers are free because the sovereign, and the sovereign alone, can do whatever it pleases without political restraint.[27] This notion of absolute sovereignty flows from his fundamentally material and antisocial view of the human race and its condition without laws: the war of "everyman against his neighbor."[28] Once again, we see in Hobbes a limited, dark, and entirely constricted view of human beings and society—and one that flies in the face of a good portion of human experience.

With Hobbes, many modern thinkers and leaders tend to think that justice is whatever policy the majority believes in and is willing to support.[29] This glorification of power, power politics, and political victory was just what Augustine's view meant: a government is simply a band of robbers without justice. Whatever law and justice exist is merely for the convenience of those striving for power. Ultimately, they are guided by a fundamentally nihilistic and totalitarian notion of justice, which reduces justice to whatever those in power can gain support to do.

The Nietzschean Ideal

One might say that the end of the modern Western Enlightenment worldview (the emergence of postmodernism) begins with Nietzsche's observation, "God is dead."[30] In his work, Nietzsche "deconstructed" the foundations of Enlightenment liberalism, reducing all truth claims, moral claims, and aesthetic claims to bids for power. In the premodern world, societies often believed that the gods founded their civilizations, and their system of government and royalty were decreed by or descended from their gods. The imperial system of Japan, as it existed at the end of the Second World War, was the last of these societies. In Western

Europe, and especially in England and the United States, even after the Enlightenment, natural law theory and the connections between natural law theory and religious faith in popular society continued to influence the legal order of society. It might be the Christian God, the Deist God of the Enlightenment, or in the Muslim world today, it might even be Allah, but in any case, the social order and law were seen as a social reflection of some kind of divine order.

Nietzsche understood that the phrase "God is dead," if taken seriously, meant that the social order of Europe had no stable foundation. In other words, if the Christian God was dead, European society, culture, morals, law, and even such mundane matters as most of its holidays had no adequate foundation for their existence. In this situation, Nietzsche proposed that the will is fundamental, and the will to power is the foundation of all morality and social order. What is needed, then, is a kind of superman who embodies a "master morality" as opposed to the slave morality Nietzsche believed to characterize the Christian culture of medieval and early modern Europe.[31]

Nietzsche's hostility towards Christianity as a "slave religion" reflects his view that Christian morality involved the attempt of the weak to gain power over the strong. Instead, he glorified the "Over-Human," i.e. those who have the vitality to impose their will on others. In practice, the result of Nietzschean thought is inevitably some degree of totalitarianism, as John Milbank notes in his book *Theology and Social Theory: Beyond Secular Reason*.[32] Nietzsche's thinking inevitably entails the view that words such as "justice" have no meaning other than that meaning given by force of will. Justice is a name that the *Ubermensch* (an "over-human" who has the vitality to impose their will on others) gives to his or her ideas of justice. Nietzsche instituted a continuing program of seeing all moral and all truth claims as simple bids for power. In his work, Nietzsche "deconstructed" the foundations of Enlightenment liberalism, reducing all truth claims, moral claims, and aesthetic claims to bids for power. Nietzsche's hostility towards Christianity as a "slave religion," reflecting the attempt of the weak to gain dominance over the strong, the *Ubermensch,* is well known. The Nietzschean notion of the will to power embeds in contemporary politics an innate tenancy towards violence and the oppression of minorities, religious, racial, and otherwise.[33]

Contemporary politics and political thinking are dominated by two underlying political ideologies in which a fundamentally power-centric ideology manifests itself: first in what might be called "materialistic, *laissez-faire* capitalist liberalism" and second in "Marxist dialectical materialistic communism." Ultimately, both extremes see politics and economics as subject to universal material laws that act in the world without reference to any transcendental moral ideal. Both ideologies discount moral and spiritual values as necessary to political or economic life. Ultimately, both have shown themselves to be incompatible with human flourishing. What is needed is a new approach, which can be provided by a *sophia-agapistic* vision of politics and the continuing search for a just society.

Peirce and Post-Darwinian Theory

One possible alternative to the incipient nihilism of the late-modern world begins with the figure of Charles Sanders Peirce. As noted, Plato considered justice an unchanging ideal, so his Republic sought to describe a stable, perfect political system. The implications of modern science and philosophy cast doubt on whether any ideal state can be achieved in history or could have existed in the past. After Darwin, philosophers struggled to defend justice within a materialistic evolutionary concept of societies governed solely by material forces, changing and adapting to new circumstances. Peirce was one of those who made the attempt.

Though not a political philosopher, Peirce set out to reconstruct a sound understanding of the world in the context of post-Darwinian America—an account relevant to political thought. A distinction between "physical existence" and "reality" is fundamental to Peirce's view of universal ideas. Things that do not have a physical existence, such as the equations of science or the theories of philosophers, are nevertheless real. They are noetic (ideal) realities constantly refined and extended in their meaning by human endeavor. As such, the ideal of justice and feelings that the justice of a particular society is imperfect is part of a never-ending process of development that continues throughout human history.

The status of abstract notions, like justice, as real is essential in constructing a political philosophy that can respond to the issues of our society. As mentioned earlier, modern thought has been fundamentally nominalist. Concepts such as truth, beauty, goodness, and the like are considered mere labels humans put on their subjective preferences. This results in the inability of modern societies to reason about moral issues, for they involve matters to be resolved by power and confrontation, not by reason.[34]

Peirce believed the lack of belief in the reality of universals was a defining weakness of modern thought, leading to the dysfunction we experience in our culture. The nominalism of contemporary thinkers undermines, among other things, the search for scientific truth with which Peirce was primarily interested. Science depends on the critical analysis of a reality that scientists seek to understand, a reality existing outside of the scientist's mind. This understanding is expressed in the laws of science, which practicing scientists discover through research and analysis. In the same way, the search for Truth, Beauty, Goodness, and Justice requires that humans believe that, in some way, they exist outside the personal preferences of individual minds and the manipulative potential of human actors. In the words of Peirce, certain truths exist whether we want them to or not.[35]

For Pierce, knowledge in general, knowledge in science and philosophy, and knowledge in the moral sciences are matters of communal endeavor. Pierce strongly believed that universal principles are products of human minds and truth-seeking communities. Peirce did not, however, subscribe to naïve idealism. Instead, drawing on Duns Scotus, Peirce took the view that while universals are expressed in words, it is not the sign but the thing that the expression signifies that is real. Thus, what is at stake in the discussion of justice is not the word but the reality behind the word as it impacts the decisions of people and societies in the search for a stable and fair society.

Critical Realism and *Sophia-Agapism*

The realism of *sophio-agapism* is not naïve realism; it is critical realism. Critical realism recognizes that, however well attested by a relevant community, any theoretical formulation is ultimately provisional. Calling such formulations "provisional" reflects the fact that future critical inquiry may require revision. This is true in science, law, philosophy, and other disciplines. Just as the decision of a court of law can be overturned due to new and conflicting evidence, any provisional claim of justice can be revised if circumstances make this appropriate. That revision does not necessarily mean that the original claim was wrong (though it might be). More likely, the discovery of additional facts in the future, social change, and other factors cause a particular social view of justice to be revised.

The "realism" aspect of critical realism means that any particular theoretical construct (formulated by a community searching for truth, beauty, goodness, justice, and the like) comes into contact with a feature of a reality existing outside of the private opinions of a particular individual or group. This "contact with reality" involves the disciplined and honest search for the value in question without prejudice and with respect for the historical techniques used to discover some aspect of reality. As Thomas Torrance puts it:

> Moreover, since reality, owing to its boundless objectivity, has the capacity to manifest itself in an indefinite variety of ways far beyond what we can explicitly predict and therefore constantly to take us by surprise, scientific statements that bear upon it inevitably have an irreducible indeterminacy or openness in virtue of which they have a built-in thrust for adaptation and for ongoing modification.[36]

Our philosophical and legal intimations of justice are objective because they exist outside of our personal prejudices and preferences. Therefore, they are subject to both investigation and revision in accordance with the nature of the reality being investigated. They also possess a fundamental openness and indeterminacy, which makes human social progress possible.

Dialogue and the Process of Uncovering Justice

Any form of human inquiry takes place in the context of an investigation adapted to its subject matter. Scientific inquiry begins with the search for the explanation of physical phenomena through scientific research. The *sophio-agapic* search for justice occurs in a much more complex environment than any scientific inquiry. Any given society's social, political, and legal institutions participate in the search. In particular, the courts, the justice system, the legal profession, bureaucratic officials, educational and other social institutions, and the like all participate in a process of investigation, research, decision, debate, and the like. Sophio-agapism believes that mere debate and decision-making, especially the power politics of contemporary society, are increasingly inadequate vehicles for wise decision-making in the public interest. What is needed is increasing dialogue and conversation within the relevant community and sub-communities to ensure that decision-makers have both a grasp of the factors involved and a better understanding of the best interests of all social groups impacted by a decision.

CHAPTER 2

PRAGMATICISM, AGAPISM & SOPHIA-AGAPISM

The life of Charles Sanders Peirce (1839-1914) was something of a tragedy. He was a prodigy, reading Kant as a youth, studying under his famous father, a professor of mathematics at Harvard, and acknowledged to be one of his generation's most remarkable and broadest minds. He received the finest education. Unfortunately, he divorced his first wife and lived with his second wife before marriage, an unacceptable situation in the late 19th century. Peirce also lacked the social skills and political instincts needed for a successful academic career. As a result, he was exiled from the most prestigious academic posts. Instead, he made a bare living writing articles for journals, lecturing, and teaching where he could. His friends, William James, Josiah Royce, and others, did their best to gain recognition for him, and they credited him with founding the school of "Pragmatism."

For a time, Pierce worked as a practicing scientist for the United States Coastal and Geodetic Survey, where he developed his theories of verification and an intuitive dislike of a kind of speculative philosophy he regarded as untrue to how human beings actually think. Unfortunately, personality conflicts ended his career there as well. Ultimately, his suffering produced a rare, lovely, and brilliant character. Although he never finished his philosophical system, Peirce made substantial contributions to the fields of logic, metaphysics, and epistemology, leaving a massive amount of published and unpublished work for generations of scholars to develop. Among other matters, Peirce's philosophy has profound applications to our current political situation and the impasses that Western societies face.

For all his failings, it is difficult not to describe Peirce as the most significant American philosopher. With Saussure, Peirce is the inventor of semiotics, which formed the basis of his philosophy. He was a logician of the first rank and was the first to outline the importance of abductive logic (reasoning from hypotheses). His views on the reality of universals were a contribution to metaphysics, as he was able to distinguish between "reality" and mere "existence." He was the first expositor of the pragmatic method and later, when he felt he needed to reject the nominalism of his colleagues in the pragmatist movement, he developed his own neglected "pragmaticism," founded on continuity with the realist tradition in Western metaphysics.

Semiotics and Human Thought

Political thought and much of the operation of political life in any society is conducted through human discourse involving words. As a result, any *sophio-agapic* view of political life is concerned with a theory of signs. As indicated above, Peirce founded the modern science of semiotics.[37] His thinking about semiotics was fundamental to his philosophical pursuits. In a letter to Lady Welby, Peirce states:

> It has never been in my power to study anything—mathematics, ethics, metaphysics, gravitation, thermodynamics, optics, chemistry, comparative anatomy, astronomy, psychology, phonetics, economics, the history of science, whist, men and women, wine, meteorology, except as a study of semiotics.[38]

Peirce realized that all human thinking, including political thinking, involves signs (*sema* in Greek). Let us suppose, for example, that I decide to challenge a zoning decision in my city and so decide to find out how this might be accomplished. First, I read the decision of the zoning commission. Then, I have some image or idea in my mind of the change in the decision I desire to make. Do I want the decision to be overturned? Do I wish it to be changed or modified? In these internal conversations, my mind manipulates and evaluates images or signs. I decide to learn more, so I research the zoning laws of our community. Once again, the book is filled with words, which are signs designed to help one learn to build things on their own. Finally, I become convinced that I cannot do this alone, so I hire a lawyer who writes a brief supporting my position. All this is done using signs. Signs, therefore, are implicated in all wise and prudent political thinking (*sophia*) and action (*phronesis*).

There are three essential elements to Peirce's semiotic theory:

1. Representamens (signs)
2. Objects (that which is being studied)
3. Interpretants (those interpreting the sign)

For Peirce, the semiotic nature of our knowledge means that human knowledge involves a semiotic process. The subject of an inquiry is an "object." A representamen is a sign representing or referring to the object to make it cognizable and communicable. The object of our thought may be material (I wonder what this table is made of?) or noetic (I wonder if this decision is just.) This is an extremely important point. Objects of thought need not be material. Interpretation involves the sign's relationship to the object by one interpreting a reality being investigated.

For Peirce, signs are of three basic kinds: icons, indexes, and symbols. An icon has a physical similarity to what it represents. A picture of a table of the type I wish to make is an example of an icon. An index has a real relationship with its object, though it is not an icon. A rough drawing of a table would be an example of an index. A symbol has a relationship with its object that is merely a matter of custom. People use the symbol "Table" to refer to a place where people can work and eat, but the name has no inherent similarity or identity with physical tables.

The triadic interpretive relationship of signs reveals something important about human thought: it is essentially communal and relational. Signs come to have a relationship with their object in the process of interpretation, which takes place within a community of interpretation. In the case of understanding signs involving the search for justice, for example, the community is politicians and lawyers, lawmakers, judges, and those who administer the laws and record decisions. Even if I am pondering a matter within my mind, there is still the object of my thought, the signs I am using, and the process in which I am engaged in a relational process. This relational process is seldom purely internal, as one thinking about law and justice inevitably converses with multiple sources. For example, even if

I am alone in my office thinking about a legal problem, I am in a dialogue with statutes, legal opinions of the past, the facts of a particular case, and the opinions of my client and others. Even when alone, I interpret in community.

All intellectual progress is progress in the development, interpretation, and testing of signs by human beings in a community. This is why the notion of a private language is ultimately meaningless.[39] Languages are vehicles for human communication, which is a social activity. While I can conceive of a private language that only I know, it would not be a genuine language. It would be more like a secret code that is useless to anyone unaware of the hidden rules of the code.

Semiotics is essential in all reasoning, including legal reasoning and political philosophy.[4] In any claim that something is just or unjust, in any decision concerning a public policy, there are always a set of external circumstances outside the interpreter (object), the words (signs) that embody an interpretation, and the interpretation of the interpreter (interpretant). The claim "Murder is unjust" interprets the words "murder," "is," and "unjust." The statement, "Murder is unjust," claims that the objective facts described as "murder" are incompatible with an idea expressed by the English word "justice."

Claims like "This was a murder" occur in a particular society with a specific legal system that evolves over time. Over many years of decisions, interpreters have sensed that there are different kinds and degrees of murder. Some murders are justified, and others are not. There are defenses to claims of murder. In other words, a justice system constitutes a long, multi-generational conversation about what constitutes justice under an ever-changing set of circumstances. Every time a new situation arises—every new pattern of facts—enriches and grows a communal notion of justice. This is not true only for murder but for all the myriad situations in which the phrases "This is just" or "This is unjust" might apply.

Consider the number of laws, administrative rulings, court decisions, and the like that already exist and are promulgated daily. One quickly sees that the notion of justice (and injustice) is a semiotic universe filled with innumerable signs, interpreters, and interpretations, all of which may bear to a greater or lesser degree on any given decision by a court, legislature, or administrative official.

Critique of Abstract, Philosophical Doubt

Pierce began his analysis of the problem of modernity with his critique of the first modern philosopher, Rene Descartes, and his program of systematic doubt.[40] Descartes founded his system on his first principle of thought: to doubt anything and everything.[41] This led Descartes to the philosophical method of doubt, to question everything except those things, if any, in which he could find no possible reason to doubt.[42] It turned out that Descartes could doubt everything except his personal act of thinking. He developed his famous maxim from this starting point, "I think, therefore, I am."[43] The principle of philosophic doubt sits at the foundation of modern philosophy—the assertion of the primacy of the individual human mind over all else. Perhaps even more importantly, it shifted the search for the truth of ideals, such as justice, from the external world to the interior reflections of the human mind.

Peirce recognized that the kind of individualistic philosophic doubt that Descartes represented was a "false" or "fake" doubt. Peirce points out that Descartes did not, in fact, doubt in his every day and professional life what he proclaimed to doubt philosophically. Therefore, his doubt was a mere "philosophic" or "fake" doubt designed to support his philosophical and religious goals. Peirce, a scientist who worked within the scientific community of his day, responds to Descartes, observing:

> We cannot begin with complete doubt. We must begin with all the prejudices which we actually have when we enter upon the study of philosophy. These prejudices are not to be dispelled by maxim, for they are things which it does not occur to us can be questioned. Hence, this initial skepticism will be a mere self-deception and not a real doubt....[44]

At this point, Peirce's pragmaticism emerges. Honest doubt is not philosophic doubt. Real doubt is doubt as to some feature of reality, which leads to an investigation to relieve that sense of doubt so that reality may be better understood and responded to appropriately. Reasoning aims to identify and remove the source of real doubt by securing an answer to the questions the doubt creates.

For Peirce, doubt is an uneasy and dissatisfied state from which humans struggle to free themselves to pass into a state of understanding or belief. All intellectual progress begins with some degree of real doubt or uncertainty. For example, a scientist is motivated to inquire by doubt that a current understanding of physical reality is complete and accurate. A legal inquiry begins with doubt that some feature of current law is fair. A moral inquiry begins with doubt that some feature of conventional morality is correct. Religious inquiry starts with a dissatisfaction with the current understanding of some feature of ultimate reality. In each case, the doubt is not hypothetical. It is real.

Furthermore, doubt cannot be permanently removed from the human situation, which is the motive for continuing human inquiry. Every understanding of any kind of reality is temporary. "Real Doubt," unlike "Philosophic Doubt," is an inevitable part of the human condition and necessary for progress in any area of human life. Descartes postulated philosophic doubt to bring an end to doubt. Peirce sees real doubt as an essential part of human life and progress.[45]

As far as political thought is concerned, doubt about whether the current state of our society is just is not a bad thing, nor can it be entirely eliminated. Human doubt about justice is the motive force that drives culture forward in the search for a more just society. For example, for generations, hardly anyone doubted the justice of capital punishment. In recent years, various thinkers have doubted its inherent justice and utility. Today, the circumstances in which capital punishment can be inflicted for a crime are restricted in ways unknown in past Western society and still unusual in many areas of the world. It was doubt about the meaning of justice as applied to capital punishment that led to the progress that has been made.

Things in Themselves and Lack of Understanding

Peirce's interest in philosophy began with his study of Kant under the tutelage of his father. He was an appreciative student of Kant but rejected aspects of Kant's philosophy, among them Kant's view that there are *a priori* (prior to experience) elements of human knowledge. Peirce rejects Kant's idea that time and space are *a priori* structures of human knowledge. Instead, Peirce regards them as results of human inquiry: the structure of physical space and time are developed as part of an empirical inquiry. Postmodern science agrees with this observation of

Peirce's since, as a result of relativity theory, time and space are relative emergent qualities of reality.[46]

For Kant, there was a fundamental distinction between "noumena" and "phenomena". Noumena are things as they exist in themselves, which Kant deems unknowable. Phenomena, on the other hand, are the appearances of things to the human senses. Since the "thing in itself" ("*Ding an Sich*," in Kant's original German) exists independently of our knowledge and perception, it cannot be known. Peirce rejects the idea that things in themselves cannot be known. In Peirce's view, while some things are not currently known, in principle all things are knowable. What Kant calls "noumena" are simply aspects of reality humans have not yet understood.

What is known at any given time constitutes "reality." However, Peirce's fallibilism results in his view that our understanding of reality can always be revised in light of new facts or new theoretical interpretations of what we know. Thus, in a letter to Lady Welby, he says, "I show just how far Kant was right, even when twisted up on formalism. Indeed, we can never attain knowledge of things as they are. We can only know their human aspect. But that is all the universe is for us."[47]

In other words, Pierce thinks that Kant's "thing in itself" is similar to Descartes' principle of doubt. In ordinary life, we do not believe we do not know the thing itself. We act day in and day out with the presumption that we know the nature of things that are the objects of ordinary life with which we come into contact. Occasionally, we doubt that our understanding is correct or complete. This does not mean that there is a "thing in itself" I cannot possibly know that is beyond human inquiry.

For example, suppose I have a business. I know my business. I spend day after day looking at financial statements, working with employees and others, finalizing business plans, looking at machinery, analyzing the assembly line, and a host of other things. When doubt appears, it is not because I do not know "my business in itself." It is because some feature of the business that is not behaving as I expect that causes me to have doubts about that business, which I take pains to resolve by investigation. When I conduct that investigation, I discover some feature of that business previously hidden from my understanding. It was not "unknowable." It was "undiscovered."

The same thing is true in law. When studying some legal problem, one begins with some feature of the legal system about which there is a lack of clarity. For example, a client receives a letter from the Internal Revenue Service denying a deduction that a law firm previously approved. Previously, the firm did not doubt that the client could take the deduction, but the activity of the IRS has caused a client, and therefore the firm, to doubt the conclusion previously reached. This begins a process of legal research involving statutes, regulations, rulings, prior case law, law reviews, and other sources. Conversations and communications are made with the IRS, other law firms, and perhaps consultants. There may be litigation and appeals. All this mental activity is caused by doubt about some feature of reality, in this case, the United States tax laws.

The pragmaticist method is inherently antithetical to the notion of a "thing in itself," for such an unknowable "noumenon" theoretically limits human knowledge and inquiry. It would, for example, place limits on science and scientific investigation. As to moral ideals and notions such as justice, Kant's formulation creates a limit that prevents complete understanding, resulting in unresolved societal conflict. For Peirce, there is always some aspect of reality that might reveal itself to us in the future, and human minds must remain open to that reality for it to be revealed. This does not, however, indicate that there is a "thing in itself" we cannot know. "The thing in itself" is fundamentally what we do not yet understand about a phenomenon. The search for better understanding is endless but not hopeless.

Peirce speaks of how the "irritation of doubt" causes a struggle to attain a state of belief, which provokes inquiry.[48] This is the pragmatic method as it applies to political thought. When our society faces difficulties adjusting to reality, it is not that we do not know our culture "in itself." We do. However, some features of our society are not working as expected or desired. Therefore, we must investigate to see if changes need to be made so that it will work again. When our society is at an impasse, it means there is some feature of our political system that we either ignore or do not yet understand. It does not mean we cannot get beyond the impasse.

This has important implications for the ideal of justice. For the nominalist, "justice" is just a word one applies to subjective preferences. This leads to a loss of faith in the reality of justice and its potential realization in a political system. This, in turn, results in social conflict. For the pragmaticist, the fact that some elements of society appear unjust or unfair indicates a difficulty that needs to be investigated, the results of which might be additional progress in achieving a more just society.

Truth, Reality, and Universals

Plato, in one of his most famous and important passages, defines reality in a way that illuminates what Peirce was trying to communicate concerning universals:

> I suggest that everything which possesses any power of
> any kind, either to produce a change in anything of any

nature or to be affected even in the least degree by the slightest cause, though it be only on one occasion, has real existence. For I set up as a definition which defines being, that it is nothing else but power.[49]

To understand precisely what Plato is saying, one must understand the Greek word translated as "power" in English. The term "*dunamis*" not only means "power" but also means "force," "strength," "ability," "capacity," or "potential." "Power" can refer to material, moral, intellectual, or spiritual power. It can also refer to the capacity or potential to impact reality in the future.

When Plato says that anything with power has "real being," he includes moral, spiritual, intellectual, material, and physical potentials. Its content includes but is not limited to material force as power. The second thing to notice about this definition is that it does not restrict itself to the active ability to produce a change in another. *Dunamis* includes the ability of ideas to impact our political decisions as possessing reality. Thus, a concept, such as "justice," that can shape human activity has a real noetic, intellectual reality.

According to Plato, not only things that can change other things are real. Things that can be changed are also real. Thus, justice is real both because it can change behavior and because the thoughts and behavior of human beings can change it. This is another way of saying that justice is a matter of relations.[50] It is a relational concept. Its meaning can and does emerge in the context of human life, human culture, human society, and human decision-making. The entire experience of human societies as they search for social harmony is a part of the emerging reality of justice in every society.

It is fundamental to a pragmaticist method that real things, material and noetic, exist independent of our opinions. That is to say, notions such as truth, beauty, goodness, justice, and the like are not purely subjective as the modern postmodernist would have it, but "real" in the sense that they can impact our behavior and adaptation to an environment, including a social setting, for good or ill. Material reality is not the only meaningful reality. Immaterial, noetic ideas like "justice" have a reality born of their capacity to enlighten and inform human action.[51]

Peirce was impressed by the diligence with which medieval philosophers investigated abstract ideas and the energy they expended in the search for truth. He understood that Aquinas studied the nature of angels and Duns Scotus the nature of God and of universals precisely because they felt they were uncovering some aspect of reality of importance to their lives.[52] Their intellectual works were not narcissistic endeavors to enforce their ideas on others; instead, they were intellectual quests designed to uncover a universal truth communicable to all human beings.[53]

For Peirce, ideas are real insofar as they exist regardless of some personal opinion. This is based on a distinction between real and fantasy:

We have only to stop and consider a moment what was meant by the word *real,* when the whole issue becomes apparent. Objects are divided into figments, dreams, etc., on the one hand, and realities on the other. The former are those that exist only in as much as you, or I or some man imagines them; the latter are those that have an existence, independent of your mind, or mine, without of any number of persons. The real is that which is not whatever we happen to think of it, but is unaffected by what we may think of it.[54]

Universal ideas, such as "Golden Retrievers are a species of canine," communicate a truth that is not dependent on what I or any one or more human beings think. The idea "Golden Retriever" conveys an abstract reality, existing noetically in the form of a concept, but it nevertheless communicates a feature of a segment of reality. Theoretical structures, such as laws of nature (like the second law of thermodynamics that holds that entropy always increases), are true regardless of what you or I privately believe about them.

The same principle applies to political ideals, such as justice. When someone claims that a policy is unjust, the word "unjust" refers to a reality of injustice that the speaker believes exists, irrespective of any specific person or thing the speaker may be addressing. The speaker may be mistaken, or those who instituted the policy may be mistaken. It is possible that the person making a claim was not interested in justice but only in advancing their private interests. Further investigation may determine who is right or point society in a completely different direction. Nevertheless, we are claiming that, if true, our claim is valid irrespective of what any particular person thinks about it.

Peirce's concept of reality is defined in contradistinction to things that are mere figments of the imagination, purely personal perceptions that have no connection to other human beings. Thus, according to Peirce, reality is essentially a communal concept:

> The real is that which is not whatever we may happen to think it, but is unaffected by what we may think of it. The question, therefore, is whether a man, horse, and other names of natural classes, correspond with anything that all men, or all horses, really have in common, independent of our thought, or whether these classes are

constituted simply by a likeness in the way in which our minds are affected by individual objects which have in themselves no resemblance or relationship whatsoever.[55]

Elsewhere, Peirce puts it thus:

The real, then, is that which, sooner or later, information and reasoning would finally result in, and which is, therefore, independent of the vagaries of you and me. Thus, the very origin of the conception of reality shows that this conception essentially involves the notion of a COMMUNITY, without definite limits, and capable of a definite increase in knowledge.[56]

To be real is to have the power of common impact on or being impacted by a community of inquirers whose opinions are not merely personal but communally tested and recognized. What is deemed real is independent of any particular thinker but impacts and constrains the thinking of all community members involved in the inquiry.[57] Thus, an abstract notion, such as "justice," is just as real as a concrete, material reality, such as "table." The difference is that the general exists as an act of thought in the mind.[58]

It is a real that only exists by virtue of an act of thought knowing it, but that thought is not an arbitrary or accidental one dependent on any idiosyncrasies, but one that will hold in the final opinion.[59]

What are traditionally called universals are "noetic realities" that possess intellectual and mental reality as they guide human life and inquiry. When embodied in a community of inquiry, they have real power to direct the community to a deeper understanding of some aspect of reality. Such reality is not, however, the same as or equivalent to physical existence. The key idea is that reality refers to things that exist independently of any one person's ideas. Thus, ideas and ideals can be real when they have the power to impact a community of inquiry and are seen as such by such a community.

The realist understands that, in the long run, an error is recognized by a community of inquirers. Going back to the claim that a particular policy is unjust, a society embracing a *sophio-agapic* approach to political thinking proceeds with the confidence that eventually it will become apparent to the courts, the legislature, and others whether a particular claim is correct. As Peirce puts it:

> All human thought and opinion contains an arbitrary, accidental element, dependent on the limitations in circumstances, power, and bent of the individual; an element of error, in short. But human opinion tends in the long run to a definite form, which is the truth. Let any human being have enough information and exert enough thought upon any question, and the result will be that he will arrive at a certain definite conclusion, which is the same that any other mind will reach under sufficiently favorable circumstances.[60]

Peirce's conceptual realism is, therefore, not naïve or absolute realism. On the contrary, it is a critical realism, always subject to revision based on further investigation, since arbitrary elements, limitations, personal prejudice, and other factors necessarily impact human thought. This is especially true in politics, where personal preference and ideological concerns can often eclipse logic in human thinking.

Peirce's approach is to adhere to a reasonable and pragmatic approach to solving political problems and correcting inevitable errors through an ongoing process. This is where fallibilism is essential. The ideas of humans may be and often are wrong. I can be wrong. My social class can be wrong. Experts can be wrong. Whole societies may be mistaken. History is rife with examples. The principle of fallibilism is a principle of humility in the face of an emerging reality. Whatever we know, however certain our opinions are, they may be considered mistaken in the future.

Three Inadequate Methods of Making Progress

In developing his version of pragmaticism, Peirce developed a notion of how intellectual progress occurs, a pragmatic idea that relies on a continuing course of inquiry by human beings. This notion of truth includes the idea that to believe a proposition to be true is not merely an intellectual commitment or removal of private doubt but, instead, a belief that includes a willingness to conduct ourselves in some way based on a truth we believe ourselves to have discovered to satisfy the desires that motivated our inquiry.[61] Peirce compares the method of pragmatic investigation with other methods of establishing truth often adapted by the human race:

1. **The Method of Tenacity.** The method of tenacity removes doubt by holding a belief irrespective of the evidence to the contrary. Interestingly, Pierce is aware that this method is used by highly successful individuals in practical day-to-day affairs. However, it does not result in progress in human understanding.

2. **The Method of Authority.** A second method establishes some power (governmental, administrative, bureaucratic, or religious) whose sole purpose is to prevent any contrary doctrine from being established or spoken. This method is used increasingly today to prevent ideas leaders feel are dangerous from being explored.

3. *A Priori Method.* The final method with which Peirce disagrees is the method of deduction from *a priori* first principles, characteristic of European rationalism. The *a priori* method does not differ from the method of authority, except that individual human reason becomes the authority. Nothing new can be discovered using this method because nothing new can ever be discovered without further information and the investigation of the results.[62]

The connection with political philosophy is evident. Governments, throughout human history, have tried to enforce their legitimacy and the wisdom of their policies by creating bureaucracies, administrative centers of power, educational institutions, and other social organs, the purpose of which is to establish and promulgate particular views as obviously true, and even *a priori* valid, and to quash opposing ideas and prevent them from influencing public policy.[63] In an important passage, Peirce sets out the terrifying nature of this approach:

Let an institution be created which shall have for its object to keep correct doctrines before the attention of the people, to reiterate them perpetually, and to teach them to the young; having at the same time the power to prevent contrary doctrines from being taught, advocated or expressed. Let all possible causes of a change of mind be removed from men's apprehensions. Let them be kept ignorant lest they should learn and some reason to think otherwise they do. Let their passions be enlisted, so that they may regard private and unusual opinions with hatred and horror. Then, let all men who reject the established belief be terrified into silence.[64]

We see this kind of behavior at work today in politics in pervasive intolerance of specific ideas. We see it in schools and universities, the media, the entertainment industry, the "cancel culture movement," the "political correctness movements," the behavior of students and faculties at various college campuses, political movements left and right, and even government.[65] The method of authority attempts to prevent disagreement with current policies by stigmatizing those with contrary views. It attempts to prevent disagreement with current policies by a process designed to avoid real thought so that ordinary persons will concede and accept the opinions of those in power. Throughout human history, this method has been used by governments, particularly those dominated by an aristocracy or an oligarchy, to prevent the expression of any views felt to undermine the power of those in authority. It is present in every kind of totalitarian regime, even in those that operate under the guise of a democracy.

Escaping Tenacity, Authority, and A Priori Thought

Having critiqued the potential for intellectual progress through tenacity, authority, and reliance on *a priori* ideas, Pearce outlines the pragmaticist alternative. He begins by noting that willful adherence to a belief by arbitrarily forcing opinions on others must be given up in a free society so that people may fix their beliefs rationally. Then, he goes on to state the main principle of pragmatism:

> Consider what effects, which might conceivably have practical bearings, we conceive the object of our conception to have. Then, our conception of those effects is the whole of our conception of the object.[66]

For Pierce, the pragmatic maxim is a logical principle connected with his idea of what counts as reality (metaphysics), the proper methodology for philosophy to undertake to resolve its difficulties (epistemology), and even moral and other questions (aesthetics, ethics, and even political philosophy). As a principle of logic, it is also inevitably a principle of the use and meaning of signs.

The pragmatic maxim was designed to cure philosophy of the habit of channeling energy toward disputes with little or no practical value in the search for understanding. For Peirce, pragmaticism is the core principle in doing philosophy and solving philosophical problems in a more "scientific way." There are no indisputable ideas. All ideas are to be formed and analyzed in relation to the results of their application in human endeavors.

Peirce's pragmatic maxim is designed to clarify our conceptions by directly relating them to actual or anticipated experiences. In broad terms, the pragmatic principle urges that thinkers anchor concepts and ideas in their potential practical application with respect to actions to be taken, including rules or modes of action to be adopted as a result of the inquiry. Transported into the language of politics and political philosophy, this maxim might be rephrased as follows:

In evaluating any aspect of political life or thought, an inquirer should consider what practical impact the adoption of a given conception might have for the government of society, and the effect of such a conception would have on some action to be taken.

A *sophio-agapic* approach to political philosophy is grounded in the potential application of ideas to substantive problems and actions to be taken to solve them. When put into practice, ideas have consequences, and the results can be evaluated. When evaluations are made, course corrections can be adopted, all in the search for a more just and harmonious society. These adjustments are all made on the basis of a logical and practical analysis of the consequences of the action. This approach is a needed corrective to the ideologically driven approaches of both the left and right in contemporary society.

Three Methods of Logical Inquiry

Most people are familiar with two methods of logical inquiry: "induction" and "deduction." Peirce introduced a third, intermediate logic called "Abduction." All human thinking, if it is to be valid, must consist of manipulating signs in one or more of these three logical ways.[67] Briefly, the three methods can be defined as follows:

1. **Induction**. Inductive reasoning begins with specific observations and proceeds to a generalized conclusion that is likely but not certain in light of accumulated evidence. For example, suppose I use bleach on my sink 1000 times and then conclude from experience that bleach is a good cleaner for sinks. This is an example of inductive thinking.

2. **Deduction**. Deductive reasoning starts by asserting a general rule and proceeds to a guaranteed specific conclusion in a limited case. If the original assertion is true, the conclusion must be true in deductive reasoning. In my example above, suppose I start with the general principle (A) that bleach is suitable for cleaning porcelain objects. Then, I observe (B) that my sink is a porcelain object. The conclusion (C) is then logically certain that bleach would effectively clean my sink.

3. **Abduction**. Abductive reasoning begins with limited and necessarily incomplete observations and proceeds to the likeliest possible explanation for what experience has revealed. It does so by the method of hypothesis, or an educated guess at an explanation, a hypothesis that must be tested against reality to be proven.

For example, I want to clean my sink with the best possible cleaner for my family. I might use plain soap, an all-natural soap my children recommend, a cleaner my wife recommends that contains hydrogen peroxide, a cleanser labeled "for porcelain" the woman who cleans our home prefers, or a cleaner that includes bleach, which I like. Each option has a proponent in my family who strongly supports its use. I initially prefer the cleanser containing bleach because my mother recommended it; however, I also try all the other cleansers recommended before concluding that, given family members' concerns, the hydrogen peroxide-based cleaner is the best choice. This is an example of abductive reasoning, which we consciously or unconsciously use in everyday life. Abductive logic yields the kind of daily decision-making that does its best with the information that can be acquired, which often is incomplete, and draws a conclusion based on the best available evidence. It then tests its findings.

Importantly, abductive reasoning is at the center of a scientific approach to understanding and at the center of other forms of intellectual progress as well. Neither induction nor deduction can provide intellectual explanations of phenomena. All scientific inquiry begins with a problem and one or more hypotheses or ideas about the best explanation or solution to the problem. This has important implications because it "dethrones" the positivist notion of knowledge as based on "the facts alone." Instead, all facts are identified within some interpretive framework. Science, for example, is interested in developing and analyzing facts. Nevertheless, those facts are identified, developed, and analyzed within a theoretical framework, a hypothesis, or a theory about how the world is organized.

The ability of a thinker to engage in a pragmatic intellectual endeavor involves thinking in what Peirce called a "scientific manner" about problems. This leads directly to understanding abduction as a logical method intimately connected to a pragmatic philosophy. The pragmatic approach is applicable in many situations where logical certainty is impossible, as is always the case with politics, where information is inconclusive and different methods have support.

In the first stage of an abductive inquiry, a hypothesis is created. For example, "I believe that shrinking the national debt without social instability is best achieved by selective tax increases on the wealthiest segment of society." In the second stage, a deduction is used to derive predictions: "If selective tax increases were to work, small but significant increases in tax rates on the wealthy should bring down the national debt without increasing social inequality." In the third stage, induction is used to verify the assumptions by searching for facts: "After enactment of a small increase in tax rates on the wealthiest one percent of Americans, it was noted that the deficit fell by X while lower and middle-class incomes and purchasing power remained stable." If the process does not yield appropriate findings to validate the hypothesis, the abductive cycle is to be repeated until a verified theory or course of action is reliably established.

Abduction and Decision-Making

More than one author has worked out the implications of abductive thinking for government, bureaucracy, and political calculation.[68] This approach for political decision-making implies that policymakers are best served by making minor adjustments to the current political reality as they test the results of their policy choices. Minor adjustments, if successful, will inevitably result in further adjustments. If they are unsuccessful, the abductive cycle of experimentation on alternative hypotheses can continue until a sound policy preference can be established.[69]

This is important because abduction is sometimes referred to as "reasoning to the best solution in unclear decision-making situations." In political decision-making, there is always an element of conflict, obscurity, and uncertainty about policy decisions and their implications. Decisions such as "Should we raise taxes?" or "Should there be a flatter tax system or a more graduated system?" provoke arguments on every side of the question, and decision-makers must make and initiate policy decisions under conditions of uncertainty. While various proponents may argue that their solution is infallibly correct, those who make decisions inevitably make decisions in a state of some degree of uncertainty. The statements of certainty so common among political figures may be little more than an attempt to avoid the consequences of any uncertainty among their followers and colleagues.

Karl Popper mounts a sustained argument for pragmatic policy incrementalism in his seminal book, *The Open Society and Its Enemies*: "Many policy possibilities lack testability. Not only does this increase the risk of failure, but it also means there is no way for the utopian engineers to improve their plans."[70] This lack of testability and potential for incremental policy change explains, for example, the continued failure under Socialist and Communist regimes of all kinds of "five year" and other plans.[71] Popper's policy preference is that of piecemeal reform, as he clearly states:

> And it is a fact that my social theory (which favors gradual and piecemeal reform, reform controlled by a critical comparison between expected and achieved results) contrasts strongly with my theory of method, which happens to be a theory of scientific and intellectual revolutions.[72]

Popper opposes vast and unverifiable attempts to fundamentally restructure society based on the theoretical ideas of experts and the resultant social planning. In his view, such programs are fundamentally irrational and impossible, since scientifically testing such plans is pragmatically impossible. When the planners' actions fail to achieve their predicted results —as Popper thinks is inevitably the case—leaders have no method for determining what went wrong with their plan. The primary problem results from an irrational approach to political decision-making.

Fallibilism and Freedom

The fact that most political and practical reasoning takes place under circumstances where there is some degree of uncertainty, obscurity, diversity of opinion, numerous facts to be explained, and no clear decision obtainable leads to another principle central to Peirce's way of doing philosophy: Fallibilism. Fallibilism is a principle of humility—a characteristic notably lacking in much contemporary political conversation. Pragmaticism does not promise absolute certainty. All theories and actions taken on such theories are subject to revision based on additional information or a better explanation of the information at hand. There is always the potential for incompleteness or error.

In other words, where rules of action are involved, opinions must be subject to change, and any theory or explanation of the facts may be wrong. In political terms, the principle of fallibilism means that any decision made by those in leadership could, in principle, be incorrect and require adjustment, however sure of success we may be at the time a policy is adopted.[73] In politics, there is an unusual degree of uncertainty concerning what unforeseen and unexpected consequences may follow any decision.

Fallibilism, or the realization that all human thought should be seen as revisable in the light of experience, is essential to another value of our society: freedom of thought and speech. If I possess the unquestionable truth about policy matters, I may ignore, suppress, or distort others' positions since my opponents are felt to be certainly wrong. If, however, I understand that I am fallible in my own opinions and policy preferences (however deeply held), then it is crucial and essential to participation in political life and to the operation of a free political system that conflicting views be able to access the public square, so that policymakers, and in a free society, citizens, can make wise judgments about matters of importance.

Freedom, therefore, finds its most secure grounding in the sense that no one person or group has access to the truth about matters of public policy, nor is everything a matter of "Will to Power," as the Nietzscheans would have it. Instead, our understanding of political reality is limited and subject to incompleteness and the necessity for change and adaptation.

One of the most attractive features of Peirce's pragmatism, as it relates to practical matters of political thought, has to do with the "critical common-sensism" he endorses.[74] Peirce bases his system on human "common sense," the fundamental reality and reasonableness of our common sense understanding of the world and its attributes. However, pragmaticist common sense is not naïve common sense. Our "common sense" understanding of phenomena is not always correct. Peirce recommends a critical "common-sensism" subject to revision based on future discovery. The potential results of criticism, doubt, and further inquiry always control the pragmaticist method. There can be no definite, established limit or end to freedom in the human search for understanding in any area in such a system of thought, including politics and government. Our "common sense" can be and often is wrong, and therefore, given human fallibility, any view is subject to further investigation.

Evolutionary Love, Political Theory and Sophia-Agapism

From 1891 to 1893, Peirce wrote a series of articles collectively known as "A Guess at the Riddle."[75] In the pieces, Peirce sets out a metaphysical understanding of the world based on chance, necessity, and love. In his view, the process of evolution, which lies at the basis of much of his thought, involves the response of creation and creatures to the circumstances of existence through orderly evolution by natural law and the impact of love.[76] "Agapism" is the term Peirce uses for the cherishing or self-giving, sacrificial love at work in creation and all human endeavors.

Chance, Necessity, and Love

In Peirce's view, order emerges from chaos, which we might call in today's quantum language "pure potentiality."[77] In modern quantum physics, this idea gives rise to the view that there is a transition from the potential to the actual when there is an observation or reduction of the wave packet.[78] This potentiality exists before the laws of nature and is the source and ground of whatever exists.[79] While Peirce emphasizes the idea of chance, I would highlight the importance of "unrealized potential." Chance exists because of the existence of multiple potential outcomes. Potential lies beneath chance as one of the possible routes that the evolution of any system, including a political system, might take.

In law and politics, the available ranges of action are much more significant and complex than the changes occurring at the quantum phenomena level. In general, societies have multiple routes open to them for addressing social problems and creating a more harmonious society. There is rarely one and only one option available. Nevertheless, some options are always either practically or theoretically unlikely to succeed. Finally, due to the inherent complexity of any society, options that initially seem likely to succeed may fail.

In "A Guess at the Riddle," Peirce expounded a theory of creation that anticipates modern cosmology in which he sets out his view that there is an evolutionary principle at work in the universe that we can call "love." As one author puts it:

> "Evolutionary Love" is one of Peirce's most fascinating philosophical writings. It describes the existence of a cosmic principle of love throughout the universe creatively supporting the formation of new evolutionary forms. This love is a cherishing form of love, because it recognizes that which is lovely in another being and sympathetically supports its existence. Peirce calls his new theory "agapism," and he contrasts it with evolutionary theories that are based on a selfish form of love; these preach "the Gospel of Greed." Peirce points out the occurrence of such selfish, greed-based thinking in the modern politico-economical structures, and in Darwin's biological principle of natural selection based on the competition of private interests. On the other hand, agapism promotes a devotion to helping one's neighbors, and is a true doctrine of Christian ethics.[80]

This quotation by Nicholas Guardiano sets out one reason Peirce's agapism is important for political philosophy: Peirce's philosophical program was partially motivated by a desire to overcome a kind of excessive *laissez-faire* capitalism prominent at the time by setting out his view of the role of cherishing love in human society. Peirce's view is that the universe itself is characterized not just by competition or the blind search for survival, but also by a kind of cherishing love. The emergence of the order of things is not merely deterministic or the result of chance; it is partially the result of the fundamental relationality of the universe, a relationality that expresses itself in a kind of love.

Peirce's notion of an agapistic aspect of the universe is reminiscent of the early Greek philosopher Empedocles. In Empedocles's view, Love and Strife are complementary agents in forming the universe from elementary components. Empedocles' views are similar to those of Peirce, whose triad of Chance, Order, and Love mirrors, in some ways, earlier ideas. Peirce's "Chance" is similar to Empedocles' "Strife," and Empedocles' Love is similar to Peirce's notion of agapistic cherishing.[81]

Regarding political society, Peirce undermines the modern fascination with power and power politics, not denying the existence and importance of power but relativizing its significance in light of something more fundamental: relationality. In other words, Peirce's approach provides an ontological basis for the role of cherishing love or a kind of deep relationality in morality and politics. This insight is given additional strength by the developments in physics and other disciplines since he wrote.

Peirce wrote before modern relativity and quantum theory, and before the abundant evidence recently provided by science that an element of relationality is built into the universe. Beginning with Einstein's insights, the notion of the world as built on independent units of matter connected by forces acting on fundamental particles has been continually undermined. Relativity theory holds that time and space are relational phenomena. According to current science, particles are waves or "excitements" in a universal field that permeates the universe. The quantum phenomenon of "Entanglement" and chaos theory point towards a *pervasive element of relationality* embedded in the universe at its most fundamental level.[82]

One can easily see that certain aspects of quantum physics call into question a mechanistic interpretation of reality on which the modern world and modern politics primarily rely.

Three are of particular importance:

1. The quantum world is discontinuous. Energy travels in indivisible units, known as "quanta," from which we take the term "quantum physics." This quantization of light means that the world does not unfold smoothly or linearly, as modernity believed.

2. Fundamental entities, such as electrons, have incompatible characteristics. Sometimes they appear wave-like, and sometimes particle-like, a phenomenon known as "wave–particle duality." In particular, the presence of an observer and the character of the observations impact whether fundamental entities take on wave-like or particle-like characteristics. In other words, the notion of an observer outside the observation is undermined. This indicates a fundamental relationality at the root of reality.

3. When fundamental entities come into a relationship with one another, they become entangled in a non-local relationship, which appears to be a non-causal form of connection. Such entangled particles act in concert, in violation of the principle that no signal can travel faster than the speed of light, a phenomenon known as "quantum entanglement." The phenomenon of "entanglement" signals an interconnected world not made up of separate entities or phenomena.

None of these principles are compatible with the modern, post-Enlightenment world's notion of a universe that can be explained in a materialistic, mechanical way.[83]

In particular, the profound interrelatedness of the universe at a fundamental level calls into question the kind of mechanical materialism that characterized modern science. Postmodern science has moved from an atomistic to a relational, holistic view of reality. This new view should impact every area of human knowing, including political thought.

The physicist Argyris Nicolaidis puts it this way:

In conclusion, a mode of thinking has been reached where the primacy focuses on an "interactive being," a being constant in relation to the other and being in continuous *ex-stasis* to reach the other. This relational mode of existence, which has been associated with creative growth, novelty, and free development is qualified as agape. Agape then is something more than an emotional state or sentimental experience it is a very principle of existence....[84]

Thus, postmodern science leaves open the idea of a fundamentally relational mode of existence that results in creativity and growth. The nature of the created order provides a basis for the evolution of a kind of love in practical politics and other areas of human inquiry.[85]

Agapism and Politics and Morals

According to Peirce, this *agapistic love* manifests itself in persons and communities in three ways:

1. Agapistic love may affect a people or a community, and its collective personality as an idea or experience is communicated to individuals in sympathy with the common connection of the group's collective mind.

2. Agapistic love may affect an individual, enabling that individual to apprehend an idea or appreciate the attractiveness of an idea due to an increase in sympathy with his community under the influence of a striking experience or development of thought.

3. Agapistic love may impact an individual independently of human affection by virtue of an attraction exercised directly on the mind before comprehension.[86]

As examples of the three kinds of experience of which Peirce is speaking, consider the post-resurrection appearances of Christ to his disciples. These were striking appearances to a group in sympathy with one another, such that the group was enlightened, changed, and motivated to action. Second, consider Peirce's own example: Paul's experience on the Road to Damascus. This striking event brought Paul into sympathy with the Christian movement.[87] Peirce calls the third kind of example "the divination of genius," by which a single individual is struck by an idea that immediately attracts them. An example is the famous incident of an apple falling at Isaac Newton's feet, giving him the immediate notion of gravity. The idea is that there are events and moments of revelation in science, politics, religion, and other areas that contain a bestowal of meaning that can and does change the unfolding future.[88]

From the perspective of political thought, all three characteristics of agapistic love are important. First, there are incidental moments of genius by which political thought is moved forward in a sympathetic group. This might, for example, be seen in the decisions of the Constitutional Convention of 1789. Second, there are times when an individual who is not in sympathy with a society or political system is struck by some virtue in that system and immediately grasps its importance. For example, this might be seen in some of those who favored communism but whose faith in freedom was kindled by contact with democracies. Finally, there are times when ideas formulated by individuals or small groups impact an entire society, as perhaps when the ideals of the Enlightenment and its preference for political democracy influenced the American nation, leading to the American Revolution and national freedom through the Declaration of Independence, drafted initially by Thomas Jefferson.

Love and the Gospel of Greed

Peirce's theory of "Agapism" can be contrasted to the "Gospel of Greed" prevalent in American society, which he thought unworthy of any human civilization. Peirce was appalled by how Social Darwinism used the scientific principles of natural selection and survival of the fittest to justify a social organization and social policy based on unlimited, selfish striving for power and position, which he called "the Gospel of Greed."[89] In Peirce's time, Social Darwinism supported a form of unrestrained economic conflict and exploitation on the grounds that a survival of the fittest kind of economic organization was the most efficient way to organize society. One reason for Peirce's support of an "agapistic" theory of evolution has to do with his disapproval of this approach to economic organization. He felt that the kind of political and economic structures that this way of thinking promoted were immoral. This does not mean that Peirce opposed free enterprise. His opposition was to a particular form that operated without an underlying morality based on a healthy relationality.

Against this "Gospel of Greed," Peirce posited his own "agapism" as involving devotion to ideas, the search for truth in community, and a way of life built on an *agapistic* personal and communal ethic. In this view, human beings do not find their fulfillment in unlimited self-promotion but as participants in a community of persons engaged in a joint endeavor. In the case of American democracy, this involves the creation of a society based on freedom, equality, and a search for the common good.

Human beings will not, however, search for the common good, or for ideals like justice, freedom, and equality, unless they believe that such ideals are real and worth the energy, physical, mental, and emotional, required for their realization. Just as science becomes impossible if one loses contact with the structures of the natural world being investigated or comes to believe that there are no real relations to be studied, so also the achievement of a just society becomes impossible if humans lose the conviction that justice is an actual state worth the self-discipline and sacrifice necessary to achieve it.

There must also be a sense that citizens are part of a joint enterprise bound together by common practical interests worth supporting, strengthening, extending, and finally expressed in a personal and unforced willingness to sacrifice for the common good. Unfortunately, modern society has failed in these areas, driven by a mechanistic view of reality and politics, in which power is the fundamental and decisive factor.

Sophio-agapism joins the pragmaticist love of truth for its own sake with an essential loving cherishing of human society, institutions, and other human beings in unbroken unity. This kind of politics values the other for their own sake. It promotes the health and flourishing of the other, not because of any underlying agreement on either fundamental ideas or policy prescriptions but because of their inherent worth. Sophio-agapism does not threaten Western individuality. It provides a framework within which human beings can flourish. In the end, agapism of any kind values the other, affirming their importance, and seeks not power over the other but a healthy communion with the other, which can only be described by the word "love."[90]

Sophio-agapism is not an emotional substitute for practical "real politics." It is not a substitute for functional institutions, capable leadership, compromise, or decision. It does not ignore or minimize the harsher realities of political life. Instead, *sophio-agapism* recognizes the importance of a rational and relational order that must sit beneath any functional social order tacitly guiding its emerging order.

CHAPTER 3

COMMUNAL FOUNDATION FOR SOPHIA-AGAPISM

C. S. Peirce's friend and colleague, Josiah Royce, was born in a small community in California. He graduated from the University of California, Berkeley, in 1875 and then did a year of postgraduate study in Germany, reading Kant and other German philosophers. In 1876, he entered Johns Hopkins University in Baltimore. Royce received his doctorate in 1878, taught in California, and then went to Harvard as a lecturer in philosophy. In 1885, he was appointed an assistant professor; in 1892, he was appointed a full professor. He continued at Harvard until he died in 1916. Royce was sympathetic to the Christian faith, and one of his significant works, *The Problem of Christianity*, attempts to create a philosophical basis for belief in the modern world. His most famous work, *Loyalty*, was published in 1908.[91]

65

Pragmatic Idealism

Royce attempted to unify the insights of idealism and pragmatism. His mature philosophy can be seen as an "Absolute Idealism" or an "Absolute Pragmatism." For Royce, human knowledge arises from the pragmatic search for the truth in which humans resolve doubt in some area of inquiry. Like Peirce, Royce views truth as the view confirmed at the end of a process of inquiry by a community devoted to such investigation. Truth is found when the community of inquirers reaches a consensus on a matter under investigation. This constitutes Royce's "Absolute Pragmaticism." It is absolute because the investigation ends when the relevant community of inquirers agree on the solution to the problem.[92]

Royce was impressed that intellectually discovered truth displays a remarkable coherence with reality. He concluded that there must be some connection between the human mind and the external world. In his famous argument from error, Royce noticed that even when our thoughts are erroneous, we intend to find something we call "truth," indicating that our search's object exists, at least in a world of ideas. This exemplifies Royce's "Absolute Idealism." Royce believed that the universe is constituted of these ideas, a kind of "noetic truth" humans seek and think they will find at the end of a process. This is true in religion, morals, and politics, as much as in science. Thus, Royce believes that

> ...whoever talks of any sort of truth, be that truth, moral or scientific, the truth of common sense or the truth of philosophy, inevitably implies, in all his assertions about truth, that the world of truth of whose type of consciousness is a world possessing a rational

and spiritual unity, is a conscious world of experience, whose experience is higher in its level than is the type of our human minds, but whose life is such that our life belongs as part to this living whole.[93]

Royce believes there is a universal mind and that the visible universe reflects that mind. This universal mind is not of the type of a human mind, which is a product of human evolution and integrated with the human body. Instead, this universal mind is the ground of those minds and our universe's intelligibility.

At this point, it is worth asking, "Does reality itself give us some reason to believe that the mind 'goes all the way down' as Royce believed?" There are several reasons to think that there is a fundamental mental component to reality:

1. First, there is the mysterious nature of mathematics. Its features indicate that mathematics has a noetic or mental reality. When making mathematical discoveries, most mathematicians think they have "found" something already there. This element of discovery seems a solid reason to believe in the noetic reality of mathematical truth.

2. Second, scientists are frequently amazed at how their discoveries explain relationships in the material world. New theoretical discoveries ideally explain an existing relationship between the constituent parts of the investigated reality. Albert Einstein's famous discovery of relativity theory expressed in the famous equation, $E=MC^2$, is a case in point. As the existence of the atomic bomb indicates, energy does equal the mass of an object times the speed of light squared. The theory expressed in equations of physics seems

to describe an existing, invisible, noetic relationship mirroring physical reality. There are many other examples. This intelligibility of the universe appears to "go all the way down," as it were, so that even at the subatomic level, where the distinction between matter and energy begins to disappear, the ability of science to uncover relationships that seem to have "always existed" is remarkable.

3. Third, and this is a feature of reality that quantum physics caused science to confront, our minds appear to be part of the universe we human beings observe. My mind is not "outside of the universe looking in" but a part of a flow of reality examining some aspect of that flow. The universe must have some form of "mental potential"; otherwise, it is difficult to explain the human mind's ability to understand the flow of the surrounding reality of which I am a part. As physicist and philosopher David Bohm said, "The mind may have a structure similar to the universe."[94]

4. Finally, and this is where we come to currently debated scientific matters, our universe is intelligible in some mysterious way because it is seemingly at least partially "made up of" information. Some physicists believe that reality is made up of information and that the universe is like a giant computer. In the words of physicist John Wheeler, "it is a bit."[95] The nature of reality indicates that information, meaning, and intelligibility are simply a part of what is at a fundamental level.

One does not need to go as far as Wheeler and some current theorists to be of the view that, in some way, intelligibility is fundamental to reality. The world as we know it is made up of matter, energy, and intelligible relationships between them. This intelligibility seems to be a fundamental component of reality, not an emergent phenomenon that "sits on top of" matter and energy. Wherever one finds matter and energy, science discovers intelligible relationships (information and meaning) that seem to mirror some aspect of the reality constituted by that matter and energy.

For these reasons, it is fair to propose that, at the end of the enterprise of human knowledge, humans will discover that "mind" or "order" or "ideality" in the form of irreducible comprehensibility is a fundamental aspect of our universe. In the words of physicist John Polkinghorne, we live in "a world of deep and beautiful order—a universe shot through with signs of mind."[96]

One aspect of the universe being shot through with signs of mind is the capacity of reasoning creatures to sense and investigate both a physical and a moral order in the universe. This mental aspect of reality in no way diminishes the importance of the physical aspects of reality, nor does it contradict the pragmaticist method of inquiry. Even noetic realities must be investigated to be understood in a manner consistent with the nature of the subject matter being investigated and the degree of certainty attainable concerning the subject matter under study.

The Reality of Universals

Like Peirce, Royce believes that universal ideas, such as "justice," possess independent noetic reality. Nominalism endangers human reason and society because it undercuts the reality of these noetic realities. As a result, Royce distinguishes between an idea's internal and external meaning. Because thoughts inevitably arise in an individual's mental world, they have an inner meaning and purpose. These ideas, however, must refer to and be validated by external actors who constitute a community of interpretation to have meaning. In a clear statement of his views concerning the external reality of social universals, Royce writes:

> The object of perception is the datum of sensation: the objects of conceptual knowledge are the universals. So also, this third kind of knowledge has its proper kind of object, *social phenomenon*. Whether the object be yourself or the community in which you belong or any social order of any type, it is by this third sort of knowledge that you know it. To this essentially distinctive cognitive process I give the name 'interpretation.'[97]

For Royce, abstract ideas are based on sensation, exist in the knower's mind, and are validated by the interpretation of a community of inquiry as it moves toward a consensus of understanding through a process of interpretation. Regarding ideals such as justice, we are faced with fundamental human reactions to social situations and internal relationships between these reactions based on the conceptual understanding of the knower and the social interpretation of the community. Within human history, the interpretive process is a continuous process of conceptual development, for the interpretation process is continuous within history. It is not completed within history, nor can it be.[98]

It is necessary to distinguish between this view and a kind of simplistic, static view of universals. Both Peirce and Royce accept the evolutionary and developmental character of human understanding of the world, including that part of the world that I term "noetic." The interpretive process by which noetic realities are uncovered and applied to concrete societies is a developmental process. "Justice" does not exist in an unchanging world of forms but in concrete, changing human societies.

Morality and Moral Theory

Royce is important partially because he carefully reconciles the idea of individualism with the notion of community. His balanced approach was indicated by his support for the First World War despite being inclined toward pacifism. He was a proponent of social and organizational change and preserving the best of the past and tradition. His work is supremely wise and balanced. If for no reason other than the last, Royce's view should be heard today.

Following the notion that there is a fundamental mental aspect to reality is the view that there is also a fundamental moral element to human life. Royce examines this moral reality in his most-read book, *The Philosophy of Loyalty*, where he set out a communal ethical theory based on the fundamental virtue of loyalty. His approach has four components:

1. The fundamental ethical imperative is "Be Loyal."
2. One cannot be loyal in the abstract but must be loyal in specific circumstances to certain causes.
3. Each individual must choose the causes to which they will remain loyal.
4. Finally, in the end, each individual must be loyal to loyalty itself, which will bring persons into an ever-expanding commitment to the virtue of loyalty.[99]

For Royce, loyalty is the willing devotion of an individual to a cause outside of themselves.[100] Therefore, causes, even if they are institutional, are essentially communal. In other words, the human capacity for loyalty is essentially social and binds humans with a community of others who share our commitment to a cause. Loyalty is a communal virtue founded on personal choice that inevitably involves the individual in a community with others.

Loyalty vs. Individual Will

This social aspect of loyalty opposes systems of virtue founded on purely individual will and self-authentication. This puts Royce in immediate opposition to Nietzsche, who is the object of criticism in *Loyalty*. All purely individualistic ethical systems based on the human will to power are doomed to failure for several reasons. First, power is always dependent on good fortune and luck, and many who begin life in the search for power will fail. Secondly, one who seeks power will never be satisfied, for the desire for power is insatiable. Third, the one seeking power puts him or herself at odds with the universe itself, inevitably leading to a clash between the power seeker and reality.[101] Power is not as fundamental to social reality as relationships. When a person or society makes power fundamental, they inevitably place themselves against the basic character of reality. In other words, the Nietzschean ideal is fundamentally flawed.

Since human beings are social by nature, one who solely seeks personal power is ultimately doomed to isolation and a failure to achieve true humanity. Think of Alexander the Great, Caesar, Napoleon, Hitler, or Stalin, all alone at life's end, often with no friends, no allies, no family, and no meaningful social relationships not based on their power and position. Since the development of Greek tragedy, wise people have understood that fate treats ill those who seek their own glory and self-fulfillment at the expense of others. As the chorus puts it at the end of *Antigone*:

> Of happiness, far the greater part is wisdom and reverence towards the gods. Proud words of arrogant man, in the end, meet punishment, great as his pride was great, until at last he is schooled in wisdom.[102]

The danger and ultimate failure of a morality based on power is true not only of military or political conquerors but also of those who worship power in business, law, and religion—in any human endeavor.

The Community of Seekers

Loyalty inevitably draws human beings from isolation into meaningful, self-giving communities. Devotion to any cause involves joining others with similar dedication. In addition, our commitments draw us into contact with those with different and perhaps opposing beliefs. As we must confront persons and groups with other loyalties, we must adjust and negotiate our allegiances to place them into a harmonious relationship. This inevitably involves the social skills of dialogue, discussion, tolerance, compromise, and growth—virtues much needed in Western society today.

Communalism does not mean extinguishing individuality. The social demands of the community in no way eliminate the importance of individuality—in fact, community presupposes individuality. Only free moral actors can exhibit loyalty. Therefore, loyalty requires the free choice of each member of the cause. Far from extinguishing individual freedom, Royce's ideas inherently support human freedom and work contrary to any attempt to force a particular morality on individuals.[103] Without freedom, loyalty cannot truly exist.

Because humans are finite, we cannot possibly be loyal to all possible causes. For example, I cannot be a loyal citizen of France, but I can be a loyal citizen of the United States. I cannot be a faithful member of my neighbor's family, but I can be faithful to my own. I cannot be loyal to every religion in the world, but I can be devoted to my own. I cannot be loyal to every company in the world, but I can be dedicated to the firm I work for. This does not mean I am antagonistic to other nations, families, religions, businesses, etc. It means that I am loyal to the communities to which I belong and in which I participate.

Limits of Loyalty and Loyalty to Loyalty

We now come to the most frequent critique of Royce: There are a lot of bad causes to which people have in the past and will give their loyalty in the future. For example, members of organized crime organizations can be incredibly loyal to their group. Many members of the Nazi Party were devoted to the party, even to death. Every teacher has seen a young person cover for a cheating student out of misguided loyalty to a classmate. The list of misplaced, negative, evil allegiances could continue forever. The fact that we can have misguided loyalties is a strong argument against the importance of loyalty as a virtue.[104]

A second negative phenomenon we observe in loyalists is that their loyalty is occasionally unquestioning and unwise. For example, a certain kind of patriotism is blind to the nation's faults and willing to defend what is not defensible. Closer to home, some parents are loyal to their children, defending behavior that is not genuinely defensible. Some businessmen exhibit loyalty to their company or firm to the point that they cannot see or oppose unwise or immoral behavior.

Interestingly, we can appreciate the value of this misplaced or misguided loyalty even while denying its ultimate importance. For example, many people, myself included, can admire certain aspects of the crime family of Don Vito Corleone portrayed in the novel and movie *The Godfather* while recognizing its ultimate evil and twisted nobility.[105] Misplaced loyalty and blind or excessive loyalty constantly threaten the true virtue of loyalty.

In response to these objections, Royce developed the notion of "loyalty to loyalty." Loyalty to loyalty requires judgment. If one is to be loyal to loyalty, it is necessary to develop discrimination as to the kinds of causes to which one will be loyal and the limitations to any given loyalty. I should not, for example, be devoted to a political party that advocates killing innocent people. I should not be loyal to a social club that denies fundamental human freedoms.

Determining how much loyalty should be given to a cause can be challenging. I may be loyal to my nation, but still called to oppose an unjust war. I may support my employer but refuse to engage in illegal or immoral behavior. The virtue of loyalty must be exhibited with wisdom and discrimination. In other words, it requires *phronesis*. Loyalty requires practical wisdom concerning the causes to which I will be loyal and the extent of that loyalty. There is a sophic (wisdom-related) aspect to any truly moral loyalty.

Another standard attack on any communal theory of morality or politics involves the fear that communal norms will extinguish personhood and personal responsibility. For Royce, the virtue of loyalty inevitably involves the willing devotion of a human person to a cause greater than themselves.[106] Any cause results in a community because causes are, by definition, social. For a cause to exist and impact society, it must be embodied in a community that advances the cause. However, this community does not diminish the personal because "[L]oyalty is the willing and practical and thoroughgoing devotion of an individual to a cause."[107] Only individuals can give free loyalty to a community. One cannot exist without the other.

There are many implications for the relationship of individuals to a community.

1. First, loyalty means "willing devotion." This implies that any human community is, first and foremost, the result of human decisions, and no true community can be created by force. According to Royce, voluntary societies have an essential role in American society and politics just because they are voluntary. They cannot be commanded into existence.

2. Second, loyalty to a cause involves "personal commitment." It is the loyalty of a human person. For Royce, the incredible diversity of people and their different families, experiences, education, vocations, hobbies, and the like means there will be many different kinds of people and causes within American society.

3. Finally, loyalty involves devotion to a cause greater than ourselves. In other words, loyalty draws us from our isolated individuality into the community. The constant need for a more significant commitment to relativize our lesser loyalties eventually leads to a vision of the "Beloved Community," a perfectly just and moral transcendental community.

Courtesy and Conflict Among Loyalists

Royce is aware that in a society such as America, with many different nationalities, faith communities, political parties, and lobbying groups, the emergence of a community can and does involve the potential for conflict. This conflict can result in disorder and violence, physical, mental, moral, and spiritual. In addition, in a complex society, people will be loyal to many causes, some of which are opposed to one another and have difficulty communicating peacefully with one another. This calls for the virtue of courtesy. Courtesy is an essential expression of loyalty:

> The true value of courtesy in ordinary human intercourse lies in the fact that courtesy is one of the expressions of loyalty to loyalty and helps everyone who either receives or witnesses courtesy to assume a loyal attitude towards all the causes that are represented by the peaceful and reasonable dealings of men to men.[108]

There's no aspect of Royce's thought more critical for contemporary American political discourse than the insight that courtesy is essential in a free society in which people join together to support sometimes differing causes. We cannot truly be loyal to our causes unless we can be courteous to those whose opinions differ. If a free society cannot teach this virtue to its citizens, it is doomed to unfaithful and unreasonable discourse. It only takes a moment's reflection to recognize that much contemporary American discourse has this characteristic. A glance at social media is sufficient to see a great deal of vulgar discourtesy and unreasonable and unpeaceful commentary.

Practically speaking, this virtue of courtesy is assisted by implementing a few simple rules:

1. First, humans should respect the loyalty that others have towards their causes, even when we do not share the same enthusiasm for the causes they support;
2. Second, humans should be more critical towards the causes to which they are loyal than to opposing causes; and
3. Third, humans should give the benefit of the doubt to those loyal to their causes.

Attention to these simple rules of sound social relations would undoubtedly enhance American politics and public life.

Life-enhancing and Life-denying Communities

Royce initially declines to discriminate among causes, preferring to begin his analysis with a definition that embraces all loyalty, misguided, evil, wise, and sound. Although all communities involve the creation of social entities, since not all causes are good causes, not all communities formed to support a cause are on equal footing. To give an obvious example, there's a considerable difference between a church formed to advance the gospel and a criminal organization created to promote a criminal conspiracy. There is a difference between a political party formed to advance the best interest of a society and a political party formed to enslave the majority of the people for the benefit of the few. There's a difference between a society formed to advance the cause of peace and one form to advance the cause of war. Communities formed for criminal, antisocial, or violent purposes are not on the same footing as communities formed to promote some legitimate benefit of society.

A community may begin its life formed for the benefit of society but later become outdated, ineffective, unable to adapt to change, or corrupt and no longer be beneficial or work for the common good of society. In other words, they become unwise. History is filled with businesses and other organizations formed to advance a public benefit that became unable or unwilling to adapt to change in the society they were a part of. History is filled with organizations that, over time, became ineffective in addressing issues. Finally, any society may become corrupted and no longer work for the benefit of the common good. History is filled with organizations that began well and ended corrupt.

In the end, Royce amends his initial definition of loyalty to give it a transcendental basis. Every concrete human loyalty is, in the end, finite and fragmented. Therefore, it is necessary to ground our loyalties in a greater loyalty. Royce's final definition is as follows: "Loyalty is the will to manifest, so far as is possible, the Eternal, that is, the conscious and superhuman unity of life, in the form of the acts of an individual Self."[109] When Royce speaks of the eternal, he speaks of an inclusive conspectus or compendium of all temporary happenings and striving in a single consciousness that fulfills the rational purposes of those who seek a particular form of loyalty.[110] In the end, all finite loyalties must be grounded in a transcendental loyalty to the truth and goodness of every kind to avoid the dangers of any finite determination. For a cause to be good and for a cause to incorporate true reality, it must transcend that which one person or collection of persons can verify in any single human life or the collective life of any finite community.[111]

An Individual Plan of Life

Avoiding misguided loyalties requires individuals to develop a "Plan of Life" for themselves. Creating such a plan is by no means easy, since our society and every society provides multiple encouragements to give our loyalty to various causes. Large portions of our life plans are unconsciously transmitted to us by our society. Every society either consciously or unconsciously steers its members into a plan for their lives. Some people think this socialized life plan is contrary to human freedom. However, there is a positive aspect to what might be called "becoming socialized into a plan of life."

Recognizing that we all need education and instruction in social norms, this socialization does not eliminate the need for individual choice:

> I, and only I, whenever I come to on my own, can morally justify to myself my own plan of life. No outer authority can ever give me the true reason for my duty. Yet I, left to myself can never find a plan of life. I have no inborn ideal naturally present within myself. By nature, I simply go on crying out in a sort of chaotic self-will, according to the momentary play of desire determines.[112]

Human beings need socialization, traditions, expectations, family instruction, and other socialization into the kinds of causes and communities that our society finds life-enhancing. However, there is a tension to be recognized and an interplay that needs to occur. Every individual has to personally own the precise causes and communities within a greater society to which they will belong and give their devotion. Our moral self-consciousness and capacity for healthy social engagement are a function of our social life. As Royce put it, "our moral self-consciousness is a product of our social life. This self is known to each of us through its social contrasts with others and with the will of the community."[113] In this view, the inevitable conflicts of social life are not inevitably negative; they are how human beings grow and develop a personal identity. As Royce eloquently puts it:

In brief, it is our fellows who first startle us out of our natural unconsciousness about our own conduct; and who then, by an endless series of processes of setting us attractive but difficult models, and of socially interfering with our own doings, train us to higher and higher grades and to more and more complex types of self-consciousness regarding what we do and why we do it.[114]

Our self-awareness and identity as human persons are established as we interact with others, who may be critical of our plans, behavior, beliefs, customs, or other social aspects of our identity. They may even actively oppose certain of our most treasured ideas and behaviors. In this way, our fellow human beings train and shape us to transcend our current level of individualization. We refine our identities and commitments as we consider and react to opposing views in our internal and external self-dialogue. As solitary beings, they achieve no social growth. We become true individuals only by entering into society and that society's inevitable conflicts and comparisons.[115]

Levels of Community

As we already mentioned, Royce discusses a problem that any communitarian social philosophy must address: the danger that members of a particular cause or community become unable to recognize the limits of their cause, turn inward, and become instruments of cultish isolation, intolerance, and even oppression. Here, we see the root of what is often called the problem of "Moral Inversion" or what might be called "moral reductionism."[116]

Moral inversion occurs when a particular individual or group makes ultimate a cause that is not genuinely ultimate.

For example, I may belong to a family and be so loyal to my family that I do not recognize my family's responsibility to its neighborhood. I may become so loyal to my neighborhood that I cannot understand the value of loyalty to my town or city. I can become so loyal to my town or city that I cannot be faithful to my state or nation. I may be so loyal to my state or nation that I cannot adequately be loyal to members of the international community. In each case, my subordinate loyalty has become something negative. This problem is especially challenging where politics and state power are involved.

To avoid this problem, Royce recognizes that there are levels of loyalty, and our commitment to any given less-than-ultimate ideal cannot become ultimate without dangers to society. Royce finds this ultimate loyalty in our devotion to loyalty itself and into the gradual merger of our lesser loyalties into the ideal community of the Beloved Community, which is a kind of secular adaptation of the nature of the Christian Church, if the Beloved Community can be separated from that heavenly vision that Christians have always celebrated as their transcendent ideal—the heavenly city come down from God.[117]

Higher forms of community create a spiritual transformation in our loyalties and a greater and deeper love of our communities, as they are relativized by what I will call the "Transcendental Community" of the ideally just society.[118] No human community or existing cause can be healthily sustained without it being related to a higher ideal that relativizes and renders penultimate loyalty. In our society, many people regard politics as ultimate and the achievement of what they conceived to be a just economic and social order to be the ultimate good. This can manifest itself in an immoral fanaticism.

Over the course of the 20th century, great evils were committed by people devoted to causes that were not evil in themselves but became so by becoming ultimate. We see today the growing danger of another outbreak of the kind of fanaticism that created the Holocaust and the great human suffering under Stalin, Mao, Hitler, Pot Pol, and other leaders of movements that became ultimate to their followers.

Healthy and wise loyalty inevitably draws us from isolation into a community. Our loyalty to a cause inevitably involves joining with others who possess a similar loyalty. Only free persons can exhibit loyalty, and so devotion to loyalty requires the free choice of each individual member of a cause. In addition, our loyalties draw us into contact with those who have different and perhaps opposing loyalties. As we must confront these other loyalties, we are forced to adjust and negotiate our loyalties to place them into a harmonious relationship with others. This inevitably involves the social skills of dialogue and discussion, tolerance, compromise, and growth. These are virtues much needed today.

From Loyalty to Beloved Community

Pragmatist philosophers struggled with a problem at the root of American democracy: "What is the proper way to coordinate between individual self-interest and the needs of the community?" Peirce leaned towards incrementalism and careful change in institutions after investigation and analysis.[119] Royce, as we have seen, sought a careful balance between individuals and communities.

Like Royce, William James was generally against largeness and oligarchic or imperialistic behavior. Despite his fundamental individualism, James supported a kind of organic, communal form of social organization:

I am against bigness and greatness in all their forms, and with the invisible molecular moral forces that work from individual to individual, stealing in through the crannies of the world like so many soft rootlets, or like the capillary oozing of water, and yet rending the hardest monuments of man's pride, if you give them time. The bigger the unit you deal with, the hollower, the more brutal, the more mendacious is the life displayed. So I am against all big organizations as such, national ones first and foremost; against all big successes and big results; and in favor of the eternal forces of truth which always work in the individual and immediately unsuccessful way, under-dogs always, till history comes, after they are long dead, and puts them on top. —You need take no notice of these ebullitions of spleen, which are probably quite unintelligible to anyone but myself.[120]

This quote expresses a preference for small businesses, small organizations, families, and individuals as opposed to "big business," "big government," "big empires," and the like. Bigness is generally less human, less moral, and less connected to the heart's deepest needs than small businesses, governments, political units, bureaucracies, etc. Here is the way one commentator puts James' view:

The problem of empires, be they imperial national projects (such as the U.S.'s presumption to control the Philippines) or conceptual philosophical totalities (such as Hegel's argument for the state form as the highest form of actualization), arises less from their content than from their size. The idea that any idea, polity, or system of meaning can encompass everything, everyone, and everywhere directly contradicts the aspirations of pragmatism, which is always provisional and partial. The politics of anti-greatness implies a turn away from totality, a theme with a particular resonance in the contemporary political realm.[121]

James was interested in the individual and in the smallest units and the elements that made up a complex system, such as a society or political organization, as well as the larger system itself. One essential lesson contemporary Americans can learn from the pragmatic approach to politics is the importance of small steps to solve significant problems, as well as small communities, such as families, small businesses, small social agencies, and even small churches. "Human-sized" institutions are essential to human flourishing and harmonious social order.

Like his mentor William James, Dewey was a defender of a kind of individualism that makes the individual, and their self-development, the supreme end of political thinking. This radical individualism translates into a radical democratic theory in which the individual becomes the center of all political calculation. For Dewey, society is composed of individuals, and it is the individual that sits at the foundation of any democratic society:

Society is composed of individuals: no philosophy, whatever its pretensions to novelty, can question or alter this obvious and basic fact. Hence these three alternatives: Society must exist for the sake of individuals; or individuals must have their ends and ways of living set for them by society; *or else society and individuals are correlative, organic, to one another*, society requiring the service and subordination of individuals and at the same time existing to serve them. Beyond these three views, none seems to be logically conceivable. (Emphasis added)[122]

For Dewey, individual and social elements are fundamental to society and exist in a mutually beneficial, organic, and "correlative" relationship.[123] Individuals are not atomistic units but are formed by a society within families and various social institutions.[124]

A *sophio-agapic* individualism is better termed "communal individualism," whereby the individual finds self-actualization as a part of society. This individualism does not deny government the ability and even duty to plan and control a great deal of the activity of individuals, especially in the economic arena.[125] Ultimately, one cannot base a *sophio-agapic* ideal on fundamental individualism or collectivism. Thinking of individuals and communities as existing in a dialectical relationship is wiser. Neither individuals nor communities are fundamental. Individuals arise in the context of human communities, and human communities are formed to meet the needs of human individuals. Where the individual becomes primary, the community begins to dissolve. We see this in our society. Where the community becomes primary, individuals are suppressed. Avoiding these two extremes involves a constant interplay and adjustment between the individual and the community.

This is precisely the position that Royce takes in *Loyalty*. In Royce, we have the most intensive discussion among the pragmatist philosophers as to the meaning of community for society. Human individual human beings are linked together in a web of loyalties, family, friendships, businesses, churches, political units, moral causes, and the like. These loyalties freely bind human actors together in causes and relationships that draw them out of an isolated individualism into a host of relationships that constitute civilized life.[126] These social relationships both constitute an individual and give human life its unique character.

Communities and Beloved Community

Communities are not all alike, though they share certain features. Nor are all loyalties equal in value or capacity to promote human flourishing. There are communities formed for small and almost unimportant purposes. There are what might be called "tribal communities" that exist for only a few persons with similar interests. Utilitarian communities are formed for limited purposes. Businesses and partnerships are examples. Recreational communities are formed to gather people together to pursue a hobby. There are all kinds of communities, important and unimportant. Therefore, it is essential to distinguish between communities.

Nevertheless, all communities of whatever type have characteristics in common. They are bound together by loyalty to a cause or undertaking, not by absolute identity or the merging of individuals. In any true community, individuals retain their uniqueness, individuality, and perspective. Communities look backward (and, therefore, have traditions), and all living communities look forward (and thus are somewhat oriented toward the future). For example, a fraternity or sorority has a tradition into which members are initiated, while also constantly taking in new pledges to sustain itself into the future. Royce calls these two aspects of communities "tradition" and "hope." These two kinds of communities are important in overcoming parochialism of vision among community members.

All natural communities have a past and anticipate a future in which their members find meaning and hope related to the subject of the community.[127] In other words, all thriving communities can sustain their fundamental values over time amidst an ever-changing and evolving reality. Communities exist in time and space and yet are always oriented in some way toward the future. As noted above, this occurs within a history that will never be complete and in which deeply held ideals will never be fully achieved.

There is also a ranking and moral hierarchy of communities. The search for a truthful, just, and life-enhancing community finds its ultimate symbol in Royce's notion of a "Beloved Community." The great danger of any communitarian philosophy, and perhaps especially political philosophy, is the danger of a kind of tribalism that enforces a limited and parochial worldview on its members. Royce attacks this danger from two distinct angles. First, as noted, in any society, there are many communities. One can be a member of a family, religious group, profession, a particular area of a nation-state, and the nation-state and world. Each of these loyalties has an ever-expanding connection and has the potential for ever-increasing tolerance to be gained.

Royce believes there is a kind of "Transcendental Community," an ideal perfect community to which human beings aspire and strive. He calls this community the "Beloved Community," a community he derives from the Christian tradition. The notion of the Beloved Community transcends and relativizes all lesser communities. My loyalty to my family, religious group, neighborhood, race, political party, nation-state, etc., are all rendered secondary by the transcendental ideal of the Beloved Community. The notion of the Beloved Community is the final guarantor against the risks of loyalties to trivial communities, secondary communities, tribal communities, false and twisted communities, and every form of secondary community.

There is no question that the Christian Church and John's vision of the "Heavenly City" is the basis and ground of the notion of a "Beloved Community" as a kind of eschatological realization of the hopes and dreams of all the lesser communities humans create. In the case of Christianity, as a community of tradition, the Church looks back through the Scriptures to the beginning of the world, formulating a community of tradition that extends backward in time to the beginning of time and space. As a community of hope, The Church looks forward to the end of history and the perfect consummation and renewal of all things in the Heavenly City, which is the eschatological reality of the community of God in which perfection of justice and human flourishing is achieved.

Thus, members of the Beloved Community look infinitely backward and forwards in time, in tradition and hope, from an imperfect past and present to a future that encompasses all of humanity and human history. This is why Royce sometimes calls the "Beloved Community" the "Universal Community": all people are invited to pledge their loyalty to and find meaning and purpose in the Beloved Community.

In the Book of Revelation, John describes this community in metaphorical, symbolic detail:

> Then I saw "a new heaven and a new earth," for the first heaven and the first earth had passed away, and there was no longer any sea. I saw the Holy City, the new Jerusalem, coming down out of heaven from God, prepared as a bride beautifully dressed for her husband. And I heard a loud voice from the throne saying, "Look! God's dwelling place is now among the people, and he will dwell with them. They will be his people, and God himself will be with them and be their God. He will wipe every tear from

their eyes. There will be no more death or mourning or crying or pain, for the old order of things has passed away." (Revelation 21:1-4).

The hope of the Beloved Community is the hope of a place of perfect individuality and ideal community joined in a kind of perfect self-giving love—a love that, for Christians, mirrors the love that constitutes and characterizes the divine Trinity of Father, Son, and Holy Spirit, each maintaining perfect individuality and joined in an ideal community. It is a place of human flourishing and fulfillment, in which the finitude and failure of this world are finally overcome. It is a world of perfect health, justice, personhood, and community.

The universal hope for the reconciliation of the human race, heaven, and earth in a kingdom of complete justice is an eschatological, not a historical, hope.[128] The Beloved Community, which I call the "Transcendental Community" of wisdom and love, represents the ultimate guarantee that narrow interests and prejudice can and will be overcome—and no attempt to "stop history" at one point with one embedded group of persons or ideas dominant can succeed. Within history, we can only hope to achieve relative ends and partial realization of our most deeply held hopes and dreams. In the end, all of the human communities to which humans are loyal must be relativized by some transcendental vision of a perfect community.

According to the realistic *socio-agapism* that this work is defending, the transcendental ideal of the Beloved Community is a real and ever-evolving guide for action in this world. It relativizes our finite loyalties to existing institutions and our existing commitments by means of a vision of a final (one might say, "eschatological") community, a vision that the human race might ultimately enjoy a world in which all human ideals, including the pursuit of justice, are perfectly realized. It is the ultimate community of hope sustaining human striving for justice in a world where much injustice survives. It is also the guarantee that fanaticism is both unwise and unloving—a false response to the defects of any given society in which justice is being sought.

CHAPTER 4

"NEW PHYSICS," PROCESS, AND SOPHIA-AGAPISM

lfred North Whitehead (1861-1947) made significant contributions to Mathematics, Logic, Philosophy of Science, Metaphysics, and other areas of thought. He was instrumental in developing a philosophical outlook known as "Process Philosophy," of which he is the modern founder. Although Whitehead began his academic life at Cambridge (as a mathematician) and then taught in London (as a mathematical physicist and philosopher of education), it was in America at Harvard that he became known as a metaphysician of the first order and wrote his most famous works. In 1925, Whitehead published *Science and the Modern World* (1926).[129] In 1929, he published his Gifford Lectures at the University of Edinburgh, *Process and Reality*.[130] In 1933, he published *Adventures of Ideas*, his most accessible work and the source of much of his "political philosophy."[131] In 1938, he published *Modes of Thought*, perhaps the most straightforward summary of his ideas.[132]

Science and the Modern World was published in 1926. Only fifteen years earlier, in 1905 (sometimes called his "miracle year"), Albert Einstein published a series of papers that introduced his theory of relativity and made significant contributions to quantum physics. Fifteen years is a short time in the history of science. Nevertheless, by 1926, Whitehead, himself a mathematical physicist, had internalized the new physics of his day and gave a philosophical account of its meaning. Whitehead's lasting importance flows from his development of a metaphysical system compatible with modern relativity theory and quantum physics.

End of Materialism

From Newton until the early 20th Century, a fundamentally materialistic worldview dominated science and philosophy. In this worldview, what is "real" is matter and material forces acting on matter. The world is something like a gigantic collection of marbles in constant motion, constantly impacting one another. The picture of the universe that emerged with quantum physics was radically different. Fundamental subatomic particles are not material in the ordinary sense of the word's meaning. Instead, they are what Whitehead calls "patterns" or "vibrations" in a universal electromagnetic field, an emerging disturbance in an underlying field of potentiality.[133] Whitehead recognized the implications of developments in physics, which meant the end of the Newtonian worldview and its materialistic premises.

In response, Whitehead developed a "process" or "organic" view of reality in which the fundamental realities are events, what he called "actual occasions."[134] Actual occasions that take on a stable form over time Whitehead calls "actual entities." Actual occasions and actual entities are not fundamentally material but a part of an unfolding universal process of becoming. Material reality is simply one manifestation of the underlying process of the universe. By making the fundamental level of reality occasions and not particles, Whitehead laid the basis for a non-materialistic metaphysical account of reality.

In defining the fundamental reality as an event or occasion, Whitehead gives metaphysical expression to the fundamental immateriality of what science believes are the basic building blocks of the universe.[135] As one author puts it:

> Whitehead marks an important turning point in the history of philosophy because he affirms that everything is fundamentally an event. What we perceive as permanent objects are events, or, better, an assortment and series of "events" that have taken up a stable form.[136]

The actual world, our world of everyday life, including politics, is not fundamentally made up of objects but instead "built up of actual occasions."[137] Things we perceive as stable objects (what Whitehead calls "enduring objects") are events with an enduring character because of their underlying structure.[138]

Whitehead's worldview is decidedly not materialistic, for fundamental events are much like the waves that constitute fundamental particles—vibrations or patterns that are not material entities but capable of becoming so. Higher-order events are built up through structured combinations of actual occasions/objects. Enduring objects are events that have developed an enduring character due to their internal organization.

A Social World

In Whitehead's thought, not only are events primary, but so is "structure," or the invisible noetic patterns discernable in actual occasions. The notions of pattern and structure are fundamental in Whitehead. This means that the idea of a social order is fundamental in reality. As occasions develop organized and orderly patterns, some kind of social order develops, even at a subatomic level. Thus, social order is fundamental, as are the enduring objects or creatures we are familiar with. For example, a human being is, in essence, a society built up of actual occasions.

Similarly, everything from rocks to complex social entities or societies of an impersonal type have a social order that gives them the capacity to endure.[139] The development of order over time is a fundamental characteristic of reality, including the existence of human societies. What we call human society is essentially a very complex social entity built up from innumerable actual occasions that have entered into a series of social relationships, ultimately resulting in the emergence of human beings and society.

In addition, all societies are deeply relational, both internally and externally. Early in the development of quantum physics, it was realized that one of its implications was a degree of interconnectedness among the fields of activity that make it up. As previously noted, Einstein's Relativity Theory, which Whitehead studied and understood, describes a profoundly relational universe in which time and space, ultimate attributes of reality in Newtonian physics, are known to be related to one another and make up a "Space/Time Continuum." Much of the argument of *Science and the Modern World* concerns the metaphysical implications of relativity theory, a subject to which Whitehead himself made contributions. In the end, the world described by relativity theory is fundamentally relational. The absolute space and time of classical Newtonian physics gives way to a notion of time and space that is fundamentally relational. Time and Space are interrelated and cannot be separated except for purposes of abstract discussion.[140]

As I have already shown, at a quantum level of reality, a deep interconnectedness is revealed and symbolized by so-called "spooky action at a distance," or what physicists call "entanglement." Reality is deeply connected at a subatomic level. This interconnectedness is also fundamental to the reality we experience. Even at the level of everyday existence, a deep interconnectedness is evident in so-called "open systems" and their tendency toward self-organizing activity—the "butterfly effect."[141] This interconnectedness is operative throughout the universe, including in and among human persons. In the case of human persons, this interconnection is uniquely present due to the intellectual and emotional character of the human person. Inevitably, this fundamental interconnectedness continues to be operative at the social level of human institutions, which are made up of persons acting in their social capacities, including political capacities.

Thus, process thought involves the idea that relationships are fundamental to reality. Actual occasions combine to form societies. The essential character of a society is determined by the relationships in which it is located, past, present, and future.[142] A society of whatever character exists as a web of relationships from which it emerged in a process emerging from the past and leading to the future state of the society involved. The relatedness of the universe and the societies that make up the physical realities we experience is not merely external but also internal to the society itself.[143] Thus, not only is physical matter secondary, but also physical power. The primary and fundamental element of a process or organic view of reality is that of relation. This is true of political reality as well as material reality.

The development process within any society emerges from past actuality, that is, the past actual occasions from which the society emerged and has been formed. This process involves both negative and positive prehension, or the actual occasions and actual entities grasping aspects of their past in an action of self-creativity. This grasping is both physical and intellectual. Intellectual prehension involves grasping universals (Eternal Objects), possibilities inherent in the universe. Actual occasions and societies both positively incorporate aspects of their past and negatively reject aspects of their past in the process of emergence.

The notion of reality as a kind of social order has important implications for political thinking. The idea of a society being built up over time by the gradual unfolding of a social order that is not fundamentally material requires a rethinking of any kind of power-based political theory. It also casts grave doubt on excluding moral and religious considerations in political decision-making. The notion of a social order emerging from and, to some degree, determined by its past, as well as choosing (positively prehending) certain elements that will be incorporated into its future, flies in the face of the kind of materialistic determinism and the power politics in our society.

Humans as an Integral Part of Process

Newtonian physics allowed for the existence of observers outside the events being observed. In addition, Newtonian physics conceived that the connections between particles are external to the particles themselves, not internal. Quantum physics revealed that the observer is a fundamental part of observed reality. Thus, quantum physics implies a universe of deep interconnection in which observers are part of the system they observe. In this vision of reality, the idea of human observations as fundamentally external to events observed falls away. All reality has a fundamental internal unity. As Whitehead puts it:

> We awake to find ourselves engaged in process, immersed in satisfactions and dissatisfactions, and actively modifying, either by intensification, or attenuation, or by the introduction of novel purpose.[144]

All human experience and action, including science and human societies, including political institutions, participate in the unfolding process of the universe to which each part is inextricably connected to each other part. Neither human beings nor human societies can divorce themselves from the totality of the process of which they are a part.

The relationship of the observer and the observed is illustrated by the so-called "double slit experiment." If a researcher shines light through two slits, a pattern emerges from the other side, revealing whether light is a wave or a particle. However, the result is, in some sense, determined by our observation. It is as if human conscious involvement creates the effect and defines the character of the photon, and the photon somehow "feels" or senses the observer's presence.

Process thought shares this view. Societies, including human beings, are not outside reality but a part of a "world process." Thus, at best, humans' attempts to abstract themselves from others are only partially successful. Humans are inevitably and inextricably connected to, and sense at a deep level, the social world we are a part of. The relatedness that permeates fundamental reality is also present within families, neighborhoods, communities, nations, and the world. What we say and do has an impact, however important or unimportant, on the world we inhabit. These connections are not just external but also internal. As Whitehead puts it, "The whole environment participates in the nature of each of its actual occasions. Thus, each occasion takes its initial form from the nature of its environment."[145]

A World of Experience "All the Way Down"

One result of quantum physics is the realization that the very act of observing—of asking the question, "Through which slit will each electron pass?"—changes the experiment's outcome. In other words, experimental results indicate that, in some way, subatomic particles "know," "sense," or "feel" the presence of the observer, which determines the outcome of the experiment.[146] Whitehead was aware of this outcome. Post-Newtonian science implies that experience is a fundamental category of existence. To be is to experience. Even at the most fundamental levels of reality (the level of actual occasions and fundamental particles), a "feeling" or "experience" of reality exists.[147]

Whitehead understood that the kind of consciousness human beings enjoy is not present in fundamental particles, fundamental molecules, fundamental forms of life, and even, perhaps, in some animal life. Nevertheless, there seems to be a form of "feeling" or awareness of connection with surrounding reality at all levels of reality. As the phenomenon of entanglement demonstrates, this awareness of connection may extend to the limits of the universe. Therefore, in some sense, reality is experiential.

Whitehead uses a technical term, "prehension," to describe this primordial feeling.[148] It is difficult for human beings to separate consciousness from apprehension. Whitehead, therefore, used "prehension" to describe a form of non-cognitive apprehension in nature. Prehension is an outgrowth of the fundamental relatedness of reality as each form of existence (actual occasions) "prehends" surrounding reality. Conscious perception is possible because we have a highly developed central nervous system. This consciousness is, however, only a tiny part of the considerable amount of potential consciousness within the universe.

It would seem that at every level of reality, there is a constantly expanding and more complex form of experience available. All living creatures have some awareness of their surroundings and of the impacts their surroundings have on them. In animal life, we see a growing form of awareness. In humans, we see still another form of awareness, but all this "experience" is built on a kind of awareness or prehension present in the most fundamental aspects of reality.

We inhabit a world of deep and beautiful order on many levels. Somehow, the world emerges from the indeterminate world of quantum reality. The nature of matter and energy at fundamental levels allowed the emergence of what we call "chemistry," the basic elements making up the physical universe and their combination, out of which emerged biology, eventually resulting in the emergence of the human species—a species having self-consciousness and the ability to reflect the order of the universe in its relations as well as the ability to create culture, societies, and social structures. From the human species emerge families, society, social organization, law, economic systems, arts, literature, music, morality, religion, and all the myriad complex social relations that make up any society.[149] All of this emergent order is deeply relational.

The various levels of reality are, in some way, interdependent. Each level possesses independent rules, regulations, laws, and order emergent from, but not identical with, the order from which it emerged. Finally, each level of reality participates in an invisible noetic order within which various levels of existence have their own unique conceptual order. That is to say, humans can investigate the underlying structures of many aspects of reality using science and other disciplines. The means of investigation depends on the nature of the order under investigation. Each part of reality must be investigated according to its own intrinsic nature and the connections by which it is constituted.[150]

This organic, interconnected, and hierarchical view of reality has implications for political philosophy and practice. Every stable society is built ahead of multiple levels of increasingly complicated participants in the social order. For example, we tend to think that our society is made up of humans who happen to be residents of the United States of America. However, the health and functioning of the society depend on its citizens and their interconnected, relational participation in a physical, social, and political environment that includes all its surrounding physical and non-physical elements.

Not surprisingly, one fundamental application of Whiteheadian philosophy has been environmental protection. The notion that the world is built up of actual occasions or objects connected by feelings and senses, which respond to one another's existence and presence, implies that the members of our society are connected with their environment: human and non-human, organic and inorganic. If this is true, then it is impossible to have a healthy society that does not consider this web of relationships in which the human participants are located.[151]

A Physical and Mental Universe

One of Whitehead's contributions to philosophy is his circumvention of the mind-body dualism inherent in modern metaphysics. According to Whitehead, every actual occasion has a mental and a physical pole. That is to say, experience and intelligibility are present in everything from subatomic particles to human beings. In Whitehead's view, every level of existence possesses mental and physical poles, including quanta, atoms, cells, organisms, the Earth, the solar system, our galaxy, and the universe up to God. For God, the whole physical universe is the physical pole, and all ideas and forms are the mental (or "noetic") pole.[152] In other words, there is no ultimate distinction between mind and matter. Mind and matter are two aspects of a single reality. The potential for the kind of consciousness that human beings possess is, thus, an evolutionary possibility within the structure of the type of universe we inhabit.[153]

There is no ultimate distinction between actual occasions that are in some sense alive (humans) and those that are not (like rocks) or between the human race and animals. As mentioned above, regarding experience, the existence of a mental pole does not imply a consciousness. Returning to the double slit experiment, when quantum physicists speak of a particle as "sensing" the observer, they do not imply that subatomic particles are conscious. This can be hard to understand, but it refers to the fact that experience and intelligibility seem to "go all the way down" in reality. Therefore, mind, matter (organic and inorganic), humans and animals, for all their differences, are also in some sense fundamentally related in an intelligible way.[154]

Applied to political philosophy and social theory generally, Whitehead's process view encourages investigators to look at the patterns of relationships that make up the society and polity in which one is interested—and to look at them as constantly changing events, not as an object frozen in time. What we sometimes call the American Experiment in Constitutional Democracy is an example. Our political system is not simply an object to be dissected and understood solely as the power applied to individuals based on its component parts. Instead, it is an event that comprises a complex of constantly changing and evolving relationships. To the extent that our society embraces fundamental values, those values must be continually applied to new and changing realities. Understanding this reality according to its intrinsic nature requires a sympathetic investigation of all of its features, some of which are moral and ethical. A merely reductionistic approach is inadequate to fully understand reality—any reality, especially highly complex social realities.

In addition, as far as political philosophy is concerned, fundamental "connectedness" implies that the tendency to divide the political world into "us" and "them" is ultimately a false abstraction. We are all part of and inevitably connected to our families, communities, nation, and world, joined in profound ways to those with whom we share all levels of human society. This includes those who agree with us and those who disagree, our political allies and our opponents. This relatedness casts doubt on the viability of any political philosophy that relies solely on power to exclude other relational factors.

Once again, when one combines the process or event focus of Whitehead's thought with its social character, one is led away from any notion of the universe as fundamentally constituted of matter and force. One is also led away from the idea, embedded in our culture through Hobbes, of society as a conglomeration of individuals related to one another by force. Power exists, but it is grounded in a deeper reality, which we shall examine later when we discuss God, Love, and the gradual movement of human societies from force to persuasion.

The evolution of the universe and human society reflects their propensity to seek the kind of satisfaction we call "Peace" or "Harmony." Whitehead believes his metaphysics has practical implications, which he outlines in his book *Adventure of Ideas*. Whitehead's metaphysics supports a view that sees justice as a kind of harmony within the social process that constitutes a society—a goal that policymakers should seek, rather than power or ideological victory in the political sphere.

Eternal Objects

To understand Whitehead's views on the movement from a society based on force to one based on persuasion, it is crucial to understand his notions of God and universals, what Whitehead calls "Eternal Objects." As mentioned above, the world in which we live and have our day-to-day existence (what Whitehead sometimes calls the "Actual World") is built up over long periods through the emergence and relationships of actual occasions.[155] Those things we perceive as stable objects (what Whitehead calls "Enduring Objects") are events with an enduring character because of their underlying structure.[156]

For Whitehead, however, two objects participate in the emergence of the world of actual occasions that are not themselves actual occasions. These are:

1. Eternal Objects are ideal entities that are pure potentials for realization in the actual world and form the conceptual ground for all actual occasions;[157] and

2. God is both an Eternal Object and the primordial actual entity; God is not an actual occasion but is present in all occasions.[158]

According to Whitehead, eternal objects are the qualities and formal structures that define actual occasions and related entities. An infinite hierarchy of eternal objects defines each actual entity. This feature permits each real entity to be experienced by future entities in essential ways.

1. Eternal Objects participate in the causal connection of individual entities, functioning as private qualities and public structures. They characterize the growth of actuality in its rhythmic advance from private, subjective immediacy to public, extensively structured fact.
2. Eternal objects are ideals conceptualized by historical actual entities. As such, they are potential elements that ensure that nature's process is not deductive succession but organic growth and creative advancement.[159] This characteristic is essential for understanding political notions such as justice.

Eternal objects are primordially realized as pure potentials in the conceptual nature of that one unique actual entity that we call "God." As realized in God, eternal objects are ideal possibilities or potentialities, ordered according to logical and aesthetic principles, that can be realized in actual occasions. As realized in God, Eternal Objects transcend the historical actual entities in which they are realized.[160]

Persuasion Instead of Force

For Whitehead, God is "actual" (an actual entity) but non-temporal, the source of all creativity and innovation, who transmits his creativity in freedom and persuasion.[161] Whitehead's God has two poles of existence: a transcendent pole, which is primordial, and a consequential or physical pole. The transcendent pole is the mental pole of God, wherein one finds the existence of eternal objects. As primordial, God is eternal, having no beginning or end, and is the ultimate reason for the universe.[162]

God's consequential or physical pole implies that God is present in the universe and in all actual occasions, which are the physical poles of God's existence. In this physical pole, God experiences the world and the actualization of eternal objects in actual occasions. Because of God's physical pole, God can be impacted by and experience actuality. Thus, Whitehead's God experiences and grows with creation. Process Philosophy uniquely contributes to philosophical and theological ideas in postulating a physical pole to God.

For Whitehead, God is not an all-powerful ruler, a cosmic despot. God is intimately involved in the universe of actual occasions and impacts the future not by force but by persuasion.[163] Thus, Whitehead states, "More than two thousand years ago the wisest of men proclaimed that the divine persuasion is the foundation of the order of the world, but that it could only produce such order as amid the brute force of the world it was possible to accomplish."[164] This divine persuasion, the slow working of God in history as love and wisdom, is the hope of the world that the constant resort to force and violence in human affairs can be overcome.

Writing before the Second World War, before Hiroshima, and the wars of the late 20th century, Whitehead saw the critical role of faith and all religious groups as instruments for the evolution of the human race towards a more harmonious world based on persuasion, reason, and love rather than brute force.[165] In a much-quoted and beautiful passage, speaking of Christianity in particular, Whitehead writes:

> The essence of Christianity is the appeal to the life of Christ as the revelation of the nature of God and of his agency in the world. The Mother, the Child, and the bare manger: the lowly man, homeless and self-forgetful, with his message of peace, love, and sympathy: the suffering, the agony, the tender words as life ebbed, the final despair: and the whole with the authority of supreme victory. I need not elaborate. Can there be any doubt that the power of Christianity lies in its revelation in act of what Plato divined in theory?[166]

One does not have to be a Christian to capture the importance Whitehead placed on God as the author of love and the power of persuasion in the emergence of a just and peaceful civilization.

The Victory of Persuasion over Force

Like Whitehead, Plato taught that the divine agency is persuasive, relying on reason, not coercion, to accomplish the world's creation. Plato also taught that it was a part of the reordering of the human person by virtue to recover the primordial reliance on reason and persuasion by which the world was created and by which human beings recover an original reasonableness and harmony. This view has obvious implications for political philosophy and political practice. Human freedom and flourishing depend on the emergence of ever-greater harmony and reasonableness in human society, including its political organization.

For Whitehead, "The progress of humanity is defined as the process of transforming society to make the original Greco-Roman/Judeo-Christian ideals increasingly practicable for the individual members."[167] The project of every human society and political institution is, therefore, advanced by achieving the victory of persuasion over force.[168] Recalling the words of Plato, Whitehead writes:

> The creation of the world—said Plato—is the story of persuasion over force. The worth of men consists in their liability to persuasion. They can persuade and can be persuaded by the disclosure of alternatives, the better and the worse. Civilization is the maintenance of social order by its inherent persuasiveness as embodying the nobler alternative. The recourse to force, however unavoidable, is a disclosure of the failure of civilization, either in general society or in a remnant of individuals.[169]

Against Hobbes, Whitehead holds that persuasion has always been a part of human society and denies that force is the defining characteristic of human society. He disagrees that human society is "a war of everyone against everyone else." The social and persuasive side of society is older and more fundamental than the recourse to force. The love between the sexes, the love of parents for children and families for one another, and even the communal love of small groups are all probably older than brute force as a fundamental aspect of human society. In other words, Whitehead sees that a philosophy compatible with the best understanding of reality must, in every area, abandon the Newtonian emphasis on material objects and force.

This does not mean, however, that force is not an inevitable characteristic of society, for there is and always will be a need for laws, structures, and their enforcement and defense. Forms of social compulsion are an outgrowth of the need for social coordination but are (or at least should be) of themselves the outgrowth of reason.[170] Interestingly, Whitehead believes that commerce is an essential component in the movement from force to persuasion, for commerce depends on private parties reaching agreements without recourse to force, which tends to build the capacities for reason and persuasion that a free society requires.[171] The importance of persuasion is consistent with the emphasis on the role of love, cherishing, conversation, and dialogue in human society.

Freedom and Order

Whitehead believes freedom of thought, speech, and action is fundamental to social progress. However, there is always a social need to balance what he calls Individual Absoluteness and Individual Relativity.[172] Generally, Individual Absoluteness refers to the scope of human freedom in a society. Individual Relativity refers to the inevitable need for individuals to limit their freedom for the good of society and other human beings. In this dichotomy, there is a recognition that social organization and harmony require some limitations on human freedom.

The creation, in a free society, of a harmonic balance between the desires and wills of individuals and the maintenance of a sense of social solidarity requires an understanding of the relational environment from which the individual emerges and the need for stability in the midst of unfolding change, and how individual freedom results in the emergence of a gradually evolving society. There is inevitably an element of chance in how societies evolve, and the resolution in any given community of the tension between freedom and order can seem merely the arbitrary result of chance—as it sometimes is.[173] The rate and size of social change can vary within a society over time. If existing institutions are working well, and the citizens and centers of power are relatively content, the rate and scale of change may be slow. In other situations, the rate of change may be significant.[174]

Adjustments required within a society are determined mainly by what Whitehead calls Instinct, Intelligence, and Wisdom. Instinct, which relates to what Peirce calls "habit," are inherited modes of organization and action that have become customary for society due to inheritance, individual, and environmental factors. Intelligence includes those theoretical factors that are uncovered by human rational inquiry. Wisdom refers to how instinctual and theoretical elements intertwine in the practical accomplishment of social progress. Wisdom can be of greater or lesser effectiveness depending on the ability to coordinate and incorporate the primary facts of human existence in decision-making. [175]

In the end, social progress occurs when human actors in the social arena make wise decisions impacting the evolution of human societies, including their political organization. In the same way, social regress occurs when human actors make unwise decisions concerning the development of human society, including its political organization. Finally, there is no avoiding this result because every human decision, great and small, impacts the universe somehow, creating a future, opening up some possibilities and closing down others.

In the midst of all this, human actors make decisions. These decisions impact the human society in which the actors are located for better or for worse. The activity of free human actors is the foundation of all human thought, and any form of tyranny is antithetical to the emergence of a harmonious social order. In a significant passage, Whitehead notes:

> A barbarian speaks in terms of power. He dreams of the superman with the mailed fist. He may plaster his lust with sentimental morality... But ultimately, his final good is conceived, as one will imposing itself on other wills. This is intellectual barbarism.[176]

It takes a little imagination to see what is meant by this passage. Whitehead is referring to Nietzsche. Writing in the United States on the verge of the Second World War, with the terrible political results of Nietzschean thought evident in Germany, Whitehead understood, as we sometimes forget, that freedom requires a willingness to love, reason, persuade, and forgo all forms of force unless required by the circumstances. The example of Nazi Germany and the various disasters of totalitarian regimes in the 20th century are clear arguments for adopting a "politics of reason and relationship," which I call *sophio-agapism*.

Conclusion

Ultimately, Whitehead believes that four factors govern the fate of social groups, including our society:

1. The existence of some transcendent aim or goal greater than the mere search for pleasure;
2. Limitations on freedom that flow from nature itself and the basic needs of human beings;
3. The tendency of the human species to resort to compulsion instead of reason, which is fatal to social growth and flourishing if extended beyond necessary limits; and

4. The importance of persuasion that relies on reason and agreement to resolve social problems. In the end, it is the way of persuasion that holds the hope for social and human flourishing.[177]

Whitehead is critical for a *sophio-agapic* analysis of justice. Through his concept of eternal objects, Whitehead is a noetic realist. He believes that values have a form of reality that can impact events and the evolution of any society, especially a complex political society. As a logician, physicist, and philosopher, his work in developing his metaphysical system indicates an orderliness to reality that can be examined by science and other disciplines, including political philosophy. Finally, his notion of "divine persuasion" is similar to Peirce's notion of an *agapic* aspect of reality, including social reality. For Whitehead, human reason and emotions are essential to a flourishing society, including its political organization. Whitehead's organic, relational view of reality extends to his view of society and encourages attention to the relationships that make up society beyond mere law and power.

In setting out his organic and social vision of reality, Whitehead is sympathetic to a harmonic idea of society and the goal of social justice. What is sometimes referred to as a harmonic theory of justice is also an aesthetic theory of justice.[178] In the end, Whitehead is captured by a vision of the search for beauty that dominates all efforts to create a better society in every area. Thus, he states:

Science and Art are the consciously determined pursuit of Truth and Beauty. In them, the finite consciousness of mankind is appropriating as its own infinite fecundity of nature. In this movement of the human

113

spirit types of institutions and types of professions are evolved. Churches and Rituals, Monasteries with their dedicated lives, Universities with their search for knowledge, Medicine, Law, methods of Trade—they all represent that aim at civilization, whereby the conscious experience of mankind preserves for each use the sources of Harmony.[179]

In the end, Whitehead's vision is a *socio-agapic* vision of a world in which the human search for truth and beauty is a search for personal and social harmony. Human society is a never-ending evolutionary project in which each person and society can participate in unfolding a better and more just society.

CHAPTER 5

INDIVIDUALS, SOCIAL SELVES, AND SOPHIO-AGAPISM

eorge Herbert Mead (1863-1931) is the least known of the American pragmatists. His classic work *On Social Psychology* was published after his death as a compilation of writings.[180] One reason Meade is not well-known as a pragmatist is that he is better known as a founder of the discipline of social psychology. He was a student of Josiah Royce but developed his own unique interpretation of Royce's communitarian thought along naturalistic grounds. He taught philosophy at the University of Chicago, and was a popular teacher there. Mead is also important because he represents a communitarian approach to pragmatism in the lineage of Alfred North Whitehead, with whose work he was familiar. His approach to social thought is evolutionary and informed by the notion that society is always in process.

Finally, Mead derives a degree of recognition from being a friend and disciple of the philosopher John Dewey. He is important for a *sophio-agapic* philosophy because of his emphasis on how human selves emerge from communities, beginning with the family, and then powerfully impact those communities. Nevertheless, Mead does not stand directly in the tradition of Peirce and Royce due to his materialistic approach to the issues of social organization and his nominalism. His closest philosophical ally was John Dewey, whose work will be discussed later.

Mead, Royce, Peirce

Mead studied under Josiah Royce and was impacted by Royce and Peirce. Mead's understanding of the human self was significantly influenced by the work of Peirce, particularly his semiotic approach to human thought. Mead developed the term "gesture" to show how language develops from our human capacity to point and make gestures. Languages are "gestures" converted into signs. The development of language was a pivotal moment in human evolution. Mead believed that humans develop intellectually primarily due to their capacity to manipulate signs and communicate using various languages. Mead saw the process of language, the ability of human beings to think in signs, as essential to the unique capacity of human beings to have both an 'I' and a 'Me,' that is, to have a distinct self and a social self.

Because using signs is a social activity, Mead saw human thinking as a fundamentally and inextricably social experience. Human beings achieve selfhood through interacting with the social circumstances in which they are born. The growth and development of human beings and societies are mainly due to the human ability to use signs and develop intricate and constantly expanding sign systems to understand and create personal and social realities, including political and social institutions.

Selves, Society and Civilizations

Mead understood that human beings do not make themselves. Human beings become selves in the context of human society. Civilization is made possible by the generalized social attitudes of various societies, which individuals internalize. Nevertheless, human beings are not automatons determined by their society.

> Human society, we have insisted, does not merely stamp the pattern of its organized social behavior upon any one of its individual members, so that this pattern becomes likewise the pattern of the individual self; it also, at the same time, gives him a mind, as the means or ability of consciously conversing with himself in terms of the social attitudes, which constitute the structure of his self and which embodied the pattern of human societies' organized behavior, as reflected in that structure. And his mind enables him in turn to stamp the pattern of his further developing self (further developing through his medical capacity), upon the structure or organization or organization of human society, and thus in a degree to reconstruct and modify in terms of his self the general pattern of social or group behavior in terms of which his self was originally constituted.[181]

Human societies both constitute individuals and are constituted by them. Society and culture, including political institutions and conventions, form individuals and are formed and transformed by them. Thus, a constantly unfolding interplay exists between individuals and society, resulting in constant social change.

Mead recognized that human social institutions exist at various levels of scale. He notes that Americans, with their native love of size and success, have long given institutional priority to larger institutions.[182] This love of the large and our intuitive belief that size and universality are both critical and positive can lead to a failure to understand that the large and universal can undermine the smaller foundations on which they rest. Larger institutions, such as nation-states, rest on the stability of smaller units, families, neighborhoods, communities, cities, etc.

This recognition of the value of the small does not mean that Mead underestimates the value of larger institutions. The modern fascination with scale impacted Mead. Mead created his version of Rousseau's notion of "The Will of the People," which implies the gradual emergence of a "Universal Will of the People" and institutions that reflect that universal will. For example, in his view, the League of Nations represented an attempt to create an organization in which a universal will could be institutionalized.[183] The formation of the League of Nations and the development of the United Nations after World War II can be seen as attempts to institutionalize this universal will. Perhaps more importantly, creating a host of international administrative agencies, courts, service organizations, NGOs, and the like reflects the same impulse.[184]

Ancient writers focused on ideas like "The General Good" or "Public Peace" (transcendent public goods built into the nature of human society).[185] Rousseau developed a notion of a "General Will" of the people—a notion Mead incorporates using the idea of a Universal will of an enlightened humanity. Unfortunately, the notion of a "general or universal will of the people" has embedded within it a lack of any rational basis to limit the misbehavior of majorities, a failure that has had catastrophic consequences in modern history. This makes it one foundation of the contemporary tendency towards tyranny on a large scale.

A humbler ideal might recognize that our human finitude and self-centeredness makes it impossible to fully achieve a general or universal will. Under such circumstances, seeking relative peace and harmony within society is enough.

Rousseau was aware of the problem with an unrestricted general will and tried as best he could to find a reasonable way to protect freedom. He recognizes that the fundamental problem of the General Will is to provide for social cohesion while maintaining some idea of personal freedom.[186] The problem is that the social contract, as conceived of by at least Hobbes and Rousseau, requires that the individual grants all personal rights ("whole and entire") to freedom and property to the state and receives back in return their rights to share in the public good.[187] This results in a union of persons "as perfect as possible."[188] Unfortunately, it has little place for the freedom of minorities.

This highlights a fundamental weakness in the modern project for social organization: having reduced human society to atomized units (individuals) united not by social bonds of love but by "contract," the union is one of force imposed by power— the power of the majority. The idea of a balance of powers and limited government is the inevitable result of this movement since power is, by its very nature, absolute and susceptible to abuse.

Paradoxically, in Rousseau's view, giving oneself to the whole amounts to giving oneself to no one.[189] Thus, Rousseau says:

Finally, in giving himself to all, each person gives himself to no one. And, since there is no associate over whom he does not acquire the same right that he would grant others over himself, he gains the equivalent of everything he loses, along with a greater amount of *force* to preserve what he has. If, therefore, one eliminates from the social contract everything which is not essential to one once finds that it is reduceable to the following terms. Each of us places his person and all his *power* in common under the supreme direction of the general will; and as once, we receive each member as an indivisible part of the whole. [190]

A close analysis reveals the difficulty with both Rousseau's General Will and Mead's Universal Will. It is not coherent to say that people can both give themselves to an idealized whole and not give themselves to anyone. Human actors sit at the top of any social organization and are subject to all the temptations to abuse power that history clearly illustrates. Mead's theory assumes that the universal whole will have the same interests as any given individual and respect the rights and humanity of the individual, which human experience shows to be unlikely.

The experience of humanity with dictatorships of left and right, from the French Revolution to contemporary societies, shows that this is not the case. In every totalitarian, communistic, or oligarchic state, whoever is in control has abused those who are part of the "indivisible whole" they lead. The problem is easily identified by using terms like "force and power." Any sovereign of unlimited power will almost certainly abuse that power unless human nature changes dramatically from what the unvaried experience of the human race throughout history shows to be likely. Force and power do not give space for personal freedom; love and respect for the human individual do. This is where a *sophio-agapic* approach to political theory holds a distinct advantage.

The notion of a universal will of the human race is simply incoherent in modern, large, bureaucratic nation-states. Rousseau's theory was formed with small, socially bonded, racially homogenous, religiously Christian Geneva in mind. Modern multicultural societies are much too complex for any such notion to be a helpful guide to political life and leadership. Any General Will easily becomes the "Will of the Majority," to be effortlessly manipulated by revolutionaries and oligarchs in every age.

A *sophio-agapic* approach to political theory rejects notions like a universal will of the human race or general will of the people in favor of pragmatically seeking social harmony by balancing the various interests of groups in society, which cannot be united under a single formula of the general or universal will of the people. Instead, political leaders have the challenging job of balancing the wills of various groups while seeking to adjust social institutions and create a harmonious society.

Selves and Society

As noted previously, Mead believes human beings have a unique reflective capacity to have both an 'I' and a 'Me,' that is, to have a personal self (I) and a social self (Me). It is unique to human beings that we can mentally see ourselves as objects of our own thought. This is a reflexive capacity. We can reflect on ourselves, our beliefs, actions, successes, failures, character, and lack of character. This reflective capacity is essential to developing our social and individual selves. Human beings have a capacity lacking in lower animals, which means that the characteristics of human selves and society are unique.[191]

Humans can see themselves directly and indirectly from the viewpoint of others in society. Interaction between the social self and the reflexive capacity of the individual gives human beings the unique capacity to make moral judgments, create order or disorder, and grow. Our ability to have an "inner conversation" about circumstances and decisions inevitably allows us to enter a personal and social dialogue about the desirability of any particular social change. This kind of thinking is preparatory to social action by any individual and social change in a community.

For Mead, society and social institutions emerge in a dynamic relational process by which humans ("I's") constantly dialogue with and adapt to their surrounding culture. The initial culture for most human beings is a family consisting of parents, grandparents, and others who influence the emergence of the child as a distinct person. Every child develops a self-image as it learns to adapt to the culture and perceptions of those who raise it. There is a constant internal dialogue between the emerging self ("I") and the socially endorsed view that an individual has of themselves ("Me"). For Mead, human selves emerge in dialogue with human society. The organization of the human community precedes the emergence of any particular self. Human beings are born into a social matrix that existed before they were born, before they became conscious before they began to make decisions, and before they could influence that social matrix. In other words, Mead's thought is essentially communitarian. Human beings are born into a community, and the nature of that community has powerful influences over what kind of person and what kind of event "I" that person becomes.

This dialogue between self and society continues throughout life as humans (Me's) adapt to their ever-changing environment. In a complex society such as ours, individuals are faced with the challenging task of navigating the social expectations and customs of an ever-more-complex hierarchy of institutions, familial, economic, educational, political, and other, each of which influences and is influenced by the other. This intricate web of societal interactions and influences provides a rich, stimulating environment for intellectual exploration and understanding.

Mead was influenced by evolutionary theory and its implications for human thought and society. Like the emergence of human society, the emergence of that self is a process. This contradicts the modernist view that society is simply an amalgamation of autonomous individuals. On the other hand, it is too simplistic to believe that the human individual is merely the product of social forces. There is an interaction between human selves and society, out of which, in a dynamic process, human beings and societies emerge.

Pragmatism and Process

Mead's thought has a process aspect:

> In other words, the organized structure of every individual self within the social process of experience and behavior reflects and is constituted by the organized relational pattern of that process as a whole; but each individual self–structure reflects, and is constituted by a different aspect or perspective of this relational pattern, because each reflects this relational pattern from its own unique standpoint, so that the common social origin and constitution of individual selves and their structures does not preclude wide individual differences and variations among them, or contradict the peculiar and more or less distinctive individuality, which agent of them, in fact possesses.[192]

This aspect of Mead's thought is essential to understanding individuals' capacity to be founded in a specific social context and dynamically change it. While it is true that individual selves emerge from a social context, the individual self is also a distinctive part of the pattern of society as a whole. First, and fundamentally, each human being has a particular genetic makeup, so each self has the inevitable result of changing society and the capacity to change that society intentionally. Second, each self has a perspective somewhat different from every other self in a society. As human selves emerge through a process of dialogue with society—that is, as the "I" continues to be in dialogue with its social self (Me)—that individual self has the inevitable result of changing society and the capacity to change that society intentionally. Not everyone who participates in a large society, such as ours, makes a tremendous difference, but each individual does make a difference.

Order and Change

The order of society is a constant tension between what might be termed the forces of revolution and the forces of order. Mead put it like this:

> That is the problem of society, is it not? How can you present order and structure in society and yet bring about the changes that need to take place, or are taking place? How can you bring about those changes in an orderly fashion and yet preserve order? To bring about change is seemingly to destroy the given order, and yet society must change. That is the problem to incorporate the method of change into the order of society itself.[193]

Here, we see the impact of evolutionary thinking and the French Revolution on Mead's thought. Mead considers human society to be a constantly evolving organism. He is, in this way, influenced by Darwin. He sees that the institutions of any given society must change. On the other hand, he also sees that change in any given society cannot occur in such a way that it destroys its fundamental order. The results of this way of thinking were evident in the French Revolution and are apparent in our own culture today. As a pragmatist, Mead is interested in discerning how change can be managed in an orderly process in which human beings can continue to flourish and there can be harmony in an ever-changing social order. In the tradition of Peirce, Mead believes that the best method for societies to move forward is a scientific way of managing change: an orderly process of investigation, hypothesis, trial and error, and change.

Finally, Mead distinguishes evolution as it occurs in nature and the kind of evolution one sees in society. Natural evolution is, by its very nature, purposeless. On the other hand, human social evolution can be both orderly and purposeful because it is the product of decisions by rational human beings. Because human beings can reflect, they can adapt to change in an orderly manner that protects the interests of society and its participants.[194]

Religious and Economic Universality

Mead believes that human history reveals two universalizing processes reflecting this tendency. First, there is the emergence of "Religious and Economic Universality," a phrase that refers to the impulse to achieve a universal or all-encompassing order in religious and economic contexts. From the beginning of human civilization, a tendency has existed to seek political universality as kingdoms and empires sought to expand their boundaries. Examples are the movements from the Assyrian, Babylonian,

Medo-Persian, Greek, and Roman empires in the Middle East and Mediterranean areas in the ancient world. The British Empire and the so-called "Pax Americana" are examples of this tendency in the modern world.

Similarly, there has always been an impulse to expand economic influence and trade throughout history. Marco Polo's story is one of hundreds of stories of ancient trade explorers. Throughout history, wherever a political subdivision has been created, a kind of economic universality emerges within that empire—and beyond—as that empire seeks to expand its economic life. These same impulses can easily be seen in contemporary world politics. The expansion of American economic power after the Second World War and the current expansion of Chinese power are examples.

Mead also examines the expansion of religious groups with a universalizing tendency as they claim or desire universal scope. Mead uses Islam as an example of a religion that uses all available social means, political, legal, cultural, and military, to achieve a universal Islamic society.[195] In reality, many religious groups have expanded their reach, often following the path of armies or economic expansion: Christian, Buddhist, Taoist, Islamic, and others. How Islam finds its way to Indonesia is a story of a religion following ancient trade routes. Similarly, European and American missionaries followed the European nations' economic and political expansion. However, I believe religious expansion is a secondary phenomenon in most cases.

The great empires of human history represent universalizing tendencies. The Greek city-state, for example, was succeeded by the Macedonian Empire of Philip and Alexander the Great. These empires were created as societies expanded and tried to universalize their institutions and culture. The same might be said of the Roman Empire. Human history provides many examples of groups seeking to dominate other groups and universalize their particular social beliefs, forms, and organization. As communities come into conflict, there is a constant impulse to seek domination.[196]

Nevertheless, there is a limitation inherent in my analysis that needs to be brought out. A tendency towards fragmentation has always counterbalanced this universalizing tendency. There were indeed many great empires in the history of the world. It's also true that they all disintegrated over time. This was true of Alexander's empire, the Roman Empire, the British Empire, and increasingly true of the American Empire created after the Second World War. While Mead's analysis explains the emergence of empires, his theory is not so clearly applicable to their inevitable decay and decline.

Conflict and Integration

Underlying society's constant turmoil and change is the continual interplay between the self and culture—and, in the case of most individuals in a complex society, between selves and the innumerable societies in which they participate. In the Western world of Mead's day and our international community, there is a constant interplay and adjustment of individuals and groups to one another. Often, this is expressed in terms of military activities. One thinks of the current struggles in Gaza and the Ukraine as examples. Just as human beings seek to assert their egos in private life, in the life of nations, governments struggle for superiority and domination. With domination comes a degree of affluence and other kinds of social superiority. This, in turn, provokes additional conflict. Nevertheless, in the struggles of various societies for dominance and security, there is the potential for rational and non-violent accommodation and negation.[197]

The process of social interaction and the drive for greater and greater social organization results in conflict in and among all human societies. Anyone who has been married understands that even the smallest family unit cannot avoid periodic conflict. In analyzing the role of conflict in human societies, Mead makes a distinction between two different social situations that impact the degree and dangers of conflict:

1. Conflict within and among groups with some degree of commonality
2. Conflict between groups where there is either no degree of commonality or outright hostility.

The first situation occurs where some degree of common life, social solidarity, and friendliness exists. Conflict arises within an underlying framework of shared values and cooperation in such situations. In the second situation, the factors that tend to moderate and make rational accommodation possible are either absent or weak. As a result, there is a degree of hostility, distrust, and a lack of common life, social solidarity, and friendship.[198]

This distinction illuminates the difficulty the United States is having at the current time. Since the Second World War, especially since the late 1960s, there has been a decline in common life, social solidarity, and friendliness among social groups. There are many reasons for this. Two that come to mind are the increasing lack of shared religious and moral values and the increasing inequality of wealth and power in society. The lack of shared spiritual and ethical standards and economic disparity make it challenging to feel that social and political life is fair or just. At the same time, a historically unique kind of conflict among classes, races, religions, and other groups has emerged in America. This situation points to a need to rebuild the common life of the nation in such a way as to increase the fragile bonds of common life, social solidarity, and friendliness.

Mead recognizes an inevitable degree of hostile behavior in any society, including the modern nation-state. A society's legal system usually moderates this inevitable latent and actual conflict.[199] The ability of any legal system to curb conflict is dependent on (i) an underlying degree of lawful cooperative behavior in situations where there is or might be conflict, (ii) a degree and extent of conflict that existing institutions can handle, and (iii) a degree of trust in the fairness of existing institutions. I believe here, too, we see room for improvement and a warning concerning our current tendency to tolerate certain forms of unlawful behavior, an increasing level of social conflict, and the erosion of trust in the fundamental fairness of the legal system.

Many of the worst episodes of human violence are rooted in the human desire to achieve a perfect world within the boundaries of human history. This has been true throughout human history—and sometimes true of Christians. In the 20th century, the cataclysmic barbarity of Lenin, Hitler, Stalin, Mao, and a host of others found its roots in the mistaken belief that we can create a perfect world. Since the Enlightenment, human beings have been increasingly entranced by an unfounded hope that human beings can create an ideal society. On the left and right, politicians promise to work for such a world, and perhaps occasionally, they do so. The results are uniformly disastrous. Churches and religious leaders can and have fallen into this trap. We can create a better world with wisdom and love for one another, but humans cannot make a perfect one.

Hope for a Universal Human Society

Near the end of his discussion of conflict and integration, Mead states the following:

> The human social ideal—the ideal or ultimate goal of human social progress—is the attainment of a universal human society in which all human individuals would possess a perfected social intelligence, such that all social meanings would each be similarly reflected in their respective social consciousness—such that the meanings of any one's social acts or gestures (as realized by him and expressed in the structure of his self), through his ability to take the social attitudes of other individuals toward himself and toward their common social ends or purposes would be the same for any other individual who responded to them.[200]

Several aspects of this statement must be unpacked before we examine Mead's views on achieving his notion of a universal human society.

1. Mead accepts the Enlightenment notion of the inevitability of human progress, including human social progress towards a universal culture, which implies a universal political society.

2. The world is evolving by the laws of nature, and human society is evolving according to the unwritten law of progress. In this, Mead reflects Darwin's influence without fully applying the difference between cultural and biological evolution. In the case of biological evolution, all that is promised is survival of the fittest. In cultural evolution, such a

"tooth and nail" notion ignores that humans can create a worse future for themselves and the human race.

3. At the core of Mead's philosophy is the belief in human perfectibility, or more specifically, our capacity for a degree of "perfected social intelligence." This term encapsulates our ability to understand and interpret social meanings and to align our actions with these meanings for the betterment of society.

4. A perfected human social intelligence involves a unity of the acts and gestures of one's self ("I" and "Me"), the social self of all other individual selves, and the social self of society as a whole regarding commonly held social ends or purposes.[201]

In my view, none of this is realistic or attainable, and an attempt to implement it can result in foolish behavior, a loss of freedom, and suffering—the exact opposite of what those who make such an attempt desire. In fact, in the West, we increasingly see elites in education, politics, and media supporting a decline of freedom of speech among certain groups in the attempt to create a perfect human society based on a perfected human social structure. [202]

Underlying Mead's argument is the human capacity to identify with one another in what he would call an "organized social life process."[203] Mead understands that modern democratic societies have not reached the point where individual citizens can put themselves into the attitudes of those with whom they have relationships and whom they affect.[204] His argument, however, is based on the presumption that it is at least theoretically possible, although there are obstacles, and no society today has achieved the kind of social solidarity he envisions.

At this point, I think it might be good to put another word to this phenomenon: empathy. Empathy is the human ability to sense how another person feels and what they may think, and intellectually to be able appreciate the reasons for another human's behavior. Empathy is crucial because it allows human beings to enter the emotional and thought world of another human being in a limited way. It is fundamental to such diverse practices as leadership, counseling, and even writing a popular book.

It doesn't take a lot of experience to know that human empathy is limited. Every parent understands that they have some capacity to feel the pain and suffering of their children, but it's imperfect. Every spouse knows the same. As one gets further from familiar relations, the problem gets even more severe. Pastors understand that they cannot fully enter the pain and suffering of counselees, so they must be careful about what they say and do. Business leaders understand that it is impossible to empathize with the problems of employees completely. Government leaders have the same experience. Our human capacity for empathy is limited, not just by our individuality but also by our selfishness and self-centeredness.

Societies cannot be built on the hope that humans can fully enter into one another's experiences on a social basis. We cannot. We can hope for a degree of wisdom and love in how we treat other people, even though our interests and understanding will never be fully aligned. The problem is not that neither modern democratic societies nor any other societies have developed the capacity to understand and identify with each other fully. The problem is that it's impossible.

There is another reason why a viable society cannot be built solely on human empathy or the human ability to enter into another individual's mental, physical, and other worlds in a self-giving way: human sin, finitude, and brokenness. The human problem isn't that some people do not have sufficient empathy. The human problem is not that some people act in selfish ways. The human problem isn't that some people suffer from excessive anxiety and grasp too much money and power. The problem is that we all do.

Children and Castes

Mead continues his analysis by examining the relationship between children and adults, especially between educators and children.[205] To be effective, teachers must empathetically enter the life world of those they teach. Interestingly enough, when an adult teacher fully identifies with the children they are teaching, they regress emotionally or fail to mature as they should as adults. They get stuck in immaturity. I have seen this repeatedly during my professional career. Once again, this does not mean that we do not respect children, including respecting their limitations, emotional, physical, and mental. Any good teacher does. However, no good teacher believes it is enough to empathize with the student.

The second category Mead discusses is perhaps even more problematic. He begins to speak of "castes." Most people are familiar with the Indian caste system, an absolute, impenetrable, and humanly unfair system of social stratification. Mead takes this concept and extends it to other relationships, particularly economic relationships. Once again, motivated by the best possible intentions, he muddies the waters instead of clarifying the situation. There's a significant difference between "castes" and "achievement-oriented positions."

Most of the time, an elite is in churches, businesses, governments, academia, and other institutions. Much of the time, that elite has earned its way to a position. Of course, anyone who has worked in any organization understands that political, social, and other injustices occur. Such injustices need to be addressed. But it's a mistake to think that achievement-based excellence involves a caste that unfairly excludes other people.[206] Mead seems to understand the limits of his analysis. For example, he notes, "Insofar as specialization is normal and helpful, it increases concrete, social relationship relationships. Differences in occupation do not themselves build up castes."[207] Yet, his analysis leaves the impression that much of modern Western society's social and economic inequity stems from this problem.

Selves and Societies

At the root of human social organization is the unbridgeable distinction between self and society. Although human beings depend on one another and civilization depends on our ability to unite in common endeavors, human self-centeredness and selfishness inevitably color human social integration and render it partial. In a wonderful passage, Mead analyzes this problem:

> The "social" aspect of human society—which is simply the social aspect of the cells of all the individual members taken collectively—with its concomitant feelings on the parts of all those individuals of cooperation and social interdependence, is the basis for the development and existence of ethical ideals in that society; whereas the "asocial" aspect of human society—which is simply the asocial aspect of the cells of all human members taken collectively—with its concomitant feelings on the part of all these individuals of individual individuality,

self-superiority to other individual selves, and social independence is responsible for the rise of ethical problems in that society.[208]

Understanding what he is saying and its limitations is essential to unpack this paragraph.

1. Mead defines the social aspect of a society merely in terms of the collective interaction of individuals. This is a classic statement of the modern view that individuals exist in purely external relationships with other individuals. Any such view inevitably defines the existence of individuals in terms of power.
2. Ethics is based on a social consensus, the collective views of individual decisions concerning morality.
3. Society's ethical problems stem from "asocial" aspects of human life instead of the social aspects of human life.

Mead indicates that humans grow out of social institutions, beginning with the family. If this is to be taken seriously, human individuals have no priority over human societies. Societies and human individuals exist in a kind of dynamic relationship. Individuals and societies are both important and influential. There cannot be a healthy society without healthy individuals, and there cannot be healthy individuals without a healthy society.

Second, the modern world was built on the belief that human reason would be able to identify a set of human ethics agreed on by all reasonable people. The history of the last 300 years shows this hope to be delusional. No consensus has developed among either societies or elites, and there would seem to be little hope of a change in this situation. One need only look at divisions over abortion and sexuality in Western societies to see that a certain amount of moral and ethical diversity is inevitable if human beings are to remain free to hold and express their moral views.

Finally, it doesn't seem to me that you can say that the problems of human society stem from the "asocial" aspects of society unless you want to use the word asocial as a synonym for human self-centeredness, sin, and anxiety infinitude. If one accepts the inevitability of an asocial element to human relations, you can't consider aspects of human nature as being potentially overcome and extinguished. Instead, human asocial tendencies must be dealt with and coordinated in the search for social harmony. The writers of the Constitution had such a view. The whole system of checks and balances of American democracy arises from the view that no one is trustworthy. Therefore, everyone has to be subject to constraints and limitations.

Selves and Dialogue

There is an essential connection between Mead's concept of the social nature of the development of human and social institutions and the idea of dialogue. The development of the human self involves constant dialogue between the I and the Me. Similarly, the development of society involves constant dialogue between individuals and society as a whole. The human capacity for self-reflection and the social capacity for interaction means that a kind of dialogical interaction between individuals and social groups inevitably determines the development of society. To solve human social problems, it is essential to consider all social facts that would impact the decision. This inevitably involves the need for individuals to communicate and discuss various options and their likely consequences. For this to be done rationally, there has to be a non-violent method (dialogue) in which the parties can reach a reasonable conclusion on policy alternatives and their likely impacts.

Mead understood that human beings are inevitably embedded in time and space and are therefore limited in their reasoning by their position in the space-time continuum. Humans always perceive the present based on the past and always understand the past based on the present. In other words, there is no unfiltered, "scientific" understanding of the past. Our past is a constantly changing mental construct, as we've reflected on it, as is our anticipation of the future. Even our current perceptions are immediately colored by all of the relevant perceptions from our past.[209]

This has powerful implications for wisdom in public life. We are all colored by the attitudes, education, prejudices, and other factors of our past in our political views. Our hopes also influence our current political views for some future political situations. But we live in the present and must act in the present. The only way to overcome those prejudices is to adopt a pragmatic and dialogical attitude toward politics. As we think about past situations, we have to scrutinize them to be sure that we have the best understanding of what occurred and how effective a former policy was that we could have. We have to overcome our partial knowledge of that past. On the other hand, as we gaze at our preferred future, we also must act wisely. Instead of making massive changes, we must experiment and ensure our hoped-for future can be obtained.

Since Darwin's time, all philosophy has been influenced by and must account for evolution. Mead represents one attempt to do so in the area of social psychology. Lurking behind his notion of emergent universality is the idea that human social organization is "going somewhere" in an evolutionary process. Human societies demonstrate a form of development analogous to biological evolution. Mead understands that the evolution of human societies is not the same or subject to the same forces as natural evolution. The evolution of human societies involves the activities of human beings and the choices they make. The impact of human freedom on the evolution of human society means that it cannot be conceived of as inevitably progressive or even inevitably adaptive to social situations and forces. History is filled with societies that passed away simply because they did not creatively adapt to the future. Furthermore, there is no reason to believe that contemporary, modern Western society is exempt from the risk of extinction.

A *sophio-agapic* approach to political theory does not deny an evolutionary context to human social organization. It does not even deny the application of the metaphor of evolution to human social change. However, it does insist on the impact of both human reason and the capacity of human beings to cherish and develop social institutions. This means that there is no certainty to social evolution. Rather than being evolutionary in a materialistic sense of that term, it is evolutionary because of the choices human beings make or do not make to improve the condition of society in the search for a social order.

CHAPTER 6

THE RATIONAL POLITICS
OF PRAGMATISM

John Dewey (1859-1952) was undoubtedly one of the most influential political and philosophical American thinkers. His work as a philosopher included educational philosophy, political philosophy, and other fields. He popularized pragmatism as a method, a way of looking at the world, and a mechanism for social change. Dewey's experimentalism incorporates Peirce's belief that philosophy ought to emulate science as a fallible enterprise of solving concrete theoretical problems in which defined, limited, and provisional problems are solved experimentally and scientifically. This pragmatic view of reason is vital for a *sophio-agapic* understanding of politics.

John Dewey was born in Burlington, Vermont. After completing undergraduate studies at the University of Vermont, Dewey earned a Ph.D. from Johns Hopkins University, where he studied under Charles S. Peirce. After that, Dewey taught at the Universities of Minnesota, Michigan, and Chicago. After a dispute in Chicago, Dewey finished his career at Columbia University in New York City, where he chaired the philosophy department until retirement. After his retirement, Dewey lived another twenty-two years. He continued writing articles and books on philosophy, logic, art, education, science, and social and political reform. Among his many books are *Democracy and Education*, *Reconstruction in Philosophy*, *The Public and Its Problems*, and *Freedom and Culture*.[210]

Individualism

Dewey was a defender of a kind of individualism that makes the individual and their self-development the supreme end of political thinking. This radical individualism translates into a democratic theory in which the individual is the center of all political calculation. Nevertheless, Dewey's individualism might be better termed "communal individualism," whereby the individual finds full self-actualization as a part of a society. This individualism does not deny the government the ability, and even duty, to plan and control a great deal of the activity of individuals, especially in the economic arena.[211]

As indicated, for Dewey, society is composed of individuals, and it is the individual that sits at the foundation of any democratic society:

> Society is composed of individuals: this obvious and basic fact no philosophy, whatever its pretensions to novelty, can question or alter. Hence these three alternatives: Society must exist for the sake of individuals; or individuals must have their ends and ways of living set for them by society; *or else society and individuals are correlative, organic, to one another*, society requiring the service and subordination

of individuals and at the same time existing to serve them. Beyond these three views, none seems to be logically conceivable. (Emphasis added)[212]

For Dewey, both the individual and the social are fundamental to society and exist in a mutually beneficial, organic, and "correlative" relationship.[213] However, individuals are not atomistic units but are formed by society within families and various social institutions.[214]

Pragmatic Communitarianism

One review of his thought describes Dewey's philosophy as follows:

> Dewey elaborates a version of the Idealist criticisms of classical liberal individualism. For this line of criticism, classical liberalism envisages the individual as an independent entity in competition with other individuals, and takes social and political life as a sphere in which this competitive pursuit of self-interest is coordinated. By contrast, the Idealists rejected this view of social and political life as the aggregation of inherently conflicting private interests. Instead, they sought to view individuals relationally: individuality could be sustained only where social life was understood as an organism in which the well-being of each part was tied to the well-being of the whole. Freedom in a positive sense consisted not merely in the absence of external constraints but the positive fact of participation in such an ethically desirable social order.[215]

In Dewey, a complementarian relationship exists between the individual and social institutions, each relying on the other for its full and healthy expression. Individuals cannot emerge without a sound society in which they can flourish, nor can society flourish without well-formed individuals.

Mediating Institutions

The modern bureaucratic and administrative nation-state, a relatively new institution in human history, tends to represent the same set of powers in all of its various instantiations. It emerged from a long struggle of society to liberate itself from subservience to feudal and other ancient and medieval social orders. In contemporary free societies, the state exists, at least in part, to give support and freedom to other social institutions:

> As the work of integration and consolidation reaches its climax, the question arises, however, whether the national state, once it is firmly established and no longer struggling against strong foes, is not just an instrumentality for promoting and protecting other and more voluntary forms of association, rather than a supreme end in itself. Two actual phenomena may be pointed to in support of an affirmative answer. Along with the development of the larger, more inclusive and more unified organization of the state has gone the emancipation of individuals from restrictions and servitudes previously imposed by custom and class status. But the individuals freed from external and coercive bonds have not remained isolated. Social molecules have at once recombined in new associations and organizations. Compulsory associations have been replaced by voluntary ones; rigid organizations by those more amenable to human choice and purposes—more directly changeable at will. What upon one side looks like a movement toward individualism, turns out to be really

a movement toward multiplying all kinds and varieties of associations: Political parties, industrial corporations, scientific and artistic organizations, trade unions, churches, schools, clubs and societies without number, for the cultivation of every conceivable interest that men have in common. As they develop in number and importance, the state tends to become more and more a regulator and adjuster among them; defining the limits of their actions, preventing and settling conflicts.[216]

Because human beings are social animals by nature, the freedom humans gained during the modern era did not change society's fundamentally relational and communitarian nature. What changed is that, instead of *externally* imposed social relationships, the foundation of society came to consist in *voluntary* social relationships and societies through which human beings develop and express their capacities. The government's responsibility is to secure the status and freedom of the many voluntary societies of which any given political unit is composed.

Once a nation, like the United States of America, has achieved its status as the supreme governing body over a territory, it becomes the duty and primary responsibility of the governing body to secure the freedom and security of the various persons and social groups of which it is composed. Governments should not be monopolists of either political or economic power, as they are under both Communism and National Socialism, but regulators and guarantors of freedom for all persons and institutions within their boundaries. In essence, governments must learn to serve the social organs of the country, especially what we would call "mediating institutions."

Society as a Process

Dewey is steadfastly committed to Darwinism and a vision of nature and society embedded in continuous change and development. This involves a vision of human maturation and human society as unceasingly in a state of dynamic change:

> The tendency to treat organization as an end in itself is responsible for all the exaggerated theories in which individuals are subordinated to some institution to which is given the noble name of society. Society is the *process* of associating in such ways that experiences, ideas, emotions, values are transmitted and made common. To this active process, both the individual and the institutionally organized may truly be said to be subordinate. The individual is subordinate because except in and through communication of experience from and to others, he remains dumb, merely sentient, a brute animal. Only in association with fellows does he become a conscious centre of experience. Organization, which is what traditional theory has generally meant by the term Society or State, is also subordinate because it becomes static, rigid, institutionalized whenever it is not employed to facilitate and enrich the contacts of human beings with one another.[217]

Individuals are embedded in society so that ideas, emotions, values, and other features of a healthy culture are transmitted and made "common." As human beings join cooperative enterprises, they free themselves from static, rigid conformity and are enriched in the process of social progress. Members of a society must be willing to change and grow as society adapts to an ever-changing and evolving environment. This adaptation involves inevitable change in society and in certain of its institutions. "Freedom for an individual means growth, ready change when modification is required."[218] This fundamentally evolutionary and process orientation derives from Dewey's dynamic view of society and social relationships.

Democracy and Education

Dewey was not only a political philosopher but also, perhaps even primarily, an educational philosopher. His best-known work is on education, *Democracy and Education*.[219] The book's fundamental premise is that personal death requires societies to have education systems. One generation succeeds another, and any form of social progress involves the transmission of past experiences to a future generation:

> The primary ineluctable facts of the birth and death of each one of the constituent members in a social group determine the necessity of education. On one hand, there is the contrast between the immaturity of the new-born members of the group—its future sole representatives— and the maturity of the adult members who possess the knowledge and customs of the group. On the other hand, there is the necessity that these immature members be not merely physically preserved in adequate numbers, but that they be initiated into the interests, purposes, information, skill, and practices of the mature members: otherwise the group will cease its characteristic life.[220]

The necessity for education born of human finitude is true of even the simplest of societies, but as society grows more complex, education becomes even more critical. A society continues only so long as it transmits its underlying values to a new generation. This explains a great deal of the difficulties our society is having at present. Our educational systems have failed to transmit the underlying understanding of and appreciation for the values of our society to succeeding generations. Focusing on what is wrong with the American experiment and society has been taken to such an extreme that the succeeding generations do not understand the history, democratic tradition, personal and social skills, and other elements needed for our society to endure.

Human beings and society depend on the communication of the aims, beliefs, aspirations, knowledge, shared understanding, and the like so that a functional degree of "like-mindedness" exists among society members.[221] Communication between parents and children, children and adults, teachers and students, managers and workers, artists, admirers, etc., is essential for a society to continue and prosper. In placing communication at the center of society, Dewey is not merely talking about communication of information, but also communication of meaning and purpose, a communication of the heart of a society as well as raw information about that society, its institutions, and past accomplishments and failures.

While all persons and institutions in a society bear some responsibility for communicating the past to the next generation, there must be some form of formal education in a complex society. Certain institutions must be formed, and people must be recruited to transmit what is essential for society to continue. A complex society has no alternative but to create a system or systems of formal education:

> Without such formal education, it is not possible to transmit all the resources and achievements of a complex society. It also opens a way to a kind of experience which

would not be accessible to the young, if they were left to pick up their training in informal association with others, since books and the symbols of knowledge are mastered.[222]

As a pragmatist, Dewey is committed to the notion of community and its importance in human relations, including its importance to logical and scientific thinking. Thus, he argues:

THE ENVIRONMENT in which human beings live, act and inquire, is not simply physical. It is cultural as well. Problems which induce inquiry grow out of the relations of fellow beings to one another, and the organs for dealing with these relations are not only the eye and ear, but the meanings which have developed in the course of living, together with the ways of forming and transmitting culture with all its constituents of tools, arts, institutions, traditions and customary beliefs.[223]

In this concise paragraph, Dewey masterfully introduces the intricacies of decision-making in the political sphere. He underscores the challenges politicians face in making decisions within a specific cultural environment. This environment is a complex tapestry of societal artifacts, traditions, customs, beliefs, and attitudes towards governance and each other. Altering this inherited cultural milieu is a Herculean task that often spans generations. In the brief tenure of any policymaker, this is a reality that must be acknowledged.

Dewey agrees with Aristotle that human beings are social animals by nature. As social animals, humans create situations and social environments that emerge from the natural world, but exist on a distinct level of reality. The human capacity for thought, logic, creativity, moral decision-making, and like make human beings a distinct and unique creature and human cultures different from the natural environment.[224] Sitting at the root of human uniqueness is the fact of human languages. Human beings can develop sign systems and communicate information through those sign systems.[225]

> Language occupies a peculiarly significant place and exercises a peculiarly significant function in the complex that forms the cultural environment. It is itself a cultural institution, and, from one point of view, is but one among many such institutions. But it is (1) the agency by which other institutions and acquired habits are transmitted, and (2) it permeates both the forms and the contents of all other cultural activities.[226]

Human language is the basis of human culture and every cultural institution, including any society's political and legal institutions. Language is the agency by which these institutions can be created and maintained.

Human languages have multiple uses, two of which are of particular significance in politics:

1. Sitting at the base of all specialized languages is what might be called the common-sense language of a people. The common-sense language of a people refers to those largely unexamined fundamental concepts that a group holds tacitly and subconsciously inform its judgments. For example, in America, it's taken for granted that individuals should be free, and this freedom involves the ability to say and do what we please. This is a tacitly held

fundamental, common-sense idea of almost all Americans.

2. The second kind of language is what we would call scientific language. Our language is subject to experimental testing regarding its validity and limits. Contrary to common sense language, what Dewey calls "scientific language" is what we might call "examined language." Examined language has been scrutinized and clarified to see how far common sense is correct and can be applied. For example, in the law, the fundamental common-sense notion of freedom finds a restriction when I use my freedom to scream 'fire' in a crowded theater.

On examination, limitations are inherent in our common-sense ideas, and some are even proven false. These limitations are relevant to political discourse. Dewey analyzes the difference as follows:

The resulting difference in the two types of language meanings fundamentally fixes the difference between what is called common sense and what is called science. In the former cases, a group's customs, ethos, and spirit are the decisive factors in determining the system of meanings in use. The system is one in a practical and institutional sense rather than in an intellectual sense. Meanings that are formed on this basis are sure to contain much that is irrelevant and to exclude much that is required for intelligent control of activity.[227]

In addition to the limits of common sense, human beings are not merely rational, sign-producing, and sign-using biological computers. In the human person, there is a unique role for emotion and (I would say) the full range of moral and spiritual constituents of the human personality. Dewey put it this way:

> Another phase of the problem is brought out by the part played in human judgments by emotion and desire. These personal traits cook the evidence and determine the result that is reached. That is, upon the level of organic factors (which are the actively determining forces in the type of cases just mentioned), the individual with his individual peculiarities, whether native or acquired, is an active participant in producing ideas and beliefs, and yet the latter are logically grounded only when such peculiarities are deliberately precluded from taking effect.[228]

In other words, human decision-making is inevitably impacted by organic factors and by the entire emotional makeup of human beings. In my judgment, Dewey makes an error when thinking that logic must preclude these factors from impacting decisions. What logic should do is seek to be sure that the emotional and spiritual components are, in fact, rational. As everyone knows, not every emotional, spiritual, or moral conclusion of human individuals is rational. This does not mean that they should be excluded from the realm of logical inquiry or, in the case of political inquiry, from public debate.

Abduction and Reasonable Inquiry

Most people are familiar with two methods of logical inquiry: "induction" and "deduction." As previously indicated, Peirce introduced a third, intermediate logic called "abduction." All human thinking consists of manipulating signs in one or more of these three logical ways. Abductive logic yields the kind of daily decision-making that does its best with the information that can be acquired, is often incomplete, and draws a conclusion based on the best available evidence. It then tests its findings.

For Dewey, like Peirce, abductive reasoning is at the center of a scientific approach to understanding and at the center of other forms of intellectual progress as well. Neither induction nor deduction can provide intellectual explanations of phenomena. All inquiry begins with a problem and one or more hypotheses or ideas about the best answer or solution to the problem. This has important implications because it "dethrones" the positivist notion of knowledge as based on "the facts alone." Instead, all facts are identified and interpreted within some interpretive framework. Science, for example, is interested in developing and analyzing facts. Still, those facts are developed and analyzed within a theoretical matrix of reasonableness based on the scientific method.

Science is not the only area of life in which one has to reason from a hypothesis to a conclusion that can be tested against the facts. For example, in solving a crime, one makes a conjecture as to possible culprits based on factors such as motive, means, and opportunity, and then collects evidence to verify or refute the conjecture. In business, this approach is essential when launching a new product. Based on initial research and trends, one hypothesizes that the new product will be successful in the market. However, before committing significant resources, it is crucial to conduct comprehensive market research to validate this hypothesis and ensure that the investment will yield the expected returns. Similarly, in law, a lawyer might theorize that a particular legal structure is the most appropriate for a transaction. To confirm this theory, the lawyer must thoroughly examine relevant legal precedents, regulations, and implications to ensure the structure is legally sound and beneficial for the client. In government, policymakers might propose a strategy such as raising taxes to address a fiscal issue. However, it is necessary to investigate and analyze economic data, historical outcomes, and public opinion to substantiate this policy recommendation and to forecast its potential impacts accurately.

Deep within the logical views of Peirce and Royce is the notion that all thinking is tripartite. First, outside of myself, a reality is being investigated (the object). Second, my ideas (or those of my group) about that object exist. Finally, there is the interpretation of my ideas (or my group's) of that reality by a third party, the interpreter. In many ways, this is the most complicated aspect of public discourse. In a nation of 300 million people, there are countless interpretations of the same reality. There are many different interpretations of any one group's ideas about any political reality. If they are to act logically and wisely, public officials have to somehow analyze, usually in groups, that reality and all the various ways in which it is interpreted and, from that, develop a course of action (the policy choice). This is where Dewey's logical theories become important. It is not enough for there to be dialogue. That dialogue must be such that it allows a society to reach rational conclusions about matters of public policy. This leads to an examination of the role of logic in Dewey's thought.

The Logic of Dewey

Dewey considered his view of logic as "instrumentalism."[229] That is to say, logic exists as an instrument by which human beings make decisions. Because Dewey was a materialist, he considered that our notions of logic have two sources:

1. **Nature:** The universe's evolution created species that survive a way of looking at reality that was pragmatically useful for survival. That pragmatic way of looking at reality in the quest for survival is a natural source of logic.

2. **Society and Culture:** All human beings exist in an evolved human society. Specific ways of thinking and looking at reality were conducive to that society's success and challenges. Thus, culture is also a source of logic.[230]

In other words, logic does not emerge from a pre-existing ideal realm of pure reason, as Plato might have thought. Instead, these forms of reasoning evolved as humans faced reality and tried to adapt successfully to that reality and the challenges it presented. If we go this far with Dewey, we can see a natural connection between logic and political theory. Demanding that our public debate be rational and logical is just part of demanding that it successfully leads to policies that serve the common good.

Because logic emerges from the character and evolution of the universe and human cultures, it is inevitably a progressive and evolutionary discipline.[231] Like other forms of human understanding, logic constantly unfolds as it adapts to new and different circumstances. This is important for a constructive, postmodern, *sophio-agapic* view of logic. Currently, the logical theories prominent in the late 19th and early 20th centuries are gradually being superseded by "postmodern logic," which incorporates the logical discoveries occasioned by quantum theory and other scientific advances. Postmodern logic is a non-classical probability calculus resting on a non-classical propositional logic.[232] In this kind of logic, the law of the excluded middle, for example, is superseded in some situations by the existence of more than one alternative future state of the logical system.

This changing and progressive nature of human logic's unfolding does not undermine the universe's fundamental rationality. The universe itself displays an inherent rationality. We see evidence of this rationality logically developed in the mathematics of, for example, quantum physics. This rationality embedded in the universe is in some way prior to human evolutionary rationality and human culture. Nevertheless, the rationality considered final by any given society may come to be superseded as a deeper understanding of reality emerges.

This does not undermine human rationality or the evolutionary impact on human rationality. On the assumption that evolution and the gradual development of human culture were built into the universe's potential from its inception over millions of years, the rationality we observe in the universe and human culture gradually emerged. The British physicist turned religious scholar John Polkinghorne put it this way:

> Certainly, our powers of thought must be in such conformity with the everyday structure of the world that we are able to survive by making sense of our environment. But that does not begin to explain why highly abstract concepts of pure mathematics should fit perfectly with the patterns of the subatomic world of quantum theory or the cosmic world of relativity, both of which are regimes whose understanding is of no practical consequence whatsoever from humankind's ability to have held its own in the evolutionary struggle.
>
> Nor does the fact that we are made of the same stuff (quarks, gluons and electrons) as the universe serve to explain how microscopic man is able to understand the

microcosm of the world. Some fairly desperate attempts have been made along these lines nevertheless showing how pressing is the need to find an explanation for the significant fact of intelligibility.[233]

The universe as we experience it is intelligible, but the precise forms, mathematical and linguistic, are appropriate to describe that intelligibility evolves as progress is made in understanding reality. This reality is, as has been shown, both material and noetic. Our understanding of the invisible noetic realities progresses, as does our understanding of material reality.

Common Sense and Political Deliberation

Dewey distinguishes between common sense language and scientific language. I would call the latter "examined language," which includes language we would call scientific, that is, language that has been subject to the kind of inquiry and verification we associate with science. Our common-sense view of many situations almost amounts to a presupposition to see certain things in certain ways. Dewey talks about common sense as follows:

The use of the term common sense is somewhat arbitrary from a linguistic point of view. But the existence of the kinds of situations referred to and of the kind of inquiries that deal with the difficulties and predicaments they present cannot be doubted. They are those which continuously arise in the conduct of life and the ordering of day-by-day behavior. They are such as constantly arise in the development of the young as they learn to make their way in the physical and social environments in which they live; they occur and recur in the life-activity of every adult, whether farmer, artisan, professional man, law-maker or administrator; citizen of a state, husband, wife, or parent. On their very face they need to be discriminated from inquiries that are distinctively scientific, or that aim at attaining confirmed facts, "laws" and theories.[234]

Ordinary human life would be impossible without common sense. Where common sense begins to deteriorate, social chaos almost always ensues. For example, in nearly all of their deliberations, lawmakers have to rely on common sense or what might be called traditional interpretations of the Constitution. There are times when changes need to be made, and those fundamental assumptions, those common-sense ways of looking at things, must be questioned. But most of the time, they do not. This view of common sense is similar to Michael Polanyi's understanding of tacit knowledge.[235] Human society and any form of human inquiry rest on a foundation of tacitly held beliefs about how a particular phenomenon works. Tacit understanding sits behind all other inquiries as a foundation for intellectual, moral, or spiritual progress.

This particular insight casts doubt on what is sometimes called the postmodern deconstructionist project. This project deconstructs common sense and social customs, exposing them as mere bids for power. In this view, social institutions and legal principles simply reflect the decisions of elite groups. A *socio-agapic* approach, on the other hand, holds that every society must have such common-sense tenets, many of which reflect a generational understanding of what works in human society. This is fundamental to what I have called a *socio-agapic* view of politics. That is to say, the idea that the family is essential, that children should take care of parents, and that parents should take care of children, that people should work hard for a living, and a vast number of critical social ideals and institutions reflect the common sense of the human species over millennia.

Dewey makes an excellent point when he observes that much of common sense is qualitative.[236] Much common sense concerns the quality of human life regarding fundamental matters. These qualitative decisions are not necessarily subject to the same form of scientific inquiry as other policy decisions. This does not mean that they are irrational. Even our qualitative judgments are subject to an examination appropriate to the nature of the subject matter under investigation.

Just to give one example, the prohibition against murder was not simply a prejudice enacted into law by a group of people to subordinate the views of another group of people who happened to believe in murder. Murder is prohibited because it has been the universal human experience that murder causes social instability and violence. To control violence, murder needs to be controlled. This is a simple and obvious example, but many other examples are not so simple, nor are they so obvious. Legal systems have developed complex theories of law that define the contours of murder, the kinds of things that constitute an acceptable taking of life, the kind of punishments appropriate to various infractions, and a variety of other adaptations, all in the search for a just and harmonious society.

Dewey properly recognizes that there are limits to common sense, and being a modern post-enlightenment thinker, he is not inclined to grant common sense its full range of applicability. Partially, this is due to recognizing the cultural variability of many common-sense ideas. Dewey recognizes that common sense varies from culture to culture in some ways. The virtues of nomadic tribesmen in seventh-century Arabia are not necessarily the common-sense virtues of a person living in Los Angeles, California, in the early 21st century. His point is as follows:

> One has only to note the enormous differences in the contents and methods of common sense in modes of life that are respectively dominantly nomadic, agricultural and industrial. Much that was once taken without question as a matter of common sense is forgotten or actively condemned. Other old conceptions and convictions continue to receive theoretical assent and strong emotional attachment because of their prestige. But they have little hold and application in the ordinary affairs of life.[237]

Dewey has a point here. However, his point can be, and often is, overstated in our society. For example, there's no question that many of the sayings of the Old Testament were created in a culture far different from ours. Nevertheless, they continue to guide everyday life in almost every matter of daily existence. The same could be said of Oriental wisdom literature, the wisdom literature of the ancient world, and other world religions today. Fundamental notions such as the importance of honesty, sobriety, hard work, faithfulness, harmonic human relations, and other aspects of common sense may not have a hold on ordinary life, but they should have. It is not the case that all of the verities that common sense urges on human beings are outdated simply because they are ancient in their origin.

In his book *The Abolition of Man*, C. S. Lewis used the Chinese philosophical term "Tao" to encompass what he considers to be the broadly accepted, traditional moralities of both Eastern and Western cultures—including Platonic, Hindu, Taoist, Christian, and others.[238] The Tao assumes a ground to objective value in which certain attitudes and beliefs are true and others false. By "true" and "false," we mean true or false to the kind of thing the universe is and the kind of things human beings are.[239] This Tao or "Way" is described by Lewis as follows:

> It is the reality beyond all predicates, the abyss that was before the Creator Himself. It is Nature, the Way, and the Road. It is the Way in which the universe goes on, the way in which things everlasting emerge, stilly and tranquilly, into space and time. It is also the Way which every human being should tread in imitation of that cosmic and super-cosmic progression, conforming all activities to that great exemplar.[240]

Lewis argues that this Tao, or Way, is the basis for all objective principles and human virtue. In short, in his usage, the Tao refers to the belief "that certain attitudes are true, and others false, to the kind of thing the universe is and the kind of things we are."[241] Throughout *The Abolition of Man*, Lewis argues that the modern abandonment of a belief in the historical ground of ethics and public morality endangers society. That is to say, many items of wisdom and morality are not entirely matters of conventional common sense; they are embedded in the way things are, and the fact that different societies construct specific moral and practical issues differently does not in any way eliminate the reality of common-sense solutions to human problems developed over centuries.

Instrumentalism and Public Policy

It should be evident that the notion that reason has an instrumental function and that logic is instrumental has significant consequences for the development of public policy and the conduct of public debate. Rational public discourse cannot simply involve an attempt to gain enough public support that one's ideas can be enacted into policy. From a *sophio-agapic* point of view, public policy formation begins with identifying a problem. Subsequently, it is finally about adopting strategies and tactics that will lead society to a better state.[242] As to justice, public policy is finally about the gradual evolution of a more just society in a way in which all citizens' rights are protected and enhanced. As such, it is an essentially logical process. Dewey put it this way:

> It is reasonable to search for and select the means that will, with the maximum probability, yield the consequences which are intended. It is highly unreasonable to employ as means, materials and processes which would be found, if they were examined, to be such that they produce consequences which are different from the intended end; so different that they preclude its attainment.[243]

Applied to the realm of public discourse, this principle can be stated as follows:

> *Public policy is unreasonable if it adopts policies and processes that, under examination, are likely to produce consequences contrary to the public good and the intended result.*

Political actors must be willing to subject their views to criticism and modify their policies where the best evidence indicates that the public good intended cannot be acquired by the means chosen. This inevitably involves a logical and reasoned approach to public policy development, not simply enacting policies that more special interest groups favor.

Wise public policymaking involves using all the forms of logic. Political actors must guess what the wisest public policy is (hypothesis). They must gather facts that either support or do not support our hypothetical public policy. Finally, in reaching our conclusions, we must ensure they're not deductively incoherent. This is part and parcel of proving or disproving the hypothesis.

Deliberation and Enhanced Common Sense

We have already seen that abductive logic proceeds from a perceived problem to a hypothetical proposal for the solution of the problem to a testing of that problem. Where ideology is allowed to determine the adoption of solutions to political issues, preconceived notions are improperly allowed to determine results. Dewey states the problem in the following terms:

> But in social matters, those who claim that they are in possession of the only sure solution of social problems often set themselves up as being peculiarly scientific while others are floundering around in an "empirical" morass. Only recognition in both theory and practice that ends to be attained (ends-in-view) are of the nature of hypotheses and that hypotheses have to be formed and tested in strict correlativity with existential conditions as means, can alter current habits of dealing with social issues.[244]

Here, we see the fundamental problem with much modern political discourse. Those on the political left who favor collectivist solutions and those on the right who favor unlimited personal freedom believe they possess the only scientific solution to political problems. Therefore, they do not see the need to consider their proposals as hypotheses that must be checked against reality to ensure they work in practice.

It is not enough to have debate, discussion, argumentation, or even conversation and dialogue. The conversation has to be conducted to evaluate public policies and choose rational means to test them before adoption, or at least before adoption, in such a way that the consequences might be disastrous. In this vein, moral judgments cannot be excluded from the evaluating process since they are part of the matrix of existential and potentially observable and recordable material that makes up the facts of the case.[245] Wherever political conclusions are taken to be *a priori* true or determined by ideological, philosophical, or other commitments, the process of rational policy determination is bypassed.[246]

Conclusion

As sympathetic a reviewer as Bertrand Russell noted that, in the end, Dewey's philosophy is about power, and in that sense, "Nietzschean," though not as crudely Nietzschean as that of Nietzsche.[247] Reason is merely instrumental—an instrument of human will. In this sense, Dewey's philosophy is "modern" in that it is dominated by a materialistic application of Newtonian and Darwinian principles to society and politics. The pragmaticism of Peirce and Royce is missing.

This does not mean that Dewey should not be taken seriously in a *sophio-agapic* understanding of political life. Since all human reasoning, including political reasoning, must be conducted logically and in the search for truth, restrictions are placed on dialogue. It is also fundamental to a solid understanding of politics that decisions should be tested to be certain that they are correct before being implemented on a grand scale. As Dewey puts it: "Unless the decision reached is arrived at blindly and arbitrarily, it is obtained by gathering and surveying evidence appraised as to its weight and relevancy; and by framing and testing plans of action in their capacity as hypotheses: that is, as ideas."[248] In other words, dialogue alone is not a sufficient guarantor of good decision-making in politics, just as in any area of inquiry.

Dialogue alone is not enough; dialogue must be conducted reasonably and rationally with a view to solving some problem or finding a solution to some disagreement. This takes us back to the fundamental meaning of dialogue. The Greek roots "dia" or "through" and "logos" or "reason" indicate that dialogue is not a mere sharing of opinions. Instead, it is sharing logical views to reach a deeper understanding of the truth about a matter under deliberation.

Like Peirce, Dewey has a "scientific and instrumental" view of knowledge that includes a kind of fallibilism that recognizes that our ideas, however well attested by reality and comprehensively accepted, can always be wrong and need revision. This excludes any sympathy for totalitarian undertakings in philosophy, politics, education, or any other field of inquiry. This part of Dewey's philosophy is of increasing importance in our society, in which there are so many loud voices, left and right, who are sure of the truth about their own opinions and are contemptuous of the views of others.

Dewey, like Mead, is included in this study, not because of his fundamental agreement with a sophio-agapic approach to political decision-making and the reality of ideals like justice but because of his importance in underscoring the role of community, logic, and scientific inquiry in the process of political dialogue. Politics is not conducted in the abstract world of spiritual ideals but in the real world of investigation, accommodation, negotiation, and decision-making.

CHAPTER 7

CRITICAL REALISM, TRADITION, & SOPHIA-AGAPISM

ichael Polanyi (1891-1976) worked as a research chemist after receiving doctoral degrees in medicine and science and made important discoveries as a practicing scientist. Polanyi was familiar with quantum physics and its application to chemistry. After Hitler rose to power, Polanyi, of Jewish descent, emigrated to Britain and became a Professor of Physical Chemistry at the University of Manchester (1933-1948). Eventually, concerned about the condition of Western culture, Polanyi determined to turn his attention to philosophical pursuits. Because of his interest in and contribution to social sciences and philosophy, Polanyi was made Professor of Social Sciences at the University of Manchester (1948-58). He also lectured as a visiting professor or senior fellow at Chicago, Aberdeen, Virginia, Stanford, and Merton College, Oxford.[249]

Dangers of Politicization of Science and Learning

The overt politicization of science in Nazi Germany, and the collectivist destruction of science in Communist Russia, made a profound impact on Polanyi. He observed first-hand the distortions of science that totalitarian regimes create. In his little book, *Science Faith and Society*, Polanyi outlined the problem of politicized science and his proposal for the freedom of science from political manipulation.[250] In so doing, he set out the fundamentals of his ideal of a free society—or perhaps more importantly, a free society composed of communities devoted to the search for truth at multiple levels of reality. Given the current loss of belief in the truth in Western societies, which Polanyi experienced in Germany and Eastern Europe, his work is of contemporary relevance.

In the Soviet Union, science was conducted in an atmosphere of what we would call "extreme political correctness." It was an article of faith that Marxist dialectical materialism embodied the ultimate scientific explanation for and guidance to society. No scientific inquiry could be done that did not advance the cause of the creation of the perfect socialist state. There was nothing like "pure science" in any area of scientific endeavor. Eventually, nearly all scientific work was brought under the control of Communist ideology.[251] Scientific efforts were required to serve the state as the embodiment of the will of the people and the revolution. Non-scientists, pseudo-scientists, and politicians directed the course of science with disastrous results. In the process, the Soviet Union devastated their scientific community, especially in biology and the "human sciences."[252]

It is hard to overestimate the impact of Marx on modern Western society, even among intellectuals who would disclaim that they are "Marxists." Marxist ideology and a fundamentally materialistic and Marxist approach to political thought lie deep in the modern intellectual psyche. Many people base their decision-making on the assumption that material forces govern the world and socio-economic forces control history. This way of thinking often comes out in political discussions on matters of great public importance. The idea that history has an inevitable, materially determined conclusion is a remnant of Marx, even when held by those who have never read him and by some who disagree with him. Such a view is destructive of both human reason and freedom. Contrary to this way of thinking, a *sophio-agapic* approach to politics holds that human beings are morally responsible for the societies they create, their decisions, and the future they bring about through their actions.[253] Polanyi believed restoring a balanced human approach to all human endeavors was essential instead of the currently prevalent materialistic vision of human society and political action.

A False Ideal of Objectivity

Under the influence of the principle that reality is composed of only matter and energy, during the 19th and early 20th centuries, the idea developed that all actual knowledge was scientific and that objective observers could, by scientific investigation, uncover all (and the only) truth about reality. This thinking took an extreme turn with what is sometimes called "logical positivism" under the influence of the philosophers of the so-called "Vienna circle." According to this way of thinking, statements are meaningful only if empirically verifiable (using the techniques of science) or tautological (*logically necessary*).

Polanyi, on the other hand, believed logical positivism set up a false idea of scientific knowledge based on the notion that science consists of a set of statements, which are objective in the sense that they are entirely determined by observation.[254] This false ideal of objectivity ignored the reality that science is profoundly shaped by theory—including at the level of "objective observation." It also ignores the active participation of investigators within the reality they are studying and seeking to understand. As Polanyi points out, the abstract theories held by participants in inquiries are the source of objectivity, for they are the publicly stated views of scientists subject to criticism and correction.

Knowing the Truth

For Polanyi, all knowledge is personal. People search for knowledge, attempt to uncover new aspects of reality and acquire knowledge about the facts in which they have a personal interest. This is true in science and all other areas of human inquiry. Just as modern quantum physics has uncovered the role of the observer in science, human inquirers are fundamental to all areas of human knowledge. Human culture involves humans as integral parts of the "world system" that can be investigated at many levels: physical, moral, aesthetic, theoretical, etc. The prejudices, abilities, cultural heritage, level of training, and many other aspects of the human observer impact every area of inquiry, including understanding the political life of a society.

For Polanyi, humans believe something to be true when we think the order, or symmetry, we have discovered in some reality will manifest itself in future observations. This capacity to be revealed in the future is not restricted to material phenomena. Polanyi believes that we expect many unseen things to reveal themselves. Truth, Justice, Beauty, God, and all the values that make human life worth living exhibit an immaterial reality expected to show itself in the future by those who have dedicated themselves to the search for truth.

The scientist in a laboratory, the painter in a studio, the moral philosopher at a computer screen, the physicist in a laboratory, the judge writing a decision, and the priest praying at an altar serve an invisible reality they believe will reveal itself to the determined seeker. These seekers believe a new truth, solution, or discovery will be revealed. Each seeker believes their endeavor will lead to discoveries and expand our experience and knowledge of Truth, Beauty, Justice, and God. In this way, scientific knowledge is no different than, or superior to, other forms of knowledge. This idea of a community dedicated to the search for truth can also be applied to political communities.[255] Faith in the immaterial, noetic reality of justice can guide people, communities, nations, and societies into a brighter future and manifest themselves as emergent realities to those who diligently seek them.[256]

When a scientist publishes the results of a research project, they make a public declaration to their community of inquiry concerning what they have come to believe is valid about a matter under investigation. Similarly, when a lawyer finishes a brief, a painter finishes a painting, a writer finishes a novel, and a pastor finishes a sermon, they publish to the world their work—for which they will be held personally accountable by their peers. Progress is made if some aspect of truth, justice, beauty, or goodness is revealed. If a mistake has been made, it will be pointed out. In publishing a work in any area, a person submits their work to the critical judgment of the community as a whole and takes personal responsibility for it.

Traditions of Inquiry

A crucial aspect of Polanyi's communitarian view of science is his emphasis on tradition as how any community of inquiry maintains its project into the future. For most Western people, the term "tradition" connotes an inherited set of beliefs resistant to change. The Latin word "*traditio*" refers to a teaching, belief, or practice handed down from generation to generation. It means to "hand over." The Greek word from which the Latin root derives is more precise and includes the idea of a gift or charitable bestowal given to another. Traditions are inherently communal because a community is required for a practice to continue and be passed on from generation to generation. Traditions are also inherently personal because people participate in a tradition as it unfolds.

A tradition involves handing over specific teaching, ideas, skills, and methods from one generation to another. The development of science has proceeded in this way. It can also mean handing over a way of life from a generation that has lived it to another emerging generation that inherits it from its predecessors. Religious communities typically pass forward a way of life, for example, prayerfulness or meditation, to succeeding generations. The skills required to maintain a way of life often do not involve mere knowledge. Instead, they include character traits, habits, instincts, and abilities that cannot be reduced to information, for they are learned by apprenticeship. This is also true in the context of political realities.[257]

For example, while practicing law involves specialized knowledge and knowledge that can be passed down intellectually, it also involves skills, habits of work, relational skills in managing clients, and a host of habits and character traits that cannot be intellectually specified but must be learned under the tutelage of an experienced practitioner.[258] Moreover, such life skills and habits can only be earned through an apprenticeship where one generation trains another succeeding generation in a personal relationship in which a mentor or guide teaches a subsequent generation.

Although Polanyi's primary training was as a scientist, he understood that law and other professions require similar mentoring in a tradition. Lawyers, for example, attend law school, where they learn a way of thinking about legal problems and the basic principles of various areas of law. Subsequently, in practice, the new lawyer develops practical skills and habits and the way of life involved in being a lawyer. This often involves working with and for another lawyer, a firm of lawyers, or some public agency. This way of life learned in the community of practicing lawyers constitutes the tradition within which law is practiced.

In connection with the practice of law and the search for justice, there are many, many members of the legal community who work together to make the legal system work. Legislators, judges, members of the executive branches of government, administrative officials, private and public lawyers, members of all branches of government, and various bar associations combine to maintain, extend, and defend a legal system and, hopefully, the search for justice. How people become trained and participate in creating a fair and just society is as varied as the personal and societies comprising a more significant political community.

To give another example, let us assume that a young person in high school conceives that they would like to become a judge. Such a person would need to attend a college or university and then law school. In law school, the person would learn the basics of legal reasoning and research and writing techniques. In class after class, they would come to understand the basic principles of various areas of law and the procedures used by courts in applying the law. During the summers and the school year, they would clerk for a firm, court, or public agency. Before graduating, they would apply for various federal or state clerkships, and after graduation, would take such a clerkship if offered. After completing such a clerkship, the person would join a public agency or firm and practice law, learning the skills of a trial and appellate lawyer. Finally, after years of practicing law, our example would be ready to seek an appointment as a judge or run for office. Once elected or appointed, they would hear criminal cases or cases in contract, tort, property, estates, and other areas of the law. Over time, that judge would make their contribution to the law and the communal search for justice in our society.

A modern government and the administration of its laws involve a highly complex tradition, passing on knowledge, skill, and a way of living, all of which are important to the tradition. Our imaginary judge is but one of the myriads of persons and organs of government that comprise and govern a modern political state. The current government's executive, legislative, and judicial branches have many different members. Their skills, talents, and abilities are many and varied. No person or group can possess the talents, abilities, skills, and experience necessary for such governments to create and maintain a just society. It requires a community of communities to pass down skills to succeeding generations.

The Body Politic as a Self-Policing Community

In response to the specter of the totalitarian and materialistic models he encountered, Polanyi defends the importance of political, scientific, and religious human freedom in the search for truth. He carefully walks a path between the objective pole of human knowledge and the inevitable subjective or personal elements of human knowledge. He begins by examining what it means to "know the truth." Polanyi was concerned about how

Western intellectuals had become seduced by various totalitarian ideologies, left and right, and the descent into nihilism, which is evident in our politics and prevalent among scholars. His goal was to provide an intellectual foundation not just for scientific freedom but also for political liberty.[259] Polanyi believes a free society requires a disciplined community practice free speech (discussion and dialogue) with a common faith that:

1. There is such a thing as truth;
2. Members of a community love the truth and are committed to searching for it;
3. Members of such a community internalize a personal obligation to pursue the truth; and
4. Members of a truth-seeking community must have the ability to undertake the search.[260]

In searching for the truth in any area, a truth-seeking community must practice two virtues: fairness and tolerance.[261] Fairness is the ability to listen to the opinions of the community members with an open mind, attempting to be objective in judging the argument's merits. Tolerance is the ability to engage sympathetically with different, and even hostile, views and to grant those views the respect they deserve. No free society can endure without dedication to the pursuit of truth, justice, and the other ideals of the human heart in a fair and tolerant way. This pursuit engages the best qualities of its citizens, whose upbringing and education have prepared them to have the character needed to be free citizens of a free society.

Polanyi recognizes that the nature of a truth-seeking community is not merely intellectual. A shared conviction about the nature of reality and the subject under investigation is necessary, but so is a shared form of life, a shared cooperation in that life, and some kind of structure, order, and discipline.[262] What is true in science is also true in society. It is not enough that a community have a shared legal system; it must have shared values, a shared commitment to fairness and cooperation, and a degree of shared social life. Where this begins to break down, there will inevitably be conflict and decay of social institutions. What Polanyi calls conviviality and the institutions necessary to maintain it are required for any functional society.

Critical Realism and Fallibilism

Over and over again, Polanyi points out that science is motivated by a belief in the reality of its discoveries and the theories that explain them. When scientists make a discovery, they believe they have made contact with some feature of reality outside of an individual's perception. Although primarily a philosopher of science, Polanyi understood that his ideas had an application beyond science.[263] Thus, in *Science, Faith and Society*, he remarks about the application of his ideas to other disciplines:

> We can generalize this to other modes of discovery, in literature, in the arts, in politics. All these can advance only fragmentarily by the efforts of individuals within a community organized essentially on the lines of scientific life. The community must guarantee the independence of its active members in the service of values jointly upheld and mutually enforced by all. The creative life of such a community rests on a belief in the ever continuing possibility of revealing still and hidden truths.[264]

In every area of human inquiry, progress is made by those who believe in the reality of the phenomena being investigated, including those who attempt to advance the social search for justice.[265] Those who believe in the reality of justice make progress in unveiling its hidden reality through investigation. In the case of law and politics, this involves the fair and wise enactment and enforcement of law and policy. In enacting and enforcing laws and policies, participants can avoid fanaticism, error, and abuse by holding to the principle of fallibilism. Like Peirce, another critical realist, Polanyi is a fallibilist. While every inquirer or political actor is entitled to hold their notions of justice with confidence and universal intent, it is also necessary to recognize and accept that the inquirer or actor might be mistaken.

The Problem of Moral Inversion

Polanyi famously critiqued what he referred to as the "moral inversion" that often characterizes modern radical political movements. He sees moral inversion as a perversion that arises when the moral idealism of the Christian faith is cut off from its deeper roots and becomes secularized. Polanyi believes the strong demand for moral perfection characteristic of Christianity, combined with the materialist reductionism of modern thought that ends in an objective moral nihilism, results in a destructive form of moral reason.[266] In *Logic of Liberty*, Polanyi describes the phenomenon (speaking of Russian Communists and German Nazis) as follows:

> In such men, the traditional forms for holding moral ideals had been shattered and their moral passions diverted into the only channels which a strictly mechanistic conception of man and society left open to them. We may call this the process of *moral inversion*. The morally inverted person has not merely performed

175

a philosophic substitution of moral aims by material purposes, but is acting with the whole force of his homeless moral passions within a purely materialistic framework of purposes.[267]

By nature, humans have a moral sense that must be developed to reach maturity. When denied an intellectual ground for moral passions by education or training, these passions, like a river that has breached its banks, flow in an uncontrolled flood into whatever channel lies conveniently at hand. In modern, materialistic societies, that channel has been revolutionary action designed to create a new society along strictly materialistic lines. Communism or some form of National Socialism has often been the preferred channel when these destructive energies are unleashed. The political disasters of the 20th and now 21st centuries are frequently powered by moral energy resulting from this destructive rechanneling of moral passions

What Polanyi calls "moral inversion" might better be called "moral reductionism" or "moral absolutism." The problem is often not with whether the underlying idea of morality is immoral or moral, but with the fact that one moral ideal is sought to the exclusion of other important ethical principles. For example, Lenin, Mao, and their followers were willing to destroy human life and engage in great cruelty in pursuit of the goal of an economically more just society, but at the expense of the equally important value of human freedom and human life. This phenomenon involves not so much an inversion as a kind of reductionism or absolutization of one value to the exclusion of others. This same thinking is embodied in the modern slogans of "right to choose" and "right to life." The attempt to reduce the moral quandary to a single maxim oversimplifies the moral reality.

Dynamo-Objective Coupling, Moral Inversion, and Hypocrisy

According to Polanyi, the false ideal of objectivism, when coupled with the moral urges of humankind, creates a "dynamo-objective coupling," whereby alleged "scientific assertions" of a group are accepted because they seemingly satisfy the moral passions of human beings.[268] In other words, the dynamic power of moral impulses can be perverted by a denial of conventional morality coupled with an objectivist excuse for unleashing moral energy in service to a particular cause. Paradoxically, this is precisely what Marxism, Nazism, and a host of modern "isms" can achieve, particularly among the young.

There is no critique of Christianity more common than the complaint that Christians are hypocrites—that is to say, Christians do not live up to the high moral ideals of Christ, which they profess to admire. This is, of course, true. One only needs to read the Beatitudes to see that Christ upholds a moral standard we may aspire to but can never obtain. In Polanyi's view, the perfectionistic impulse of the Christian faith is responsible for a great deal of the moral progress of Western civilization. Unfortunately, among those afflicted with a loss of faith in any moral or spiritual ideals, the deeply seated moral urge to achieve moral objectives can become a breeding ground for moral inversion powered by a feeling that all traditional morality is hypocritical.[269] This potential for the emergence of a kind of moral inversion is not limited to Western society. The criticism has been leveled at other traditional ethical systems as well.[270] The postmodern charge, however, makes this more dangerous, because of the claim that all moral claims, whatever their source, are merely bids for power.

Beginning with the Enlightenment and its exaltation of critical reason, virtually all forms of faith and morals, including the social ideal of justice, have been placed under the dissolving power of reductionistic, critical thinking. The materialism of the modern world, with its reduction of all reality to material particles and forces acting on that reality, eventually led to Nietzsche's critique that God is an illusion, Christianity is a slave religion, and the Will to Power is the final characteristic and justification of sound moral reasoning. This thinking leads directly to the appalling irrational immorality of contemporary politics, where winning is everything, and any immoral action is justified if it furthers a moral ideal held by a particular group.

The reductionist character of modern thought is seen in the tendency of the left and the right to reduce and constrict moral thinking to personal preferences. It is a short step from this position to a decision for a single materialistically inspired moral good to the detriment of other, seemingly less important, moral goods.[271] In contemporary society, we have seen played out the view that some moral ideal held by one particular group is the supreme moral good. Other ethical duties, such as protecting the rights of the accused to a fair trial, the responsibility of the prosecutors to investigate carefully before bringing charges, the rights of businesspersons to their property and businesses, the rights of the public to safe streets, the need of children and others for secure homes, *etc.* can and should be abandoned in the search for some single moral good urged by a particular group.[272]

It should be evident that the extreme views of many contemporary political groups, the violence of rioters and looters, and a media egging them on are incompatible with the freedoms they purport to be advancing. A society built on terror is a terror to everyone: good, evil, rich, poor, powerful, and powerless. I was able to travel to Russia just after the fall of Communism. Soviet Marxist Communism was physically, ecologically, morally, and spiritually impoverishing to everyone in Russian society. What we see playing out on the streets of our cities in America is unfortunately similar to the phenomena that led to millions of deaths under Hitler, Stalin, Mao, and Pot Pol, all of whom played on the unsatisfied moral sentiments of their people and created unmitigated horror and suffering.

Historically, the French Revolution is the most dramatic illustration of how moral inversion and revolutionary ideology can result in human tragedy as it becomes irrational and ungrounded in a tradition of reason. A year or so after the French Revolution began, Burke published his *Reflections on the Revolution in France.*[273] This was before the Reign of Terror and the worst excesses of the revolution, which Burke foresaw and sought to prevent. In the end, Burke's views were seen as accurate and prophetic.

In Burke's view, the French Revolution resulted from the various "estates," the various groups of people that made up all the citizens of France, failing to keep faith with one another in matters of importance. In so doing, the government of France reached a point of revolution:

> The constituted parts of a state are obligated to hold their public faith with each other, and with all those who derive any serious interest under their engagements, as much as the whole state is bound to keep its faith with the separate communities: otherwise competence and power would soon be confounded, and no law would be left but the will of a prevailing power.[274]

In Burke's view, the government, the nobility, the clergy, and the people owed reciprocal duties to one another. It was, for example, a breach of public trust for the nobility, clergy, and crown to saddle the Third Estate with a tax burden they could not meet and condemn the majority of the people to poverty. The failures of the nobility and clergy were not just a violation of the social compact (though it was). They were also a violation of natural law and exposed France to revolution. In the end, all that was left was power, which, in the case of the French Revolution, fell into incompetent, corrupt, radical, and violent hands.[275] This breach of duty was by both those whose mismanagement provoked the revolution and those who conducted it.

In one of the most critical and pertinent arguments of *Reflections on the Revolution in France*, Burke argues that the British and American revolutions could be distinguished from that in France by the absence of a sense of continuity and inheritance:

> The Revolution (of 1688) was made to preserve our *ancient* indisputable laws and liberties, and that *ancient* constitution of government which is our only security for law and liberty. If you are desirous of knowing the spirit of our constitution, and the policy that predominated in that great period which secured it to this hour, pray look in our histories, in our records, in our acts of Parliament and journals of Parliament.... We wished at the period of the Revolution, and do now wish, to derive all we possess as an inheritance from our forefathers.[276]

This notion that the institutions of a stable government that protects the rights and property of its citizens are "an inheritance" is an essential aspect of Burke's organic view of government. He believed that a wise constitutional order works after the "order of nature," like a parent bequeathing an inheritance to a child. Thus, a sound constitutional order is an inheritance from those who established that order. This inheritance is to be received, built on, and improved by subsequent generations. Burke's notion of an "order of nature" is consonant with the view that human history is an evolving process in which each generation receives the benefits of civilization, and transmits that inheritance in either better or worse, but certainly different, condition that it was received.

The French Revolution, and increasingly the condition of many nations, reflects a failure of the various social groups to exercise their respective powers, duties, and obligations in ways that sustain wise decision-making and social cohesion. Contemporary society is very different than French society at the end of the 18th and beginning of the 19th century. Instead of three estates, we have created modern, diverse states in which academia, corporations, government, the media, political parties, private wealth, and many other groups all have reciprocal duties to one another. A *sophio-agapic* view of politics holds that each social group and all individuals making up society have mutual obligations to deal with one another in wisdom and concern with proper relationality, intending to create a harmonious society.

Socio-Agapism and Polanyi

Those who make discoveries and detect the hidden rationality of the universe, at whatever level of reality, have in common the faith that they and those with whom they share the journey of discovery are making contact with something real. However, the theoretical explanation of that contact always remains subject to revision based on new information. This is not to say that what is discovered is mistaken. Like any discovery, subsequent discoveries may supersede it in whole or part.

Those who investigate any feature of our world must believe that the world is rational, not just concerning science but also concerning aesthetics, ethics, political philosophy, and religion. The form of rationality differs at different levels of reality, and each level of reality must be investigated by the appropriate means and methods. The mathematical description possible at the level of subatomic particles is not possible at the level of human relations, including political thought. Nevertheless, provisional knowledge, including provisional justice, is possible in every area of human life.

The fallibilism inherent in critical realism establishes the virtue of humility in every area of human investigation, including political discovery. The knowledge that I might be wrong in my views and opinions—and indeed the likelihood that I will in the future be shown to have been mistaken in some respects—allows me to sympathize with those who have gone before and are now being superseded. It also enables me to sympathize with those whose political solutions I currently disagree with. Understanding the frailty of human wisdom and the tentative nature of human knowledge frees one from the necessity to correct or to judge harshly those with whom we disagree in the search for knowledge and a just society.

CHAPTER 8

WHOLENESS, FRAGMENTATION, AND DIALOGUE

ontemporary physicist and philosopher David Bohm (1917-1992) was deeply concerned with the condition of modern society and the absence of authentic dialogue among people. Bohm was born into a Jewish family in Wilkes-Barre, Pennsylvania. Educated in the United States, Bohm completed a Ph.D. in physics at the University of California at Berkeley, worked on the Manhattan Project under theoretical physicist J. Robert Oppenheimer, the "Father of the Atomic Bomb," and taught briefly at Princeton. In 1951, having been investigated by the McCarthy Committee for alleged Communist activities, Bohm left the United States, and subsequently lived in South America, Israel, and Great Britain. While a graduate student, Bohm had an experience that later began the development of his unique view of the wholeness of the universe. He noticed that once electrons are placed in a plasma, they cease behaving like individual particles and start behaving as if they were part of a larger and interconnected whole.[277]

In 1951, Bohm published a fundamental work on quantum physics, defending the Copenhagen Interpretation, which implies an indeterminate universe. While working on the book, he developed doubts about the prevailing Copenhagen interpretation and began developing an interpretation of quantum mechanics that would preserve causality. As a result of his conversations with Einstein, he began to work on a causal interpretation of quantum mechanics, today known as the "Bohmian" or "Non-Variable Approach" to quantum physics.[278] Bohm's approach to quantum physics assumes the existence of underlying, subtler levels of reality.[279] These underlying levels of reality are "implicate" in the perceived universe and "unfolded" in space and time through the evolutionary process in which the world is engaged.

Our Participatory, Relational, and Undivided Universe

For Bohm, three aspects of quantum physics are vital, as they call into question the mechanistic interpretation of reality on which the modern worldview is based:

1. The quantum world is discontinuous. Energy travels in indivisible units known as "quanta," from which we take the term "quantum physics." This quantization of light means that the world does not unfold smoothly or linearly.

2. Fundamental entities, such as electrons, exhibit contradictory characteristics at different times. Sometimes they appear wave-like, and sometimes particle-like, a phenomenon known as "wave–particle duality." In particular, the presence of an observer and the character of the observations

impact whether fundamental entities take on wave-like or particle-like characteristics. In other words, the notion of an observer outside the situation observed is undermined.

3. When fundamental entities interact with one another, they become entangled in a non-local relationship, which appears to be a form of connection that does not rely on mechanical, physical causation. This phenomenon is known as "quantum entanglement" (as discussed previously). Such entangled particles act in concert, violating the principle that no signal can travel faster than the speed of light. The phenomenon of "entanglement" implies an interconnected world not made up of separate entities or phenomena.

None of these principles are compatible with the modern, post-Enlightenment notion of a universe that can be explained in a materialistic and mechanical way.[280]

Bohm understood that Einstein's theory of relativity undermines a mechanical interpretation of the universe. For example, relativity theory implies that no coherent concept of an independently existent particle is possible, either one in which such a particle would be an extended body or one in which it would be a dimensionless point. Basic assumptions underlying Newtonian physics were shown to be limited in their possible application to reality as a whole.[281] At its fundamental level, reality is relational.

Bohm defended a process-oriented view of reality consistent with the insights of Peirce and Whitehead, though he developed these insights in his own way. Rather than a universe resembling a machine, the influence of relativity theory and quantum physics led to a picture of the universe more analogous to a process or organism.[282] The universe appears to be one unbroken whole composed of interrelated quantum fields. Particles are best described as localized ripples or pulses in these fields, ultimately forming an undivided universe's material basis.[283]

The universe is fundamentally a unified unfolding process made up of matter, energy, and information.[284] Ultimately, the universe is filled with differing information levels (levels of reality) gradually unfolding in space-time. These levels of reality are meaningful based on different levels of analysis appropriate to the level of reality they represent. In addition, these differing levels of reality unfold as the universe develops. The explicit order we observe is an unfolding of an implicate order characterized by information and meaning, which unfolds into the explicit order of reality.

In Bohm's view, all the fragmented, separate objects, entities, structures, and events we perceive in the visible or explicate world are projections originating from a deeper, implicate order of unbroken wholeness.[285] Bohm uses the analogy of a flowing stream:

> On this stream, one may see an ever-changing pattern of vortices, ripples, waves, splashes, etc., which evidently have no independent existence as such. Rather, they are abstracted from the flowing movement, arising and vanishing in the total process of the flow. Such transitory subsistence as may be possessed by these abstracted forms implies only a relative independence or autonomy of behavior rather than absolutely independent existence as ultimate substances.[286]

Thus, Bohm sees reality as a process or "flow-movement" of deeply interconnected events in which no particular event can be seen as independent of all others.[11] His view is consistent with Whitehead's process view and implicitly hostile to any mechanical interpretation of the universe.

A Meaningful Universe

Bohm believes the universe is filled with information at every level of which human beings have any form of conscious understanding. In other words, the physical universe is inherently meaningful. There is a mental or informational level to every level of reality. In the end, mind and matter exist in one undivided whole. To communicate this insight, Bohm coined the term "soma-significant" to describe the universe's information, bearing, and meaningful characteristics. The term "soma-significant" implies that the mental and physical aspects of reality are not fundamental:

> The notion of soma-significance implies that soma (or the physical) and its significance (which is mental) are not in any sense separately existent but rather they are two aspects to one overall reality.[287]

The universe's fundamental information and meaning-bearing character is based on a somatic order, an arrangement, connection, or organization of distinguished elements that constitute the physical structures we observe.[288] For Bohm, this does not imply any form of a mind–matter dualism, because there is fundamentally only one flow in the universe. Changes of meaning or the flow of meaning exist; however, there is no absolute distinction between mind and matter. The universe is one meaningful whole.[289] The flow of the universe, its organic processes, is a flow of energy in which meaning is carried inward and outward between aspects of soma and significance, but they are not separate.[290]

The reciprocal flow of meaning in the universe means that soma-significance is complimented by its inverse, a sign-somatic relation, which Bohm denotes as "signa-significance." That is to say that the information and signs that make up the universe at a fundamental level affect the physical universe, since the two are not fundamentally separated.[291] Soma-significance implies that matter impacts the mind. Signa-significance suggests the reverse: any change of significance or meaning has physical consequences in the universe.

On a physical level, this relationship is apparent. For example, if I don't sleep enough, I find it difficult to reason or write anything complex the next day. Similarly, changing my mind about some matter of importance has consequences in the physical universe. Adopting a religious belief, a moral view, a political conviction, a fundamental understanding of the universe, or any other mental event impacts how a person exists, thinks about problems, acts, and responds to environmental stimuli. This, in turn, influences the entire physical universe, since all things are interrelated. In all this, there is a fundamental element of information and meaning. This implies that the kind of mind–body dualism that characterized modern thought does not provide a reliable representation of the nature of the universe.

Our Fragmented Social Reality

One feature of modern, post-Enlightenment science that impacts our society is reductionism. Modern physics presupposed that reality can be explained by reductive analysis of the world into its fundamental units, assumed to be material in nature. In Bohm's view, this analytic side of human reason, taken to excess in our society, leads to a fragmented view of reality:

> Thus art, science, technology, and human work in general, are divided up into specialties, each considered to be separate in essence from the others. Becoming dissatisfied with this state of affairs, men have set up further interdisciplinary subjects, which were intended to unite these specialties, but these new subjects have ultimately served mainly to add further separate fragments. Then, society as a whole has developed in such a way that it is broken up into separate nations and different religious, political, economic, racial groups, etc. Man's natural environment has correspondingly been seen as an aggregate of separately existent parts to be exploited by different groups of people. Similarly, each individual human being has been fragmented into a large number of separate and conflicting compartments, according to his different desires, aims, ambitions, loyalties, psychological characteristics, etc., to such an extent that it is generally accepted that some degree of neurosis is inevitable, while many individuals going beyond the 'normal' limits of fragmentation are classified as paranoid, schizoid, psychotic, etc. The notion that all these fragments or separately existence is evidently an illusion, and this solution cannot do other than lead to endless conflict and confusion.[292]

The result of fragmentation is a society that is physically and mentally unhealthy. The various conflicts, socio-economic crises, environmental damage, and social decay our society experiences all flow from the reality of a culture that has become excessively fragmented. In particular, the fragmentation of our social institutions has reached the point where it is difficult to maintain a coherent and functional society. A different way of looking at the world needs to be developed, and Bohm believes that the implications of quantum physics are leading us to just such a way of looking at the world holistically.

Returning to soma-significance, this concept is essential because the process of information flow extends into the entire universe, including the human person:

> You can see that ultimately, the soma-significant, and the signa-somatic process extends even into the environment. Meaning thus can be conveyed from one person to another and back through sound waves, through gestures, carried by light, through books and newspapers, through telephone, radio, television, and so on, linking up the whole society, in one vast web of soma-significance and signa-somatic activity. You can say that society is this thing; this activity is what makes society. Without it, there would be no society.[293]

Our physical environment—the houses, cities, factories, farms, highways, and so on amongst which we live—are the physical result of the meanings these material objects have come to have for human beings, not just in the present but in the past as well.[294] Our entire culture is impacted by the physical, mental, and moral results of the signa- and soma-significant flows of meaning that make up human culture. These meanings also affect the physical universe, with implications for modern environmental theory and practice. Bohm goes on to claim:

Going on from there, even relationships with nature and with the cosmos flow out of what they mean to us. These meanings fundamentally affect our actions toward nature, and thus indirectly, the action of nature back on us is affected. Indeed, as far as we know it and are aware of it and can act on it, the whole of nature, including our civilization, which is evolved from nature, and is still a part of nature, is one movement that is both soma-significant and sigma-significant.[295]

From the lowest level of reality to the most sophisticated elements of human society, a continual flow of meaning and activity profoundly impacts the character and quality of human life. Human beings constantly make decisions, experience acts of will, and determine outcomes based on a web of significance, much of which can only be known tacitly at any given time.[296]

This view of reality as a flow of meaning is foundational to Bohm's view of culture. Human culture, in all of its complexity and strata, at all the levels in which humans create meanings, physical, social, spiritual, political, legal, economic, and otherwise, are essentially stratified flows of meaning. Where there are significant physical or mental impediments to the flow of meaning, such as conflict, there is a blockage of that flow and corresponding dysfunction:

One might, in fact, go so far as to say that, in the present state of society, and in the present mode of teaching science, which is a manifestation of this state of society, the kind of prejudice, in favor of a fragmentary self-world view is fostered and transmitted (to some extent, explicitly and consciously, but mainly in an implicit and unconscious manner). As has been indicated, however, men who are guided by such a fragmentary self-world view, cannot in the long run, do other than to try in their actions to break themselves and the world into pieces, corresponding to the general mode of thinking.[297]

The process of dividing the universe conceptually because of a reductive, pre-existing worldview that sees the world as physically divided into atomic units results in the division and separation of human beings from themselves, nature, and one another. This divides society into fragmented and hostile groups.[298] This kind of fragmentary thinking leads to social, political, economic, ecological, and other crises in individuals and society. The result is a chaotic and meaningless conflict in which social and intellectual energy is wasted.[299]

Dialogue as Central to Overcoming Fragmentation

To overcome modern society's dysfunction and fragmentation, Bohm believes a different approach to social problems needs to be adopted. Our society's fundamental paradigm for understanding reality (atomistic materialism and individualism) and its fundamental view of how to change that reality (material power) need to be replaced by a view of reality consistent with the discoveries of post-Newtonian science. The required change involves communication through dialogue among persons and groups. Creative transformation in which fragmentation is overcome can be achieved through dialogue.[300]

As discussed previously, the Greek roots of the word "dialogue" illuminate its meaning. The word is composed of the Greek words "dia," meaning "through," and "logos," meaning "reason." Dialogue happens when two or more persons share meaning by reasonably exchanging views. New understanding emerges as meaning is conveyed and differing points of view illuminate some feature of reality. For two people to enter into a dialogue, they must commit to a mutual exchange of ideas and information to better understand the subject. A discussion implies that the parties are humble enough to know that they must share ideas, thoughts, and perspectives to understand a matter under investigation better. Finally, dialogue automatically involves community, for it requires the willingness of people to share in a joint enterprise of learning.

Dialogue, Conversation, and Community

The word "conversation" comes from the Latin root "con" ("with") and "vertere," which means "turn" or "bend." Interestingly, like the Hebrew word for knowledge, this particular word was used in the 1500s as a synonym for sexual intercourse and also had a connotation of a household, a manner of conduct and behavior, or a way of life in a home. In other words, a conversation is an intimate, profoundly human relational communication activity at the deepest possible level. A conversation is implicitly communal and intended to create or deepen communion among persons. It involves a relationship in which two or more individuals share their thoughts and lives in a way that results in an understanding that is cognitive, emotional, and even spiritual. Hopefully, their separate ideas, thoughts, and commitments will bend toward each other in the conversation, creating communal understanding and consensus.

Humans have dialogues within themselves as they conduct an internal conversation about a decision or problem. People also dialogue with one another about problems. And, of course, we dialogue in a larger context where many people participate. Politics is not exempt from the importance of conversation and dialogue in a community. It is central to a wise and effective political process, as central as debate and decision. In fact, conversation and dialogue, so often ignored in contemporary politics, form the foundation on which healthy debate and decision can occur.

There can be honest and dishonest attempts at dialogue. In honest dialogue, new understanding emerges as meaning is conveyed and differing points of view illuminate reality.[301] For two people to enter into genuine dialogue, they must commit to a mutual exchange of ideas and information to better understand some feature of reality. Authentic dialogue involves a flow of meaning. Those involved in the dialogue are caught up in a moving flow of information and meaning. A dialogue implicitly seeks a truth that the parties are humble enough to know and requires sharing ideas, thoughts, and perspectives. If these conditions are not met, as in the case where one participant uses dialogue to manipulate the other, there is dishonest dialogue.

Dialogue is not mere discussion. "Discussion" has the same root as "percussion" or "concussion." In a discussion or debate, conflicting views are expressed with a view toward breaking down the other's argument. People try to win, debate points, and carry the day in a discussion. Discussion and debate almost inevitably increase fragmentation—especially where controversial or deeply held ideas are at stake. In genuine dialogue, by contrast, participants try to find new meanings and reach an agreement with one another.[26] In the process, fragmentation is overcome, along with its unfortunate results. Genuine dialogue goes beyond conflict and the percussive impact of debate to seek proper mutual understanding and agreement.

There are certainly limits to Bohm's notion of dialogue. This is particularly true in a democracy, where people assume the centrality of debate and discussion of topics of public interest. Nevertheless, Bohm argues that modern democratic politics, which often revolves around debate and discussion aimed at one group achieving enough power to impose its views on others, is ultimately counterproductive. He suggests that a deeper sharing of dialogue, which fosters a community capable of sustaining the impact of debate, is essential. *Sophio-agapism* agrees that, while debate and decision are essential parts of public discourse, these "outcome events" should rest on a solid foundation of authentic dialogue about matters of importance.

Participatory Thinking and Noetic Ideals

Bohm approaches the search for knowledge as an experienced practicing scientist. Science involves a continuing dialogue, or exchange of reasoning, as investigations are carried out, results and theories published, criticisms leveled, and adjustments made.[302] Within any research institution, various people meet daily, sharing the results of their investigation. People meet daily, sharing the results of their investigation. In other words, most scientific investigation is conducted as a communal and sharing effort.[303] Research programs require many participating individuals who are at once examining some feature of reality and sharing their conclusions.

This scientific way of reasoning continues (or should continue) to be used in practical activities. In sensitive areas, such as religion and politics, it is difficult to achieve genuine dialogue due to blockages—emotional, ideological, and otherwise. These blockages inhibit communication and the flow of meaning, preventing discovery and change. The result is the kind of pervasive fragmentation and conflict that characterizes modern society. This fragmentation can be overcome by participatory dialogue in which people share meanings in an attempt to understand one another.[304]

From a *sophio-agapic* point of view, ideals such as justice form an essential part of the conversation since they relativize deeply held opinions and galvanize participants into a joint search for a deeper and more profound understanding of reality. The significance of noetic ideals (or potentials) for political thought is that such ideal potentials reveal themselves to a community under concrete circumstances in a provisional but appropriate way. Each determination is provisionally valid in a specific context. There can be no permanent and unchanging specification of justice as an abstract concept, but there can be contextually reasonable approximations.[305] Because of the inner relationships among people and institutional structures, every determination of justice in a specific context is relative to and may be modified by a new emerging context and future understandings. Thus, no determination of justice can be final or fixed, but it is part of the movement of society toward a more comprehensive sense of justice and social harmony.[306]

Bohm is important for a *sophio-agapic* understanding of politics and applying a pragmaticist understanding of reality to practical affairs. Our society is decaying under the influence of a fundamentally materialistic (Newton) and power-oriented (Nietzsche) view of social reality. This blinds participants in the political process to the deep rational and relational substructure of the process of reaching wise decisions in public life. Only the adoption of a more dialogical approach, such as the one proposed by Bohm, offers a way out of the dilemma postmodernity faces nearly a quarter of the way through the 21st century.

CHAPTER 9

COMMUNITY AND SOPHIO-AGAPIC POLITICS

B y this point, it should be clear that the virtues and wisdom, truth, beauty, goodness, and justice cannot be achieved without forming and maintaining communities dedicated to the disciplined endeavor to promote them. Relationships and community are fundamentally important for a healthy human society and wise political decision-making. Just as the universe is profoundly relational and interconnected, so is any human society. At its roots, any human society is an organism, not a mechanism, as so much modern political thought assumes. While individual rights are important, and society must protect individuals and their uniqueness, this cannot be achieved if the social fabric of societies is torn apart and divided by endless conflict. Pragmaticist *sophio-agapism* provides a theoretical substructure to accomplish the twin goals of social harmony and individual endeavor.

Peirce's opposition to the radical individualism of Descartes' method and much of modern philosophy originated in his experience as a scientist. Peirce, the scientist, understood that a community of scientists typically share both a particular body of knowledge and a certain degree of communal discomfort with some existing state of affairs in their discipline. The doubt of a scientist is rarely solely personal and individual. It is usually shared. It is this shared doubt that creates a shared research program. For example, the doubt that caused Einstein to formulate his theory of relativity was partially caused by the inability of science to explain the results of the Michaelson–Morley experiment satisfactorily. Many scientists shared Einstein's doubts, some to a lesser or greater degree. However, it was Einstein who finally proposed a solution, which took some time to gain the support of the vast majority of scientists.[307]

The only reasonable hope for progress in attaining a just society (or in investigating any aspect of reality, religious, moral, philosophical, political, aesthetic, or otherwise) is by participating in historic communities of inquiry interested in understanding a specific aspect of reality.[308] In this way, pragmaticism reinstates tradition as an essential aspect of any reasoning. Humans can only reason effectively within a community engaged in a tradition of inquiry. This tradition of inquiry may change or develop, even in revolutionary ways, but it is still recognizably part of a tradition. For example, in the case of Peirce, though he is a revolutionary thinker, his thought emerges from a deep conversation with the past, especially Plato, Aristotle, Scotus, and Kant, as well as a critical appreciation of Hegel. While rejecting parts of Kant and Hegel, he sees himself as a Kantian and Hegelian of sorts. He is content to operate within a tradition that he hopes to extend and perfect by his studies.

Peirce struck a devastating intellectual blow to the individualistic idealism initiated by Descartes and his essentially individualistic standard of truth. For Descartes, what was true was that which any individual person could not doubt. His argument contained a fundamentally individualistic premise, "I think therefore I am." Notice the "I." For Descartes and much of the modern movement, the intellectual ideal is the solo individual, thinking on his own in the solitude of their study, reflecting on life, and solving problems as a solitary individual. Too often, this kind of isolated individualism restricts progress in almost every area of contemporary life.

On the other hand, Peirce's philosophy begins with a communal, semiotic, communication-oriented standard of truth. In his view, truth is a matter of the ability of our ideas, inevitably expressed in signs, to illuminate some feature of reality we and others are trying to understand. Because presuppositions, prejudices, and limitations inevitably guide and, to some degree, determine human thought, no human can ever know the complete truth about any important matter. This drives Peirce to a theory of knowledge that is essentially communal. The truth is not known in solitude but as part of a community of inquiry, or what might be called a "Community of Seekers."

If for Descartes, and much of the modern world, the ideal was the solitary individual deciding for themselves, the pragmaticist ideal is the individual scientist who, as part of a team of scientists, tries to solve some problem. Think of a research laboratory with many scientists in constant communication in the laboratory and their private lives. They read and comment on each other's work and are in joint pursuit of a breakthrough in understanding. This image is central to other areas of intellectual and moral life because all knowledge results from this kind of community of inquirers who compete and cooperate over time.

We human beings are part of an infinite number of such communities. For example, I am a family member and must understand my family and its relationships to solve problems. Every other member of our family does as well. I am a lawyer and a member of a bar association. As such, I am part of a community dedicated to understanding the principles of American and Texas law. I'm also a pastor, a part of a denomination and community interested in the knowledge of God. As I write this, I'm a citizen of San Antonio, Texas, interested in the city and the state and in understanding its culture, laws, and government. I am a United States citizen interested in our nation's government and policies. In addition to being a part of some of these things, my father grew roses. He was a member of the Rose Society and was interested in the methods and means of growing the best and most beautiful roses possible. My family members are farmers who belong to various farming groups interested in the best ways of growing corn, soybeans, wheat, and other crops. You can see that all of us are members of many communities seeking understanding.

In a paper published in 1868, Peirce described philosophical inquiry as essentially social, claiming, "We cannot reasonably hope to attain the ultimate philosophy which we pursue; we can only seek it for the community of philosophers."[309] At the end of the same essay, Peirce concludes:

> Finally, as to what anything really is, is what it may finally come to be known to be in the ideal state of complete information, so that reality depends on the ultimate decision of the community; so thought is what it is only by virtue of addressing a future thought that is in its value as thought identical with it, though more developed. In this way, the existence of thought now, depends upon what is to be hereafter, so that it has only a potential existence depended upon the future thought of

the community. The individual man, since his separate existence is manifested only in ignorance and error, so far is he is anything apart from his fellows and from what he and they are to be is only a negation. This is man.[310]

Twice in the passage quoted, Peirce speaks of the "decision of the community" and "the future thought of the community." In the beginning, Peirce speaks of "the ignorance of human beings apart from their fellow human beings." Knowledge results from a community's reasoning process, not simply from an individual's thoughts and reasoning. Secondly, he speaks of the community's dependence not just on its current thoughts but on the future thoughts of community members. In other words, there is no end within history of the expansion of meaning and progress of thought, for there will always be "future thought of the community."

As to political thought, this idea implies that there can be no "end of history" in which a particular political theory or organization will be final, complete, and universally accepted. The collaborative process of understanding will continue so long as history continues. Humans are essentially oriented toward the past, present, and future. We emerge from our past. We live in the present. And we seek a more desirable future. There can be no "end of history" within human history because the nature of the human race will always demand a deeper understanding of any reality and a more complete experience of justice in any human society.

Whitehead's notion of process illuminates the process of social evolution and the achievement of a more just and orderly society. All processes involve a reception of the past, a current decision, and a transition into a new state from which all future evolution of the society will be based.[311] The process of receiving the past involves positively accepting ideas and forms of the past into the decision-making process as a new state is achieved and rejecting others. Therefore, all social evolution involves continuity and discontinuity to a greater or lesser degree. The future is present in the past by virtue of the process by which the present has come to be.[312] But, the future of a society is always different from the past, so there is continuity and discontinuity. At any given point in social evolution, certain developmental paths have been foreclosed by past decisions. Still, there are also new and different opportunities created by the present and the future towards which society moves.

I cannot illustrate this more effectively than by reflecting on the current national debt. As I write this, the United States' national debt is about $34.83 trillion and rapidly growing. This debt has been created through a series of decisions made by successive administrations and Congresses over many years. It has funded a series of programs deemed necessary at the time the funds were allocated. Those decisions profoundly impact American society's current state, and that debt's size and character constrain future choices. Certain decisions cannot be made due to the size of the national debt, and certain decisions would be unwise to make because of the size of the national debt.

Nevertheless, the future is not totally determined. Congress can decide to continue adding to the national debt, raise taxes to control the national debt, or reduce spending. It's almost certain that any wise course of action would involve all of the above. The decision as to what policy should be adopted cannot ignore the past, but wise decision-makers will move toward a better and more financially secure future. A *sophia-agapic*, pragmaticist approach urges careful consideration of the impact of various policy proposals in choosing the one that most contributes to social harmony and human flourishing for all members of our society.

Community and Growing Political Wisdom

Like scientific knowledge, political truth is never absolute because it can be revised on the basis of the emergence of new information and insight. Nevertheless, the goal of a *sophio-agapic* approach to political life involves the continuing hope that a perception of the truth leading to greater social harmony may be accepted by a significant majority of the body politic and proven by such acceptance to have achieved a kind of "operational" (or pragmatic) certainty.

As an analogy from science, despite the disputes remaining between participants in quantum research, scientists do not doubt that quantum physics is an improvement over Newtonian physics and provides a deeper insight into fundamental reality. Although one cannot eliminate the possibility of a radical change in quantum physics, most scientists expect that any further progress will be made within the boundaries of something like the fundamental view of quantum physics now accepted.[313] Disputes between the so-called "Copenhagen" approach and the "Hidden Variable" approach to the problem of indeterminacy are all conducted within a community that is working from the same general scientific paradigm, the body of existing scientific data, and similar research programs designed to resolve the issues between them.

Politics can operate similarly. Politics is a communal effort and requires a community bound together by shared principles and a common set of values seeking to build a society for the benefit of all. In American society, those fundamental principles are outlined in our Declaration of Independence, Constitution, Bill of Rights, and the various decisions of policymakers and courts interpreting these basic principles. This is the past from which we live in the present. As a society, we are engaged in the process of applying these principles to contemporary problems as we seek the common good for all citizens.

The problem in America and much of the West is that, under the impact of Enlightenment distrust of history and tradition, societies have been unable to maintain a consensus regarding fundamental aspects of human life and human thriving. Western societies have lost that sense of communal participation in a living tradition essential for the maintenance and vitality of any society. At the same time, so-called "negative politics" and the search for a final victory over political opponents have undermined our ability to function as a cohesive society. Our education, media, and other institutions fail to educate leaders and citizens on the importance of maintaining a coherent community.

There is no way forward until our society recovers a sense of communal understanding and solidarity in the search for "liberty and justice for all" or, as the Declaration of Independence puts it: "Life, Liberty and the pursuit of Happiness."[314] The Constitution puts it this way:

> We the People of the United States, in Order to form a more perfect Union, establish Justice, insure domestic Tranquility, provide for the common defence, promote the general Welfare, and secure the Blessings of Liberty to ourselves and our Posterity, do ordain and establish this Constitution for the United States of America.[315]

These are the foundational ideals of the American community of which we are all part. These essential ideals include establishing justice, which the founders felt was a fundamental goal for America and functional societies. It should be noted that the founders did not consider that they were creating a perfect union. They were content to make a more perfect union, trusting future generations would carry on the task of creating an ever more, but never completely perfect, union.

Communal Political Life as a Tradition-Bound Process

The modern world was and is inclined to believe in a kind of "tradition-free" thinking that an understanding of science and a scientific approach to political philosophy undermines. Peirce, Polanyi, and other philosophers of science point out that most scientific thinking occurs within a tradition of inquiry conducted by a community of persons dedicated to science. At any time in history, that community has an established worldview and specific basic ideas within which reasoning occurs. There is also a need within our political process for establishing communities dedicated to the fundamental principles of democracy and our Constitution, and creating a more just society over time.

Certain core beliefs, ideas, customs, and inherited information have emerged. All of these are embodied in symbols of all kinds, which carry the meaning of the tradition forward in time and allow community members to deal with new realities. While there can be and are revolutionary changes of insight, such as the change from a materialistic to a quantum way of viewing reality, these changes are not part of the ordinary operation of science or any other tradition. Day in and day out, countless individuals work within the existing tradition to make, over time, substantial improvements in human understanding. This is true not only in science but in every area of inquiry.

Peirce, Royce, and Polanyi all defend the cause and importance of traditions of inquiry. Bohm, who was the victim of an ossified consensus around the so-called "Copenhagen

Interpretation" of quantum physics, was not so great a defender of tradition. However, he saw science in all of its periods as a tradition-bound activity. While methods and theories change over time, the ideal and the fundamental qualities of the scientist remain stable. There is a tradition of science that is deeper and more stable than any particular theory and its adherents. If it is a living tradition, it is constantly being adapted and improved over time in the search for justice and social harmony.

The same can be true of government. While revolutionary ideas cannot be rejected as a matter of course, they are not part of the ordinary function of government. Because revolutionary changes in approach cannot be ruled out, freedom of thought and speech is essential so that the public can hear and be informed of all possible approaches to public issues. In time, revolutionary changes may need to be made. Still, the commitment of a free society to freedom of thought, expression, and life will remain a constant feature of a tradition. This is harder to see in America, with our short history, than it is in older democracies like Great Britain, where centuries have unfolded since the Magna Carta and the beginning of a long march towards parliamentary democracy.

The *sophia-agapic*, pragmaticist theory advanced in this book proceeds on the conviction that there is an intergenerational, intercultural voice contained in every tradition of substance, the voice of the collective wisdom of the human race from its emergence until the present day. This voice encodes the experiences of countless thousands of people who confront concrete problems in life. For example, the wisdom songs contained in the Psalms, the pithy, short sayings of Proverbs, the problematic story of Job, the meditations of Ecclesiastes, the story of Daniel, and the letter of James represent the voice of wisdom (*sophia*) speaking through the experience of the Israelites at particular points in their history. Each time the parental voice is heard, it is simultaneously the voice of a cultural and religious tradition that extends from the very beginning of the human race, attempting to convey practical wisdom to each succeeding generation of a living tradition.[316]

A living tradition continues to confront reality, grow, adapt, and change in the quest for survival as the tradition is passed from generation to generation. It maintains itself despite changes, evolution, growth, successes, and failures. A political tradition is no different from any other scientific, religious, or other tradition. It is living because it sustains a community of faithful exploration to understand a way of life or the quest for goodness, truth, or beauty from the past, in the present, and towards the future.

In the case of political thought, this intergenerational community consists of the entire history of political and legal thought by human beings. It is both *cultural* (embedded in the so-called Eastern or Western traditions) and *cross-cultural*, for in contemporary society, no individual culture or political system escapes fertilization by the thoughts and experiences of other systems and cultures. This last aspect is essential for understanding how a community's tradition is impacted by its dialogue with different communities. For example, Western democracy has impacted societies with little of the cultural background that dominates the West. More recently, the West has been affected by its dialogue with the East. To say that a tradition is engaged in conversation, dialogue, and learning is not to say that it does not remain faithful to its unique perspective and calling.

Consensus, Conflict, Hope, and Community

The process of inquiry within a community always seeks a consensus in which all members commonly recognize a particular position or theory as true. This is the hope of any community of inquiry: that doubt will be eliminated for all participants. However, this consensus is typically a future hope, not an experienced present reality. This is especially true in the political arena. In a private letter to a critic, Peirce acknowledged this essentially incomplete and future-oriented hope of any community:

> We cannot be quite sure that the community will ever settle down to an unalterable conclusion upon any given question. Even if they do so for the most part, we have no reason to think the unanimity will be quite complete, nor can we rationally presume any overwhelming consensus of opinion will be reached upon every question. All that we are entitled to assume is in the form of a hope that such conclusion may be substantially reached concerning the particular questions with which our inquirers are busied.[317]

No community of inquiry devoted to a subject like government, law, or politics is ever complete within human history as regards things that are complex and not subject to a unanimous decision. As previously mentioned, such an endeavor is a fool's errand that dooms any society that undertakes to end debate to decay and almost certainly despotism.

In an excellent ending to a dissertation entitled *The Haunted Animal: Peirce's Community of Inquiry and the Formation of the Self*, Jacob Librizzi makes the following point:

No one is radically independent and self-supporting in this life. Rather, we are all sentimentally entwined with others in our thoughts and deeds. As such, to treat the memories of others poorly as means alone, and not equally as ends in themselves, is to falsely acknowledge one's own existence as merely a means toward an end indifferent to its makings. Such a paradoxical, life negating thought—seeking radical independence and autonomy—achieves only to explain the self by explaining it away in isolation.[318]

Much of modern politics, left and right, is guilty of precisely this mistake, a mistake that St. Augustine pointed out long ago: treating those we should love as ends in themselves as means, and thus cutting ourselves off from the essential communal aspects of human life.[319] Isolated individuals, unconnected to a greater community but only responsive to the needs of those who think and feel as they think and feel, are always unwilling and unable to act in the best interests of all members of society, for they lack the vital social connection necessary for such a task.

The most significant political challenge Americans face today is to recover shared communal commitments that can sustain a democratic and free society while protecting minorities, including religious minorities. This inevitably involves finding a way out of our cultural fixation on radical independence and autonomy, which breeds conflict and increasingly prevents us from being able to solve serious social challenges. Despite our differences, common sense and commitment to community calls for the redevelopment of a society bound together by cherishing love for a shared project to achieve the common good for all.

Josiah Royce, more than any other American philosopher, emphasizes the role of community for human society, human individuals, and the advancement of human culture and knowledge. The notion of community appears in nearly every aspect of Royce's thought. In science, religion, and all other forms of reasoning, Royce emphasizes the need for a community of interpretation within which rational thinking and progress in human understanding can occur. For a community to exist, there must be what Royce terms "loyalty," a shared commitment to the enterprise, a love for the subject matter and the community, and a disciplined search for a proper interpretation.[320] As seen below, a healthy community cannot be forced. It can be created only by the choice of free individuals to give themselves to a community that embraces goals larger than a single human life.

From Individual Self-Seeking to Community

Peirce saw that individualistic self-centeredness, selfish tendencies, and the human propensity to error had to be tempered and checked by community bonds. Peirce was especially critical of Social Darwinism and the "Gospel of Greed" that Social Darwinism engendered.[321] Against the Social Darwinist position, Peirce believed that the universe, though involving chance and regularities, also involved a social, "agapistic" (love) component. Human individuals are inevitably self-centered.

Each of us tends to see the world through the physical, perceptual, and interpretive center of our self. This unique "self" is the social product of our life experiences, lessons, and learning. This historically constructed, evolving self can become trapped in intellectual and moral isolation. No one else shares precisely the same perception or interpretation of reality as any other individual. We do not have access to the hopes, dreams, and knowledge of others that we have of our own hopes, dreams, and understanding. Our communication with others, even others to whom we are close, is distorted by the inevitable differences between what we intend to communicate and how another person interprets what we have shared.

The *sophio-agapic* pragmaticist approach recommended does not dismiss individuals' importance and unique contribution to knowledge. However, individuals, left to their resources, rarely make significant progress in life or any intellectual or practical discipline.[322] How do humans overcome the inadequacy of solitude and the danger of misunderstanding and misinterpretation? The answer lies in the constant need for interpretation, correction, and reinterpretation, all of which are social enterprises.

This is not just true in intellectual life but in every area of life. Human beings need the sympathetic correction of others to perceive the world. Sympathetic modification and reinterpretation require communities of interpretation where any complex subject matter is involved. Royce puts it thus:

> And the social environment that most awakens our self-consciousness about our conduct does so by opposing us, by criticizing us, or by otherwise standing in contrast with us. Our knowledge of our conduct, in all its higher grades, and our knowledge of ourselves as the authors or guides of our own conduct, our knowledge of how and why we do what we do, –all such more elaborate self-knowledge is, directly or indirectly, a social product, and a product of social contrast and opposition of one sort or another. Our fellows train us to all our higher grades of practical knowledge, and they do so by giving us certain sorts of social trouble.[323]

Science is a paradigm of a truth-seeking community. At any given time, there are always things scientists believe they understand, other matters which they do not yet understand, and matters about which there are disputes within the scientific community. Eventually, someone discovers new facts or develops a new theory and publishes the results to the scientific community. Other scientists will do the same. Still others examine and either verify or critique the new experimental results or theory. Out of this process of research, interpretation, theorizing, and publication, eventually, a consensus emerges concerning the best interpretation. This process, in the case of science, has been going on for centuries, with many changes and improvements in our understanding of the world.

Community, the Developing Self, and Values

The development of moral character and social ideals is profoundly communal. Humans are born into a social environment, including family and the greater society. By interacting socially, individuals develop the character and values that hold together a community. Thus, Royce notes that:

> In brief, it is our fellows who first startle us out of our natural unconsciousness about our own conduct; and who then, by an endless series of processes of setting us attractive but difficult models, and socially interfering with our own doings, train usto higher and higher grades and to a more and more complex type of self-consciousness regarding what we do and why we do it.[324]

In the same way, society develops its unique cultural attributes through its members' constant interaction in various social relations, political, social, business, religious, artistic, and otherwise. The social will of society is developed and maintained through this complex interaction between institutions.[325] All aspects of this complex web of relations and interaction are central to developing the uniqueness of any particular individual or group. There will be opposition, conflict, misunderstanding, unfair critique, etc. All this is simply a part of any social life or endeavor. As Royce so eloquently states, our opponents, and perhaps our political and economic opponents are our greatest asset, since they force us to refine and improve our ideas, policies, and actions.

Relationships grow, develop, and change over time. For example, after the Revolutionary War, the original states were bound together by the Articles of Confederation. However, this agreement instituted a flawed system of government. The central government could not tax, so it was constantly near bankruptcy. There was no guarantee of freedom of commerce between the states, and some states used their powers to prevent competition. There was no central military command structure, so the nation was weak.

Eventually, the Constitution Convention was held. In the beginning, there were vast differences of opinion about what should be done. The original Constitution was drafted and submitted to the states through a series of compromises and accommodations, followed by the original Bill of Rights. This process is often, in my view, mistakenly criticized. The founders were not privy to the social realities of the early 21st century, the critical advances of the 20th century, or the crucible of the Civil War and the Industrial Revolution. They made the necessary compromises to make social progress in their day. They did not act to solve every social problem, past, present, or future. They left much for future generations to do.

What is often missed are the first words of the Constitution: "We the People of the United States." The thirteen original states already viewed themselves as one "People" and were willing to compromise, even conceding on points that were important to them. Some states eventually joined the union, even though they disagreed with aspects of the Constitution. The Constitutional Convention, the various state conventions that ratified the Constitution, and the process followed reveal multiple communities of people, all gathered with a common purpose, searching for a common, better solution than permitted by the current state of affairs. Since its original adoption, the Constitution has had to be revised on several occasions to meet the demands of the times.

Sophio-agapic pragmaticists understand that American life takes for granted a certain amount of tension, struggle, search for power, differences of opinion, and jockeying for position. There can be no complete elimination from politics of the struggle for power. However, this aspect of American life can lead to the dissolution of our national community unless complemented by dialogue, conversation, and compromise. In fact, during the Civil War, it did. The only solution to the problem of warring factions is creating a community of many individuals who join together in the common search for a just, fair, and orderly society. Without the willingness to debate, discuss, dialogue, and compromise, a solution must eventually be imposed by force.

The impulse at work in the violence in our politics and some of our cities today reflects a lack of trust in the American community and its fundamental values and structures. The result is the loss of a national sense of being part of a community where we do not always get exactly what we want but are willing to join others in the patient search for a solution that is as reasonable and fair as possible to all.

Royce understood that such a community can only be formed and maintained through a committed form of mutual respect and love, which he called "loyalty." Loyalty exists when an individual voluntarily participates in a community and seeks the community's common good with and above their personal preferences in giving to the community. Loyalty involves personal sacrifice for the common interest and a willingness to explore the best solution to the problem of human progress.

Faith, Community, and Progress

All knowledge depends on a prior communal act of faith. Scientists, lawyers, artists, philosophers, pastors, and the like are part of communities of people who believe in scientific truth, justice, beauty, God, wisdom, and other values. They trust that the endeavor they are engaged in can be successful and hope even for a final success at some point. In each case, community members prepare by becoming a part of a community of those who believe in its values, are skilled in its techniques and disciplines, and act as role models for newer members. Whether we are speaking of Isaac Newton (science), Oliver Wendell Holmes (law), Picasso (art), Pope John Paul II (religion), Michael Polanyi (philosophy), or others in various fields, there is always a community seeking the kind of knowledge the community exists to further. In each case, there is a process by which a person who wishes to become part of the community gains the skills needed to contribute.

Well-formed communities of inquiry are self-policing. They do not require external governance or any form of totalitarian compulsion to uniformity.[326] For example, there are respected journals in science, theology, law, and other areas of inquiry.

Not everyone can write for them. There is a process of gaining credibility. In addition, those journals will likely print articles exposing readers to more than one view in controversial areas. For example, several possible interpretations in quantum physics have well-known backers, especially the Copenhagen Interpretation and Bohm (Hidden Variable) Interpretation. There is no consensus as to the better explanation. Both receive space in well-respected journals and are the subject of articles, seminars, discussions, and the like.

Traditions can and do take steps down what turn out to be blind alleys. In law, some decisions breed more and better decisions in an area, while others breed inconsistencies, unforeseen injustices, and incoherencies. When a precedent is overturned, judges become convinced that a better or different rule must promote justice for parties and society. Frequently, this occurs after lengthy discussions in journals, seminars, educational events, political writings, etc. Research projects may change in other areas as certain research avenues become less fruitful.

Persons and Community

In addition to the *communal nature* of the search for Truth, Beauty, Goodness, and Justice, there is also a *personal aspect*. Every discovery, every new work of art, and every new moral intuition is the product of a human person. Over and over again in science, men and women struggle in an area to remove some inconsistency or problem in theory, only to await the insight of a single mind. Such was the case with Einstein's theory of relativity and the discoveries of modern quantum physics. In each case, after a long struggle with conflicting data that could not be easily reconciled with the current theory, a discovery was made through personal insight.[327] When this insight was reached, the scientist (in this case, Albert Einstein) published his results to the rest of the community, expecting both criticism and support. Every community is also a fellowship of individuals who have become part of the community and believe in its fundamental tenets and values. To maintain those values, participants in that society must be able to communicate and adjust their differences wisely.

CHAPTER 10

CONVERSATION, DIALOGUE, AND SEARCHING FOR JUSTICE

The importance of dialogue and conversation for political thought and practice can hardly be overestimated in the quest for wise social policy. The meaning of these terms illuminates the difference between the idea of truth as the result of critical analysis and a relational model of truth emerging from human community and interaction. The need for conversation and dialogue can sometimes be difficult to understand in a democratic society, where the ideals of debate and majority rule are fundamental. In such a society, debate can dominate decision-making.

Debate occurs when two sides of an issue present their case before a decision. There is no question but that debate and discussion are critical to a free society. However, underneath debate and discussion, and ontologically prior to them, a community exists and must be respected and nurtured. Conversation and dialogue are needed within that community to maintain mutual understanding amid political conflict. Unfortunately, insufficient attention to community building, dialogue, and conversation among differing views has resulted in a decline in the political community in the West. This results in dysfunctional government and poor policy choices.

Many commentators have written about the lack of effective dialogue in Western society today. In Congress and State Legislatures, open hostility and unwillingness to compromise and dialogue about serious problems are endemic. More concerning is that dialogue has become increasingly impossible in families, neighborhood associations, churches, and other mediating institutions and organizations. Even debate is ineffective if no one is listening or, as is increasingly the case, everyone has decided before the debate begins. A lack of authentic community dialogue results in poor decision-making and gridlock. It is also responsible for the increasing alienation of many people from the values of a democratic society.

Reliance on debate and the external features of the political process is inadequate, given the current state of our society. The term "debate" has an interesting derivation, for it comes from an early usage that means to quarrel, dispute, combat, fight, or make war. Moreover, debate comes from combining a prefix that means "from or down, off of" and a verb, "battaure" in Latin, that means to strike, beat violently, to hit with a mallet or battering ram. In other words, debate is a word that implies conflict as opposed to consensus. Therefore, it is unsurprising that a society that honors debate more than dialogue would have difficulty maintaining an integrated and healthy community.

"Discussion" has the same grammatical root as "percussion." A discussion exists when more than two people or groups express their views, each trying to convince the other that theirs is the correct view.[328] Discussion typically involves merely an attempt to persuade or intellectually force agreement. Both debate and discussion are subject to the postmodern critique that all truth claims are simply bids for power. Although dialogue can disguise a mere bid for power, the intention is not winning but a free agreement among participants.

Bohm was aware of the danger of dialogue becoming one more way in which conflicting groups seek power over one another. In our society, with its fascination with power, control, and mastery, there is always a danger that the quest for power will interfere with creating meaning and a more just society.[329] Nevertheless, healthy dialogue does not degenerate into mere debate or discussion with a view toward political or social advantage.

Authentic dialogue involves sharing meaning in a community and is designed to enhance mutual understanding. There must be an open willingness to hear the other person's views for dialogue to occur. Although some proponents of dialogue suggest that we must suspend, give up, or hold in abeyance our personal views to enter a dialogue appropriately, the kind of discussion needed in political conversations requires that participants continue to maintain their beliefs but remember that others do not share them. We may not be entirely correct in what we think. Dialogue does not require suspending our deepest commitments; it only requires listening charitably and sympathetically to those who do not share them. [330]

Semiotic theory implies a dialogical view of human reasoning regarding political matters. The triad of Object, Sign, and Interpreter as fundamental to human reasoning leads to the idea that all thought, even personal thought, is ultimately dialogical, using signs to communicate the interpretation and meaning of objects. Since all thinking involves signs, human reasoning involves what might be called the "flow of signs" in human culture and an individual human mind.[331] As Peirce observes,

> Thinking always proceeds in the form of a dialogue—a dialogue between different phases of the ego,—so that, being dialogical, it is essentially composed of signs, as its Matter, in the sense in which a game of chess has the chessmen for its matter.[332]

Whether thinking is done individually or in a community, reasoning advances through a dialogue or a conversation, leading to knowledge, information, or a decision. As far as political communities are concerned, the flow of signs in communication and decision-making is essential to reaching sound conclusions that support social harmony and human flourishing.

Understanding the communal nature of all thought leads to understanding the importance of dialogue in political inquiry and the search for justice. Pragmaticism fundamentally suggests the need for a community of inquirers jointly investigating a problem in every area of human inquiry. When scientists approach a problem, a program eventually emerges, and is advanced as people conduct investigations, formulate conclusions, and share those conclusions with a community of believers who are also investigating the problem. Usually, findings are shared in community interactions and relevant journals. This exchange involves listening to and understanding the results of the conclusions of other investigators in preparation for additional research and conversation. Thus, the advancement of science involves a continuing relationship and dialogue between scientists concerning the aspect of reality they are investigating.

Dialogue occurs with those who are not following and may be critical of such a research program but who enter the common conversation to express their views.

In politics, as in science, the search for resolution of a particular problem begins with doubt concerning some matter of importance. This doubt is not a disembodied doubt but a substantial doubt about a matter of importance to the community. Doubt involves an uneasy state of mind from which a person or community seeks to free themselves.[333] Community members enter into some form of inquiry to eliminate doubt and the unease it causes because of some policy issue or decision that must be made.[334] The investigation aims to move from doubt, confusion, and unease about a matter to a state of belief, a state of ease where the inquirer has resolved his apprehension ("the irritation of doubt") sufficiently to move forward in some way.[335] Any inquiry aims to remove doubt and substitute some degree of at least provisional understanding of a problem. In a democratic society, the goal is to achieve a shared way forward while maintaining the health and cohesion of the community.

When we have an idea that we hold accurately, our thoughts, behavior, and living habits are somehow impacted. When we begin to doubt that idea, our intellectual and practical habits are upended in some way. We enter the inquiry stage to eliminate the doubt and discomfort we feel, which may be achieved by forming a new habit or attaining information that allows a human being to choose and develop a new guide for action.[336] The danger is always that we human beings will use violence, law, or bureaucratic power to eliminate doubt and discomfort by force, thus damaging the communal search for the best and wisest solution to a problem. This is why, despite the role of power in any society, creating shared values, achieving mutual consent, and maintaining social cohesion are of primary importance and hold priority over merely achieving a policy victory.

In the case of politics and political philosophy, the signs are predominately a natural language, or if scientific studies are included in the conversation, mathematics is important as the primary language of science. The goal of inquiry in matters of public policy is to remove some degree of doubt so that we can move forward to create a more just society. A new policy adopted is analogous to Peirce's idea of a habit: it is a guide to behavior until supplanted by a better insight.

The interpretive process begins with a sign or set of signs designed to communicate information concerning the focus of the decision to the community involved, often in the form of a policy proposal. This information is inevitably received and interpreted by the community and its members. This interpretation then serves as a point at which the interpretive process continues, for it is a sign claiming a community and its members. It is easy to see that this process is fundamentally dialogical as it moves from the communication of signs to interpretation and back to further communication and interpretation.

Royce extended Peirce's fundamentally scientific notion of the role of community and signs in expanding human knowledge to all human knowledge, including religious knowledge. In so doing, he extends the realm of communal dialogue in the search for knowledge into every area of human endeavor. Thus, he claims:

> The will to interpret, in all of its forms, scientific or philosophical, or religious, presupposes that, somehow, at some time, in some fitting embodiment, a community of interpretation exists, and is in the process of aiming

toward its goal. Any conversation with other men, any process of that inner conversation whereof, as we have seen, our individual self-consciousness consists, any scientific investigation, is carried on under the influence of the generally subconscious belief that we are members of a community of interpretation. ... For there is the member whose office it is to edify. There is the brother who is to be edified. And there is the spirit of the community, who is in one aspect, the interpreter, and in another aspect of being who is interpreted.[337]

Within this view of communities of interpretation, there is a built-in aspect of a conversation or dialogue between the members of such a community. The nature of that dialogue will vary between communities. For example, a dialogue between a community of mathematicians will primarily occur using numerical symbols. On the other hand, a conversation among political or religious people about some matter of public policy or religious faith is likely to take the form of natural language. In each case, there is a person who makes a claim, a person who is the recipient of that claim of knowledge, and an interpreter of the claim. Through the conversation, new insight is achieved, and abstract and practical knowledge is extended.

This ideal conception of interpretation inevitably involves interpersonal and intergroup communication and dialogue. A community is formed by communication among its members. It cannot be sustained without the ability to state ideas and proposals, listen attentively, engage in a dialogue that results in common understanding, and evaluate proposals reasonably. Initially, all communities, including political communities, evolve based on a shared history, real or imagined, that binds the community's individuals together. This shared history is communicated to the young and new members of the community through a sharing of the past in the present and into the future.[338] Thus, in every field of endeavor, including politics, people enter and are part of a community of interpretation, a tradition, that embodies a shared understanding of the past:

> A community is constituted by the fact that each of its members accepts as part of his own individual life and self the same past events that each of his fellow members accepts as what may be called, a "community of memory."[339]

This community of memory begins in the past, is maintained in the present, and continues into the future as it gives meaning, purpose, direction, and hope to the community thus formed:

> A community constituted by the fact that each of its members accepts, as part of his own individual life and self, the same expected future events that each of his fellows accepts, may be called a community of expectation, or upon occasion, a community of hope.[340]

Through time and the process of interpretation, communication, and adaptation, a community, including a political community, is ultimately bound together by a shared history and the values, social institutions, and culture that have emerged from that shared history. This common history must be communicated so that it extends into the indefinite future and gives its members a sense of expectation and hope. Any community, whether scientific, philosophical, political, or otherwise, is involved in a constant conversation and dialogue among its members, including the private inner conversations of each member, discussions motivated by the belief that each member of such a society—such a "Community of Interpretation," as Royce calls it—is moving toward a common goal.[341]

Political Importance of Dialogue

The importance of dialogue for political progress should be obvious. The point of dialogue is to jointly enter into an examination of the processes of thought, the assumptions, the hidden agendas, and the logical components of the views we hold.[342] In a democracy, there are bound to be a variety of opinions, historical experiences, unnamed assumptions, and ideological preferences behind any particular policy proposal. It is the function of dialogue to go beyond debate and enter into the entire thought process so that the group can avoid fragmentation and come to some common opinion about policy matters.[343]

In the dialogue process, people from different backgrounds come together to share their opinions and uncover their hidden (or tacit) assumptions about some matter of importance to them.[344] For a society to function reasonably, people must share their private views and meanings so that they may move forward together. This is not happening in Western culture, which results in incoherent and chaotic societies.[345]

It is impossible to eliminate all conflict from political life. It is impossible to eliminate debate from a free society, nor can any form of government function without decisions. However, in our society, the level of conflict has reached dysfunctional proportions. It is impossible to heal the dysfunction without rebuilding a sense of community, a task for dialogue and communication. Any attempt to rebuild and restore a sense of community through the unbridled search for power will destroy a free society without a substratum of shared values and community. So long as political elites view power as the ultimate reality and the search for power as unconstrained by moral ideals and shared values, there is little hope for our democratic institutions. The proposal made here is that some form of wise communal love is necessary for democratic institutions to function appropriately.

CHAPTER 11

SOPHIA-AGAPISM, JUSTICE AND ESCAPE FROM NIHILISM

Western society has descended into a short-sighted nihilistic pragmatism, resulting in the decay of political institutions, among other problems. The intellectual momentum of the Enlightenment has burned out with terrible results in academic and political life. In particular, a loss of a conviction that abstract ideals, such as justice, are real and can and should constrain politics and government has resulted in a political reality that can only be described as "Nietzschean": a politics centered on the unbridled quest for power and its exercise unconstrained by noetic values, such as truth, justice, prudence, equity, and the like. This is a Hobbesian vision of a society of self-seeking individuals founded on a "war of all against all." The results can be seen in matters as proximate as the disintegration of the family and as distant from family life as the "economy of wars" that threatens the flourishing of people everywhere.

Just as science cannot exist without a commitment to investigating a reality independent of the observer, political and social life is debilitated when no underlying notion of justice and fairness guides policymakers' thinking. What is left is the will to power without effective intellectual and moral constraints beyond what political realities create in a given society. In some societies, that means little, if any, restraint.

The results of this approach, by the left and right, resulted in both dramatic political catastrophes of the 20th century (Communist and National Socialist regimes) and various lesser examples of policy foolishness and failure. The governments involved were established and managed by persons who viewed themselves as beyond the childishness of traditional standards of justice and, therefore, created terrible human suffering and policy failure. They were "immoralists" beyond the constraints of good and evil or justice and injustice.[346]

As Michael Polanyi put it:

> They had rejected the overt professions of these ideals, as philosophically and sound, hypocritical and suspicious, but they had covertly, injected the same ideals into the new despotisms, which they set up. These ideals became eminent in the violence, which so ruthlessly rejected them. By virtue of this moral inversion (as I have later called it), the very immoralism of this power became a token of its moral purity.[347]

Not even the best Enlightenment democracies are free of this scourge. Losing the noetic reality of truth, justice, beauty, and goodness leads to a descent into the worship of self and possessions, power, and pleasure. Justice is reduced to the success of the stronger.[348]

The loss of confidence in noetic realities, such as justice, allows the creation of political regimes characterized by a public moral insistence that they are "on the right side of history" but whose actions are characterized by lies, deceit, corruption, and violence, all in the name of the morality they have rejected. For the true, multifaceted source of human flourishing, they have substituted forces immanent in history, resulting in the inevitable presumed progress of the human race. These leaders, empowered by romantic and materialistic thought patterns, deny universal standards of truth, justice, or morality, using "moral speak" only to gain power.[349]

Over more than a century, however, the materialistic model of the world that underlies the problems of our society and political system has been superseded by a model of the world that assumes a deep interconnectedness, rationality, relationality, freedom, and inner sensitivity. In my view, and the view of others, the older way of thinking has led modern politicians, policymakers, and intellectuals into many errors. Physicist Henry Sapp puts it as follows:

> [We] are faced today with the spectacle of our society being built increasingly upon a conception of reality erected upon a mechanical conception of nature now known to be fundamentally false. … As a consequence of this widely disseminated misinformation, "well informed" officials, administrators, legislators, judges, educators, and medical professionals who guide the development of our society are encouraged to shape our lives in ways predicated on known-to-be-false premises about "nature and nature's laws."[350]

Many problems of our society result from the adoption by lawyers, policymakers, politicians, bureaucrats, and others of this outdated, mechanistic view of reality in which people become individual objects related to each other by physical, emotional, and mental forces. The way out of this situation is adopting a new way of looking at reality characterized by an organic, process, and noetic view of reality and its operation. This way does not entirely cancel the older Newtonian/Hobbesian way of looking at political reality, but it does supersede that way of thinking as limited by a deeper and more profound understanding of reality.

Pragmaticism and the Reality of Justice

What Peirce called "Pragmaticism" provides a solution to the problems created by a mechanistic view of reality and politics. Pragmaticism provides a constructive yet critical way to recover confidence in the reality of human values, not as "pre-existing forms" from which all imperfect human expressions of justice are a concrete instance, but as noetic realities that develop and are enriched over time by those who seek them, believing that they will reveal themselves in the process of diligent inquiry. In this view, universals, such as justice, are potentialities that are given concrete meaning in the life of society as communities of human beings search for meaning and work for the realization in a just society; the meaning of justice is unfolded by those who seek them as part of a community of inquiry.

Peirce's defense of the intellectual reality of universals, or what I have called "noetic ideals," has an affinity with Whitehead's notion of "Eternal Objects." Noetic ideals are pure noetic potentials capable of forming actual occasions in human history, including policymakers' decisions in government and private industry.[351] These noetic realities exist in the power they have to disclose themselves to a properly formed community of inquiry as they guide the thoughts and actions of its members. For this to happen, a community dedicated to the ideal of justice and freedom is required. Such a community must be convinced that the noetic ideals underlying a free society exist and will reveal themselves in the future.[352] This kind of community needs to be renewed in our society.

Rather than seeing "justice" as a pre-existing invariant and perfect form, as Plato envisioned it, or as an invariant law of human nature or reason, as was common in early modern thinking, justice is seen as a pattern of movement or process of a relatively invariant abstract ideal (a "transcendental potential") determined provisionally in a constantly evolving society. The relative invariance of the notion of justice is composed of its present evolved meaning in a particular society. This present meaning is the current ordering of all prior decisions made by such a society in its ever changing and ever progressive process of creating justice and social harmony.[353]

This view is not nominalist nor is the choice of alternatives solely arbitrarily chosen as an act of human will. The view is closer to Whitehead's idea of Eternal Objects as potentials realized in human lives and society as new levels of meaning are achieved in the attempt to create a free and just society. Over time, a society committed to creating a just society can discover and implement compelling ideals of justice that promote social harmony and human flourishing. This evolutionary process of justice as a guide and constraint on polity involves countless actors in a free society. In particular, legislatures and judicial systems provide a crucial means by which evolving notions can be prudently put into practice and evaluated on a policy by policy, legislation by legislation, and case-by-case basis.

Freedom of Speech and Community

For the noetic ideal of justice to reveal a proper depth of meaning for a society, communities must be dedicated to the search for it—communities that believe justice can be found and are committed to the impartial search. The notion of justice, and achieving the ideal of a free society, require a community that holds particular views and ideals and feels engaged in a common quest for a just and fair society in which people can peacefully engage in their private lives. This requires a shared basic level of commitment to and faith in our society and its leadership and ideals. In short, it requires a community that creates, reinforces, and renews the basic principles of a free society.

A pattern for what such a community of inquiry should look like can be seen in the scientific community, a self-ordered society of individuals engaged in the search for truth. As Polanyi observes, "… science can exist and continue to exist only because its premises can be held in common by a community. This is also true of all complex creative activities carried on beyond the lifetime of individuals."[354] A community of inquirers exists wherever individuals subject themselves to a joint research program with a view toward understanding. This includes many groups with differing agendas, talents, and political experience. The community of inquiry characteristic of science is also present in law and religion.[355]

For a common quest to extend beyond the lifetime of an individual or small group of individuals, such a community carries forward in thought and action a tradition in which members place their faith. Such a tradition must also be embodied in institutions that transmit the accomplishments of the past and guide the achievements in the future. In a free society such as the United States, a vast number and variety of institutions must be engaged in maintaining, transmitting, and expanding the tradition of inquiry. It includes, in addition to government, educational institutions at all levels, media, social groups, political parties, and a host of other mediating institutions. A community that maintains a democratic, free society comprises all the members of that society and all the institutions within its bounds. A single hub of power cannot govern it, but it must be guided by the hands of many separate centers of power, all committed to the fundamental ideals of a just and free society.

Freedom of Speech and Dialogue

Part of the postmodern movement involves changing how people think. It moves from an objective idea of truth, in which the observer is an uninvolved reporter, to a relational definition of truth, in which understanding is created through a relationship between the observer and reality.[356] In this way of thinking, neither an observer nor reality can be separated from the relationship they have with one another. This notion is consistent with the view that searching for knowledge is a semiotic activity that inevitably involves interpreting signs within and among a community of inquirers.

In one of his passages that has a definite bearing on political philosophy, Peirce comments:

The method of authority will always govern the mass of mankind; and those who wield the various forms of organizational force in the state will never be convinced that dangerous reasoning ought not to be suppressed in some way. If liberty of speech is to be untrammeled from the grosser forms of constraint, then uniformity of opinion will be secured by a moral terrorism to which the respectability of society will give us through approval.[357]

Those who believe that they are undoubtedly correct in their political views and those who value the maintenance of the current social order will always be tempted to use the method of authority and instruments of coercive power to secure their position in society and the dominance of their views. It is a method that has both a benefit to an existing order and a danger to human progress. However, in the end, such a method can lead only to intellectual and social decay. Therefore, there needs to be a more dynamic approach. American pragmaticists believed they had found such an approach in the pragmatic method, which begins with the logical task of ordering ideas and recognizing inconsistency and incompleteness in those ideas. It also involves further research and analysis before doubt is resolved and corrective action can be taken.

Motivated by the doubt caused by the incompleteness or inconsistency of our understanding (and a corresponding reluctance to take action based on that incomplete or inadequate information), the pragmaticist community engages in inquiry to better understand that world and how to respond to it. This can be the physical world, as in science; the moral world, as in philosophy; the spiritual world, as in religion; or the social world, as in politics and government. The exact nature of the method will vary depending on the community of inquiry and the subject matter of the inquiry. The method of politics is not the method of science or religion. Each of these disciplines has its unique adaptation of the pragmatic approach.

The goal of the pragmaticist method is to develop a course of action, what Peirce calls a "habit of action," that produces a beneficial result that is tangible and practical.[358] In one of his most straightforward statements of the pragmaticist method, Peirce urges that, in the course of any intellectual inquiry, the best course of action is to consider what possible effects having a practical bearing on the problem might result from the conceptions developed as a result of our inquiry of some aspect of reality.[359] Unfortunately, in the case of politics and social policy, careful consideration of potential consequences is too often absent from much political discourse. For example, the impact of increasing government debt is rarely seriously considered as a restraint on policy desires by whichever party is in power.

Our current ideas of justice are always subject to revision based on new evidence, which is why freedom of inquiry and speech, and respect for a diversity of opinions, including religious and other beliefs, is essential to a wise and good government. In addition, every new state of society brings new problems and opportunities for extending justice in new and unforeseen ways to new and unexpected situations.

The goal is continually discovering new information and ideas that will permit an evolving society to develop rules of action and act confidently. Historically, this involves the development of new modes of adapting to the natural and human environment.[360] In politics and government, any new rule of action is intended to solve some social or political problem that the society we are a part of faces and needs to solve to secure a more just society. In the case of politics, much of the inquiry involves understanding the various alternatives of a policy initiative and then seeking a common understanding of the best course of action under the circumstances. This involves not just debate and a vote to see who has the most significant power but also conversation, discussion, and dialogue designed to create consensus.

Defending a Sophia-Agapistic Political View

In the philosophy of C.S. Peirce, the evolution of human society, like the evolution of the world, is characterized by chance, deterministic features, and *agapistic love*. To understand what Peirce is trying to say and its practical implications, it is crucial to understand what he means by "*agapistic love*." Peirce defines agapistic love as (i) an active bestowal of energy by the lover to the beloved, (ii) the cherishing of the beloved by the lover, (iii) and a positive sympathy on the part of the lover for the benefit of the beloved.[361] Love is a kind of bestowal of energy that cherishes and seeks the best for that which is loved. This love is not just a human emotion but emerges as one of the elementary characteristics of the evolving universe.

Peirce begins his analysis of agapism with quotations from the First Letter of John, in which John concludes that "God is love" (I John 4:8,16). Peirce then proceeds to a discussion of the nature of that kind of love we see reflected in the life of Christ and to which John refers, as well as critiquing John's supposed deviations from the pure gospel of love. Finally, he analyzes its application to evolutionary theory. Peirce believed that agapism is central to the evolution of the universe and human society, and the other features of evolutionary growth, chance, and necessity are derived from this primordial love. In other words, love is a central characteristic of the world and human societies. It is not an "add-on" or a psychological reaction of certain individuals to harmonies in the world or society. It is a feature of reality itself. In another context, I described the fundamental cherishing love to which Peirce refers as "Deep Love" or "Deep Relationality."[362]

On the other hand, one should not exaggerate the role of love in a political philosophy. Just as the quantum world merges into the world of Newtonian physics (a world of material objects and force-dominated interactions,) at the level of human society, the power of love and other factors in human civilization are impacted and limited by chance or fortuitous events and by the regularity. This means that international economic and political systems, and other systemic features of modern societies inevitably involve material objects and force—physical, social, political, and bureaucratic. As to human society and human relationships, the impact of human freedom and the choices made by others cannot be underestimated. In such an environment, conflict cannot be avoided entirely, and the more irrational and unloving the other actors involved may be, the more likely it is that conflict is inevitable. Love is to be seen as a real power in political life, but it is not the only power at work in public life.

In defending a *sophia-agapistic* approach to political theory, reason moves from the phenomena of relationality embedded in the physical universe to an analysis of the human experience of relationship and then to the emergence of the various kinds of relationality in human society. The variety of ways a deep relationality impacts human culture can be unfolded by looking at various Greek terms for love as a part of the gradual evolution of the human race and society. In Greek, there are at least five different relevant terms for love:

- "eros" or love evoked by desire (ἔρως),
- "storge" or affection (στοργή),
- "philia" or brotherly love (φιλία),
- "pragma" or practical love (πράγμα), and
- "agape" or self-giving love (αγάπη).

These loves emerge from the relationality found at the root of creation, in which human beings participate. The human capacity for loving relationality evolved as consciousness and society evolved. Humanity's capacity for relationality and love has grown in meaningful ways—and will continue to do so in the future.

The Emergence of Relationality in Human Society

Reality is multilayered. At the bottom of material reality lies the principles of physics, from which chemistry and biology emerge as independent areas of reality. The human race emerged through a long process of biological and social development, with the result that religion, psychology, sociology, law, and other disciplines gradually developed over time due to the capacity of human beings to create human societies and institutions. Each level of reality depends on others yet has its degree of independence. While other levels are relevant and impact higher levels, they do not fully determine them.[363] At each level of reality, there is continuity, dependence on lower levels, freedom, and openness as new potentials arise. In particular, the unconscious relationality of the universe is now conscious, capable of infinitely more complex relationships on a mental and emotional level. This determinism, freedom, and openness characterize all levels of reality.

The emergence of human beings and human society vastly increased the range and potential of the created order, including political options for the understanding and achievement of justice in society. The deep relationality of the universe involves a preference for sound relationships, for what the Jews call *shalom*, often translated as "peace." The term has the more profound connotation of "wholeness or completeness" of order in life. The human desire and need for social interaction impact societies in the search for justice. When recognized and developed in political philosophy, "noetic potentials," such as justice, arise and can guide humans' day-to-day activities. These noetic potentials develop and "unfold" in and among different societies in different ways. Nevertheless, all exemplify the potential for order and symmetry in relationships in every social reality.

The Politics of Agapism

For political purposes, all the forms of love enumerated above have some meaning, but three are most important to any well-functioning society:

> *Philia*, which is considered the beloved part of a family or common community;

> *Pragma*, which compromises to help the relationship work over time, showing patience and tolerance in sustaining and building a relationship; and

> *Agape*, which remains committed, sacrifices, and cherishes even when the beloved is unworthy. In the case of political love, the beloved is a society.

These three loves are essential to a functional society, particularly a functioning democratic society. *Philia* is that social bond we have because of a common family with shared norms and institutions of meaning. Societies need a shared history, background, life order, etc. Humans instinctively cling to family, close friendships, fellow believers, co-workers, etc. It is more than a figure of speech when people speak of a business, a neighborhood, or even a nation as a family, or even of the "family of nations."

Unfortunately, *philia* can impact social relationships negatively, where the bonds of a common family, race, religion, or cultural heritage overcome all other relational ties and create conflict. While all societies need a sense of community, social brotherhood, and sisterhood, where historic racial and other characteristics dominate, they can lead to conflict. The conflict in the Middle East between Jews and Arabs is a striking example of this phenomenon. In this context, Royce's notions of loyalty to loyalty and loyalty to the "Beloved Community" are important. Unless all our lesser loyalties are subject to a transcendental ideal of a fully just community bound together by completely healthy relationality, they tend to produce dysfunction.

Pragma is that love that allows members of a society to tolerate differences and build a shared community that benefits all, making the necessary compromises for any society to function. *Pragma* recognizes that society requires its members to be patient and loyal, even in times of stress.[364] *Pragma* encourages compliance with laws, even those with which one privately disagrees, to advance the group's common good. Pragma is "pragmatic" in that it accepts and nurtures the other to maintain a relationship of practical value to the lover.

From a political perspective, *pragma* is an essential form of love. Within a society, it is important to build social solidarity. On the other hand, there is a *pragma* among nations and within cultures. That is to say, we inhabit one world, and in that one world, it is in the best interests of everyone to create as much harmony as possible and to avoid destructive conflict. Developing an intercultural, international *pragma* is of the first importance.

At the top of the pyramid of love is *agape*. *Agape* is that love willing to sacrifice for the good of the whole. Agape also means giving others the right and capacity to achieve their goals despite our questions concerning their reasonableness or desirability. Agape respects the freedom of the other and hopes for the flourishing of the other. Agape is a love that bestows itself on the deserving and underserving alike. Shared history or calculations of personal self-interest do not limit the love that is agape.

Agape is the highest form of Christian love but also appears in other religious traditions, such as the idea of "universal loving kindness" in Buddhism.[365] In Latin, *agape* is translated as *"charitas,"* from which we get our word "charity." This usage points to the difference between *eros* and *agape*: *eros* is a love evoked by something in the beloved that the lover needs; *agape* is a love as the free act of the lover. *Agape* is not a love evoked by desire but bestowed on its recipient. *Agape* is not a love that can be commanded or required; it must be bestowed on people and society by the action of free people. In international politics, agape is present where those with power deliberately use less than all the power at their disposal in the interest of something higher—peace and harmony among people and social groups.

Agape is not unnecessary in human affairs, even amid conflict. Wise leaders avoid conflict and when in a conflict, seek to minimize the damage and estrangement all conflict involves. As I put it in another context:

> Wise leaders shun violence and conflict. This is the virtue of avoiding violence and conflict: the ability to manage people and situations as gently as snow falls on a winter day.
>
> The best policy is this: Avoid conflict if at all possible.
>
> If conflict arises, the best policy is this: Avoid unnecessary destruction. If conflict continues, the best policy is this: Seek a just solution. If conflict reaches

a conclusion, the best policy is this: Show mercy and restore good relations.[366]

Even in conflict, the agapist approach involves self-control and the search for peace, even at personal and social cost—the cost of sacrificing to avoid and minimize violence.

Conflicts in the Middle East, Ukraine, and other areas can appropriately be analyzed using these ideas. When the conflicts are over, it will take years to rebuild the social and physical infrastructure being destroyed. In addition, because military activities breed resentment, the resentment created will be present no matter who wins the conflict. The powers involved in such situations should consider the negative consequences of conflict no matter who wins. A victory that does no more than create even more embedded social hostility is unlikely to further the cause of peace in the long run.

Just War Pacifism and Sophia-Agapism

Some years ago, I suggested a political philosophy that might be called "just war pacifism." My colleague, a professor of philosophy, disagreed with the notion that one could conceive of a form of pacifism that embraced just war theory and a form of just war theory that embraces pacifism. Nevertheless, I continue to think that this is a valuable way of thinking.

Plato, the philosopher George Santayana, and General Douglas MacArthur are all recorded as saying, "Only the dead will never know war again." War is a social reality that appears to be a permanent feature of human history. While every peace-loving person must seek to avoid conflict and war to the greatest extent possible, it is also in the best interest of every human being to see that where warfare is being conducted, it is conducted in such a way as to lead to the least possible loss of life, and especially the life of innocents, and conducted in a manner most likely to render a peaceful result, and a more harmonious social future.

As this was being written, television and media were filled with images of the results of a horrific terror attack in which noncombatants, men, women, and children were killed and, in some cases, tortured and killed. No possible construction of just war theory condones this behavior. The inevitable human reaction is to want to make the person who did this pay, leading to more violence. For some time, the citizens of Ukraine have been the subject of a dehumanizing conflict in which innocent noncombatants have become victims of violence. Violence has led to more violence. Human lives and human social solidarity are being destroyed.

Unfortunately, this gives rise to a conundrum that afflicts all just war thinking: When a terrorist organization is leading an entire social group, are the members of that society willingly or unwillingly participating in the injustice of their leaders? To what extent is there a duty to resist a terrorist regime? This is precisely the problem that Dietrich Bonhoeffer faced in Germany before and during World War II and is not, in principle, resolvable. It is only solvable in a case facing a concrete person.

Socio-agapism, when used as a principle of action in any area, is not a philosophy of weakness or inaction. It is a philosophy of wise engagement to achieve the best result for all. Even where a leader or society is in a position of power, socio-agapism establishes a principle of intelligent calculation of the best interests of all involved, believing that the best interests of all involved are also in each party's best interests in a conflict. It also establishes within society and among societies a preference for avoiding unnecessary conflict and minimizing conflict when it arises.

Socio-agapism does not provide an easy solution to all conflicts or give precise guidance to leaders. It underscores the importance of phronesis, of practical wisdom gained by experience for political leaders. Sophie-agapism suggests a path involving the relentless and sometimes costly search for social harmony and peaceful relationships within and among social groups.

The Relationship of Justice to Love

The theologian and philosopher Reinhold Niebuhr makes a distinction relevant to a *sophia-agapistic* approach to the principle of justice. For Niebuhr, "nature" refers to society's current historical possibilities of justice. These historical possibilities exist in the context of physical, historical, and other types of limitations on possible courses of action. In contrast, "grace refers to an ideal possibility of perfect love potentially present in any society."[367] In every society, the search for justice is a process whereby a set of institutions are formed, and a degree of justice is achieved. Still, there remains an unfulfilled quality of justice attained, which is constantly being further illuminated by love.

In the language of this paper, the process might be described as follows:

State A: A society achieves a degree of justice in a particular historical situation (Phase 1).

State B: The *sophia-agapistic* principle at work in a society illuminates the limitations of State A, and new possibilities of justice emerge (Phase 2).

State C: New ideas and institutions of justice are created (New Historical State).

This communal process of justice-seeking is never-ending within human history because historically bound and limited human institutions can never achieve perfect justice and social harmony (*shalom*) at any given time. In this analysis, justice is the agapistic principle at work in the process of attaining relative justice within history. The ideal of a perfectly just society is thus a transcendental goal towards which a society can move but which cannot be fully achieved under the conditions of any actual society.

Human Nature and Justice

Human nature limits the realization of justice in any specific social context. Human finitude, self-centeredness, brokenness, and the limits of reason, theoretical and practical, create barriers to achieving justice in any concrete human society. Human limitations restrict the human capacity to realize "absolute justice" in society.[368] Nevertheless, the human capacity for self-transcendence in the search for ideals creates the potential for achieving relatively just social structures in a continuing process of improving the social order.

Because of what Niebuhr calls "the indeterminate character of human possibilities" (i.e., the human capacity to transcend nature and natural instincts), human societies are intrinsically dynamic and characterized by change. *Laissez-faire* capitalism, Marxism, liberal democracy, and the various "isms" of the post-Enlightenment era view the trajectory of the evolution of human society as inevitably progressive, a view that this study challenges. To be on the "right side of history" is to apply human reason and love within the constraints of deterministic forces, whether these are visualized as economic or ideal. There is, however, no inevitable "right side of history" on which selfish and self-centered human beings will agree. There is only the slow process of wisely seeking to make changes in love within human history's constraints at any given time.

Law and the Principles of Justice

In discussing law and justice, Niebuhr helpfully distinguishes principles of justice from institutions of justice. Principles of justice are abstract ideals reflected in our theoretical notions of justice and law. Institutions of justice are concrete structures embodied in an existing human community.[369] In any given society, these institutions and the rules they administer only approximate a society's ideals regarding justice.

> Systems and principles of justice are the servants and instruments of the spirit of brotherhood in so far as they extend the sense of obligation towards the other, (a) from an immediately felt obligation, prompted by obvious need, to a continued obligation expressed in fixed principles of mutual support; (b) from a simple relation between a self and one "other" to the complex relations of the self and the "others"; and (c) finally, from the obligations discerned by the individual self, to the wider obligations which the community defines from its more impartial perspective. These communal obligations evolve slowly in custom and law.[370]

Let us take the modern Social Security and Medicare system as an example of this point. In the beginning, an individual or individuals saw the predicament of elderly parents in an industrial society when they could no longer work. Over time, a fixed principle of justice evolved, the notion that society should provide some minimum financial security for the aged This ideal sense of justice became a communal obligation seen as such by most people. In the end, concrete laws that embodied a broader collective sense of responsibility were enacted. The Social Security Administration and Medicare were formed—concrete institutions that embodied the social ideal. Over time, these institutions have evolved further, bringing drug prescriptions and other items within the ambit of the initial program intuited by society. In all this, the ideal of justice gradually unfolded in American society.

Hope for Consensus

Beginning with a sense of mutual obligation (a form of social love), intuitions of society are gradually translated into ideals of justice and then into laws and institutions embodying the initial intuition. This social process is communal and supports the continuing stability of society. In one particularly illuminating passage, Niebuhr states:

> The definitions of justice arrived at in a given community are the product of a social mind. Various perspectives upon common problems, have been merged and have achieved a result, different from that at which any individual, class or group in the community would have arrived. The fact that various conceptions of a just solution of a common problem can be fully synthesized into a common solution, disproves the idea that the approach of each individual or group is consistently

egoistic. If it were, society would be an anarchy of rival interests until power from above subdued the anarchy.[371]

Niebuhr sets out a democratic ideal amid the struggles for a just society in which people are involved, at least in the West. The "social mind" differs from the individual minds that make it up and cannot be reduced to something more fundamental. A society's social mind evolves as debate, disagreement, dialogue, and further study merge to improve a concrete set of social problems and solutions that become "common" over time. The fact that Western democracies have achieved the degree of justice they have achieved is a testimony to the human potential for change and social progress. Niebuhr includes a final warning: Social anarchy and tyranny can result if a society degenerates into egoistic self-seeking of individuals and groups. Western democracies at the time of Niebuhr had shown themselves capable of the reasoned practical adjustments required in a functional democracy. One can only hope the same remains true in our day and time.

Beyond Ideology

The modern world is bedeviled by ideological division and conflict. Interestingly, the word "ideology" was unknown before the French Revolution. A French Enlightenment figure, Antoine Destutt de Tracy, coined the term to indicate a rational system of ideas (philosophically defendable ideas) compared to irrational impulses and the like. Napoleon Bonaparte used the word to refer to his enemies, whom he accused of being revolutionary ideologues. Beginning with Marx, the term began to be used as a pejorative term associated with retrograde ideas and the resulting "false consciousness" of the bourgeoisie. In modern thought, it has come to refer to excessive partisanship that is both irrational and unhelpful.[372] It is in the last sense that I use the term.

The suggested approach embodies no specific political program but encourages wise, loving, *sophio-agapic* action to solve problems. It is ideological only because it provides a set of ideas to guide understanding and action concerning political and social issues. To the extent that our often-irrational politics is based on a pre-existing commitment to beliefs held to be certain and unassailable, a pragmaticist, *sophio-agapic* approach provides a way of approaching social issues and political decision-making that avoids errors in political judgment that can be prevented by analysis, research, dialogue, and compromise. It can also provide a non-ideological path to rebuilding community and shared values in a morally shattered society.

Contemporary political thought can profit from looking at the meaning of both "conversation" and "dialogue." These terms illuminate the difference between the idea of truth as the result of critical analysis and a relational model of truth. The word "conversation" comes from the Latin root "con" or "with" in English and "vertere," which means "turn" or "bend." Interestingly, like the Hebrew word for knowledge, this particular word was used in the 1500s as a synonym for sexual intercourse and also had a connotation of a household, a manner of conduct and behavior, or a way of life in a home.

In other words, a conversation is an intimate, profoundly human relational activity. A conversation is implicitly communal and intended to create communion. It involves a relationship in which two or more individuals share their thoughts and lives in such a way that a cognitive, emotional, physical, and spiritual understanding emerges and a deepened sense of community is created. Hopefully, their ideas, thoughts, and commitments will be "bent" toward each other in the conversation, with the potential to overcome the conflict and fragmentation of our culture.

As a part of a healthy society-wide dialogue and conversation, community can be rebuilt, shared values discovered and affirmed, and a new sense of the importance of our society's search for a just social and political system can be found. Moreover, if a sense of national conversation and dialogue exists among the various groups active in our political system, then freedom, including freedom of speech, can be maintained in a setting of mutual respect and understanding.

Our political system is subject to rampant and increasing irrationality, intolerance, emotional and social manipulation, and a host of evils that can and should be alleviated by a pragmaticist approach to decision-making. A dysfunctional degree of conflict and fragmentation is present in our society. Politicians on all sides use this fragmentation. For example, identity politics is founded on the assumption that fragmented social groups can be motivated by fear, envy, disagreement, and hatred to vote for certain politicians and support specific policies. Such politics prevents consensus and agreement, trapping our political institutions in a dysfunctional, perpetual conflict.

In politics, there is rarely certainty or complete consensus. A degree of conflict will always be present. One function of leadership is to mitigate the weaknesses of a democratic system by wisely considering and discussing policy matters with a willingness to make slow, incremental, and rational changes for the public good. Irrational conflict, public anger, demonstrations, and similar programs cannot heal the significant challenges we face as a society. The most remarkable single change we could make in American politics is to embrace such a pragmaticist approach to policymaking at all levels of government.

In summary, our society must embrace a different way of looking at political reality, one that takes account of the most profound insights of modern science, philosophy, and theories of human relations. Most importantly, there must be a recovery of a sense that we are involved in a mutual, communal enterprise of creating a just society that works for the benefit of all its members so that they can flourish and the society itself endure over time. This is the great challenge of the present.

CHAPTER 12

CONCLUDING REMARKS ON SOPHIO-AGAPISM

The modern paradigm for visualizing the world and human society envisioned the universe as made up of matter and society as made up of isolated individuals, both of which were bound together by forces. In the realm of industry, this meant technology. In the political sphere, this meant human ingenuity was put into the service of gaining political and economic power. In the thoughts of Hobbes, Rousseau, Marx, and others, there was no inherent limit to the sovereign's power. In the hands of Nietzsche, this became a recipe for disaster because all that mattered was raw power and the desire to dominate (Will to Power).

American and other political institutions have been powerfully impacted by the Newtonian worldview, a Hobbesian view of politics focused on power and the theoretically unlimited power of the state. Just as under the influence of a mechanical view of the universe, modern thinkers were predisposed to perceive the world as consisting of small units of matter held together or influenced by forces; in politics, this worldview predisposed policymakers to either extreme individualism or Marxist-influenced communalism, viewing the core governmental forces as power influenced solely by economic factors, all explicable through scientific analysis. Thus, the 20th century's most influential political and economic theories: capitalism and Marxism.

In recent years, a materialistic model of the world has been superseded by a model that assumes deep interconnectedness, relationality, freedom, and inner sensitivity. By the middle of the 20th century, at least physicists understood that the Newtonian model of the universe was limited and fundamentally incorrect. Today, scientists believe that the world, at its most fundamental level, is composed of disturbances in a wave field, with the result that every aspect of reality is deeply connected with every other aspect. Some scientists even believe that the world is fundamentally composed of information. Whichever view turns out to be correct, the fact remains that matter and forces are not fundamental. In theology, a robust analysis has emerged, suggesting that the world is profoundly interconnected and relationships are more essential than matter or energy. This basic view of reality cannot help but impact our view of human beings and society.

The insights of theoretical physics and other academic disciplines into the fundamentally relational nature of reality and the limits of a merely reductive scientific enterprise have slowly been transforming society. A newer "organic model" that sees the universe not as a machine but as an organism or a process is gradually emerging and influencing public life. As the implications of this new worldview are better understood by citizens and politicians alike, political life and the contours of our politics and political institutions are bound to change, hopefully rationally and peacefully.

The modern world is dying, and something new is emerging. What we call "postmodernism" is only the beginning of the change and might be better called "Hyper-Modernism" or "End-stage Modernism." The descent of modern thought into "hermeneutics of suspicion," "deconstructionism," and various forms of nihilism is fundamentally critical reasoning taken to an absurd end. The inevitable result will be that reason, spiritual values, moral imperatives, and the like will re-emerge as essential factors in a wise polity. The vision of the purely secular, materially driven, and scientifically managed state will wither away until it finds its proper place in a more comprehensive human polity.

Hopefully, a newer vision of political reality will emerge in its place—a constructive form of postmodernism. "Sophio-agapism" describes the philosophical proposal defended in these essays. Just as the world comprises an intricately intertwined web of reality, governments will recognize that human politics must begin with smaller units, like the family, and move organically into more comprehensive organizational units with essential but limited powers. The vision of the all-powerful nation-state that controls a territory through legal, administrative, and bureaucratic power will be proved inadequate and false. Whether this happens due to a great crisis and collapse of the current nation-state, world-state visions, or organically, through the decisions of wise leaders, depends on the decisions we all make. One thing is for sure: a wise and genuinely postmodern political order will value dialogue as much as debate and decision.

In this book, I've tried to discuss historical pragmatism and the development of a particular approach to political life and thought. In the process, I've been attempting to sketch out the contours of a *sophio-agapic* approach to political theory and social life. Briefly, the essential elements are as follows:

A Politics of Wisdom

Sophio-agapism embraces the notion that political philosophy and political action can be reasonable (the *sophio* move) and serve the common good by understanding a society's political life, the options for change available, the historical trajectory of that society, and other factors while experimenting wisely among various policy options. This is a turn away from a view of politics as primarily a matter of Will and a return to an older view that politics is mainly a matter of practical wisdom (*phronesis*). As a form of practical wisdom, *sophio-agapism* embraces the notion that wisdom comes from experience embedded in the human species' experience through the ages and from the advances of modern science and technology.

A Politics of Love

Sophio-agapism embraces a communitarian viewpoint that sees all participants in society as part of a common community bound together not just by power but fundamentally by a willingness to sacrifice for the community, whose interests must be considered in addition to the selfish interests of individuals that make up that community (the *agapic* move). In particular, nurturing families, neighborhoods, mediating institutions, and voluntary societies creates social bonds that give stability and restraint to the state's power and can accomplish goals that state power alone cannot achieve.

Political love is fundamentally a recognition that society is a joint endeavor requiring the cooperative efforts of all participants to achieve human flourishing. It is a social bond that transcends individual grasping and the search for personal peace, pleasure, and affluence. It requires confidence that the existing social order, as flawed as it may be, provides positive benefits to all members of society and should be protected while at the same time advancing in the realization of justice and human flourishing.

A Focus on Social Harmony

Sophio-agapism embraces the ideal of social harmony as the goal of political life. The modern, revolutionary focus on equality dooms political life to unending conflict among persons and classes. Political life aims to achieve progressively more significant degrees of harmony among the various participants in any society. A return to viewing social harmony as the aim of wise and just decision-making is implied by the interconnectedness of the world and the various societies humans inhabit. Equality is undoubtedly an essential component of justice, as are opportunities to achieve, the acquisition of property that one can call one's own, respect for all citizens, and a host of other components of a functional society.

The Reality of Universal Values

Sophio-agapism embraces the recovery in the public life of the notion that critical universal values, like justice, are not merely matters of the will of a majority or the choice of a single individual or ruling class but noetic realities. These noetic realities, what I have called Transcendental Ideals, can be studied, internalized, and applied to practical problems and extended in the dynamic process of the political life of a society. This requires the disciplined, fair, and impartial search for such values and their application in concrete circumstances by all the relevant players in society: private citizens, public officials, policy advisors, etc.

The kind of moral confusion we see in the West is evidence of the need to recover a sense of the reality of ideals, such as justice, and the importance of their continuing enfolding as part of a tradition of moral, political, legal, and philosophical inquiry by communities devoted to the unbiased search for justice. These Transcendental Ideals exist as ever-evolving noetic realities to be progressively revealed by a community dedicated to uncovering their nature and application.

A Wholistic Reason

Sophio-agapism embraces a holistic view of political wisdom and a recovery of classical and modern thought in guiding public policy. This means superseding the dissolving effects of critical reason as the primary source of political thinking, and combining it with a form of reasoning that involves the cherishing of people and institutions within the political life of a society. In modern political theory, will and power have become dominant factors in public life. Power alone and the Will to Power do not lead to human or social flourishing unless they rest on a substructure of caring for others and institutions.

Politics is not primarily science; it is a skill. The skills involved include the ability to choose among alternatives, forge a consensus, make difficult decisions in solving public problems, maintain the maximum degree of social harmony, and other skills that are not primarily cognitive. In addition, they are not encouraged by the dissolving effects of critical reason. Just as there is a skill beyond technical proficiency in creating a symphony, social harmony is not entirely a matter of technical ability or scientific determination. Polls, for example, can only get you so far in the search for justice.

Fallibility and Limits

Sophio-agapism embraces developing a sense of limits in public life. The historical trajectory of the political development of any society places limits on wise and caring change. The history of a society and its trajectory also opens avenues for developing the tradition of which that society is a part. The Enlightenment brought about a period of revolutionary thinking, exemplified by the French Revolution and the Marxist revolutions of the 20th century. The results are not encouraging in the search for either social harmony or human flourishing. Rather than being revolutionary, *sophio-agapism* is evolutionary. It believes that the gradual evolution of human society guided by human wisdom and love can create a better future over time. Connected with this insight is a resistance to millenarianism of the left or right, Marxist or capitalist. Humans cannot achieve a perfect society, but humans can improve on the society in which they live.

Sophio-agapism encourages a sense of limits and a recognition of human fallibility in political life. Not all problems can be solved, and very few can be solved entirely or quickly. The attempt to make massive social changes involves the risk of enormous societal damage. This demonstrates the need for an incremental approach whenever possible. Not all problems are susceptible to incrementalism, but a great many are. There is the chance of a significant cost and waste if substantial changes are made. It is hard to reverse the damage done by a massive political change. It is much easier to change course when the original action is incremental. This kind of incrementalism is not enhanced by the emotion-driven politics that currently characterizes Western democracies.

Investigation and Dialogue

Embracing an abductive (scientific) and dialectical model of political reasoning and behavior *sophio-agapism* attempts to find the best rational solution for all involved, seeking the harmony of society as a whole, and resisting political life's descent into a form of warfare by other means. Reasonable dialogue is essential for societies to recover a sense of mutual respect for differing opinions and a standard search for the best solution among available options.

Many social problems arise from illogical, emotionally driven, poorly conceived policies. From the way many governmental programs are structured to the outcomes permitted to the corruption and waste involved, these programs represent both a failure of character in leadership and a failure of thoughtful reaction to societal needs. The propensity to avoid complex problems until they are dangerously large and politically unavoidable is a risk in any democratic society. When the propensity becomes endemic in all areas of conflict, it is dangerous to political institutions.

Dialogue is important because it allows political actors to accomplish two essential goals in maintaining social harmony: the investigation of alternative policies and proposals and the maintenance of the maximum degree of unity during periods of decision. Contemporary politics is exceptionally reliant on divisive, simplistic, and polarizing rhetoric. Focus on dialogue and reason would allow political actors to maintain social harmony while investigating the best policy to adopt. It would also allow the political climate to become more harmonious.

The Importance of Transcendental Ideals

The argument for the reality of universal ideals, such as justice, leads to the importance of transcendental ideals as guides to action. The ideal of the Beloved or Universal Community, used here to denote a perfectly just and harmonious polity, is a powerful inducement to action designed to increase the level of justice and social harmony in a given society. This ideal has existence as a potential to be realized over time in important ways. However, such ideals can be harmful when combined with an unbridled attempt to create such a society at whatever cost. The experiences of the 20th century speak eloquently to this danger. Transcendental ideals are by their nature only partially and imperfectly attainable in any given society at any given point in time.

Western society has been powerfully impacted by the ideal of the perfect polity, the City of God, where injustice has been permanently defeated and justice reigns. The moral force of such an ideal must be tempered by the realization that ideals are by their nature only imperfectly achievable within the boundaries of human history and striving. Human self-centeredness, and the restlessness of human striving, render an "end of history" unachievable within history.

Overcoming the Focus on Power

Liberals and conservatives agree that there are fundamental problems in society and the human community. Interestingly, it may be a shared fundamental worldview that is at the root of the decay of public institutions. The idea that the world is fundamentally material and that politics is a matter of power and power alone is a profound source of the irrational behavior of the right and the left. If the world is fundamentally rational and relational, then all solutions that flow from a purely materialistic view of society—a view shared by extreme capitalist and socialistic theories of government, lie at the root of many of the problems we face and certainly at the root of an increasingly dysfunctional style of politics. The urgency for a new, more relational rational government ontology is apparent, emphasizing the potential importance of further developing the philosophical perspective outlined in this book. The argument made is misconceived if one considers that the intention is to deny the reality of power or its importance in political life. The point is the political power rests on something more fundamental—human and social relationships.

In order for a society to be healthy, its political system must rest upon something more fundamental than power, even the power of law. It must rest on shared values and a shared vision of political life. It is in the development of such shared values and vision that our leaders have failed dramatically. It is important to address this failure and rebuild the social, economic, and political bonds that are fundamental to healthy human society. This is the fundamental challenge for the future of free societies.

BIBLIOGRAPHY

Aquinas, *On Law, Morality and Politics* Translated by Richard J. Regan, Edited by William P. Baumgarth and Richard J. Regan, Second Edition (Indianapolis, IN: Hackett Publishing, 2002),

Aristotle, *Ethics* tr. J.K.A. Thompson (New York, NY: Penguin Books, 1955)

Augustine, *City of God* tr. Henry Bettenson (London, ENG: Penguin Books, 1984)

_____, "On Christian Doctrine" in *A Select Library of Nicene and Post-Nicene Fathers of the Christian Church.* Edited by Philip Schaff and Henry Wace. 28 First Series, Volume 2. 1886–1889. (Peabody MA: Hendrickson Publishers

Bitter, Eduardo C., "Semiotics of Law, Science of Law and Legal Meaning: analysis of the status of legal dogmatics" In Signata https://doi.org/10.4000/signata.4129 (downloaded April 22, 2023)

Bohm, David, *Wholeness and the Implicate Order* (London ENG: Routledge, 1980).

_____, *On Dialogue* (New York, NY: Routledge, 1996),

_____, *The Essential David Bohm* Lee Nichol ed. (New York, NY: Routledge, 2003)

_____, "Meaning and Information" in *The Search for Meaning: The New Spirit in Science and Philosophy* (London, ENG: Crucible Press, 1989)

Bohm, David and F. David Peat, *Science, Order & Creativity,* (New York, NY: Bantam Books, 1987)

Cicero, *On the Commonwealth* tr. George Holland Sabine & Stanley Barney Library of the Liberal Arts, ed. (Indianapolis, IN: Bobbs-Merrill Company, Inc., 1929)

Darwin, Charles, *Decent of Man* Ed, Mortimer J. Adler (New York, NY: Encyclopedia Britannica, Inc., 1952).

Descartes, Rene, "On Method" in The Great Books (Chicago, Ill: University of Chicago, 1952)

Declaration of Independence (US 1776).

Dewey, John, *Individualism Old and New* (New York, NY: Capricorn Books, 1930).

_____, *Reconstruction of Philosophy* (New York, NY: Henry Holt & Company 1920), 187 https://www.gutenberg.org/files/40089/40089-h/40089-h.htm#CHAPTER_VIII (downloaded April 29, 2022)

_____, Democracy and Education, transcribed by David Reed and David Widger (The Project Gutenberg EBook of Democracy and Education, by John Dewey https://www.gutenberg.org/files/852/852-h/852-h.htm (downloaded April 29, 2022), hereinafter, Democracy and Education.

_____, Logic: The Theory of Inquiry (New York, NY: Henry Holt and Company, 1938).

John C. Polkinghorne, Science and Creation: The Search for Understanding (Philadelphia, PA: Templeton Foundation Press, 2006), 30.

van Dongen, Jeroen. "On the Role of the Michelson-Morely Experiment: Einstein in Chicago" athttps://arxiv.org/pdf/0908.1545.pdf (downloaded December 5, 2022)

Dombrowski, Daniel A., *A Platonic Philosophy of Religion: A Process Perspective* (Albany, NY: State University of New York Press, 2005)

Guardino, Nicholas, *Charles Pierce, and the Open Court, 1890-1893: Promoting an American Metaphysician* at https://scrcexhibits.omeka.net/exhibits/show/charles-s-peirce-open-court/-evolutionary-love- (downloaded April 11, 2022)

Gelpi, Donald L., *The Gracing of Human Experience: Rethinking the Relationship between Nature and Grace* (Collegeville, MN: Liturgical Press, 2001)

Habermas Jurgen, *Knowledge and Human Interests* tr. Jeremy J. Shapiro (Boston, MA: Beacon Press, 1968, 1971).

Heisenberg, Werner, *Physics and Philosophy: The Revolution in Modern Science (New York, NY: Harper Perennial, 1962)*

Hungerford. Yael Levin, *Charles S. Peirce's Conservative Progressivism A Dissertation Submitted to the Department of Political Science in Partial Fulfillment of the Requirements for a Degree of Doctor of Philosophy* (Boston MA: Boston College, June 2016)

James, William, "Letter to Mrs. Henry (Elizabeth) Whitman, June 7, 1899.— *The Letters of William James,* ed. Henry James, vol. 2, p. 90 (1926).

_____, "Damn Great Empires! William James and the Politics of Pragmatism" reviewed in Contemporary Political Theory (2018) 17, S6–S8. https://doi.org/10.1057/s41296-017- 0103-5; published online 7 March 2017 (downloaded April 21, 2022)

Kittle, Gerhard & Gerhard Friedrich, eds. *Theological Dictionary of the New Testament* d. Geoffrey W. Bromley (Grand Rapids, MI: Eerdmans, 1985)

Kuhn, Thomas S., *The Structure of Scientific Revolutions* 2nd enlarged ed. (Chicago, IL: University of Chicago Press, 1963, 1970)

Lewis, C. S., *The Abolition of Man (*New York: Collier Books, a division of Mcmillan, 1955)

Lloyd, Harold Anthony, "How to do things with Signs: Semiotics in Legal Theory, Practice, and Education" https://philarchive.org/archive/ LLOHTD (downloaded April 22, 2023)

Loder, James E., *The Transforming Moment* 2nd ed. (Colorado Springs, CO: Helmers & Howard, 1989).

London, Scott, "Organic Democracy: Political Philosophy of John Dewey https://scott.london/reports/dewey.html (downloaded April 29, 2022)

Konvitz, Milton R. & Gail Kennedy, eds, *The American Pragmatists* (Cleveland, OH & New York, NY: Meridia Books, 1970)

Krznaric, Roman, "The Ancient Greeks' 6 Words for Love (And Why Knowing Them Can Change Your Life)" in Solutions

Journalism (December 28, 2013), at www.yesmagazine.org/health-happiness/2013/12/28/the-ancient-greeks-6-words-for-love-and-why-knowing-them-can-change-your-life/ (downloaded June 19, 2020).

Loasch, Matt, "Conceptualizing Governance Decision Making: A Theoretical Model of Mental processes Derived through Abduction" Old Dominion University Digital Commons (Summer 2019), Doctor of Philosophy (PhD), dissertation, School of Public Service, Old Dominion University, DOI:10.25777/xvpq-e948 https://digitalcommons.odu.edu/publicservice_etds/41 (downloaded, March 28, 2022)

Venneri, Eleonora "Social Planning and Evaluation: The Abductive Logic" International Journal of Applied Sociology, 4(5):115-119 DOI: 10.5923/j.ijas.20140405.01 (2014)

MacIntyre, Alisdair, *After Virtue* 2nd ed. (Notre Dame, IN: University of Notre Dame Press, 1984)

Mead, George Herbert, *On Social Psychology* rev. Ed. (Chicago, Ill: University of Chicago Press, 1964).

Milbank, John, *Theology and Social Theory: Beyond Secular Reason* 2nd ed. (Oxford, UK.: Blackwell, 2006).

Morgan George A., *What Nietzsche Means* (New York, NY: Harper & Row1941)

Morris, Randall C., *Process Philosophy and Political Ideology: The Social and Political Thought of Alfred North Whitehead and Charles Hartshorne* (New York, NY: The State University of New York, 1991),

Newbigin, Lesslie *Truth to Tell: The Gospel as Public Truth* (Grand Rapids, MI: William B. Eerdmans, 1991)

Nichol, Lee, ed, *The Essential David Bohm* (London, ENG: Routledge, 2003)

Niebuhr, Reinhold, *The Nature and Destiny of Man* Vol. 2 (Louisville, KY: Westminster John Knox Press, 1986),

Nietzsche, Friedrich, *Beyond Good and Evil* ed. Walter Kaufmann (New York, NY: Random House, 1966).

_____, *Beyond Good and Evil* tr. Marion Faber (London, Eng., Oxford World Classics, 2008).

_____, *Twilight of the Idols and Anti-Christ* tr. R. J. Hollingdale (New York, NY: Penguin Books, 1968)

Charles S Peirce, *The Essential Writings* Edward C. Moore, ed. (New York, NY: Harper & Row, 1972)

_____, *Collected Papers of Charles Sanders Peirce* Vols. 1 and 2. Charles Hartshorne and Paul Weiss eds. (Cambridge, MA: Harvard University Press, 1965)

_____, *Letter to Lady Welby*, found at Ben Chappel, "Folklore Semiotic: Charles Peirce and the Experience of Signs Folklore" Forum 30: 112 (1999) https://core.ac.uk/download/pdf/213810942.pdf (downloaded November 25, 2022)

_____, Unpublished manuscripts. Copies from Peirce Edition Project of Indiana University—Purdue University, Indianapolis.MS 298:6 found at Oliver Labs, "Dialogue in Peirce, Lotman, and Bakhin: A Comparative Study" www.researchgate.net/publication/312509433_Dialogue_in_Peirce_Lotman_and_Bakhtin_A_comparative_study (downloaded December 8, 2022)

Plato, *Republic* tr. G. M.A. Grube rev. C.D.C Reeve (Indianapolis, IN: Hackett Publishing Company, 1992)

Plato, *The Sophist* tr. Benjamin Jowett *(Oxford, ENG: Oxford University Press, 2018)*

Polanyi, Michael *Science Faith, and Society: A Searching Examination of the Meaning and Nature of Scientific Inquiry* (Chicago, Ill: University of Chicago Press, 1946)

_____, *The Tacit Dimension* (Gloucester, MA: Peter Smith, 1983)

_____, *Personal Knowledge: Towards a Post-Critical* Philosophy (Chicago, Ill: University of Chicago Press, 1961)

_____, *The Logic of Liberty* (Indianapolis, IN, Liberty Fund, 1998)

Pole, David, *The Later Philosophy of Wittgenstein* (London, ENG: University of London Press (Athlone, 1958)

Polkinghorne, John, *The Way the World Is: The Christian Perspective of a Scientist* (Louisville, KY: Westminster/John Knox Press, 1983)

_____, *Exploring Reality: The Intertwining of Science and Religion* (London, ENG: SPCK, 2005)

_____, *One World: The Interaction of Science and Theology* (Philadelphia, PA: Templeton Foundation, 2007)

_____, *Quantum Physics and Theology: An Unexpected Kinship* (New Haven, CT: Yale University Press, 2007)

Polkinghorne, John, ed, *The Trinity and an Entangled World: Relationality in Physical Science and Theology* (Grand Rapids, MI: William B. Eerdmans, 2010)

Popper, Karl, *The Open Society and its Enemies* (Princeton NJ: Princeton University Press, 1994)

Popper, Karl, Philosophy of Science: Methodology in the Social Sciences" in the Internet Encyclopedia of Philosophy, at https://iep.utm.edu/pop-sci/#H4 (downloaded April 21, 2023)

_____, "Reason or Revolution" in *The Positivist Dispute in German Sociology: Adorno, Albert, Dhrendorf, Habermas, Pilot and Popper* tr. Glyn Adey I David Frisby (London, ENG: Heiemann 1969, 1977)

Pratt, David "David Bohm and the Implicate Order" at https://www.theosophy-nw.org/theosnw/science/prat-boh.htm (downloaded April 12, 2023).

Puzo, Mario, *The Godfather* (New York, NY: Penguin, 1969)

Royce, Josiah, *Loyalty* (Long Island, NY: Sophia/Omni Press, 1908 [2017])

_____, *Metaphysics* Richard Hocking & Frank Oppenheim eds (New York, NY: State University of New York Press,1998).

_____, *The Problem of Christianity* (Washington, D.C.: Catholic University Press, 2001) Rozema, David, "Lewis's Rejection of Nihilism: The *Tao* and the Problem of Moral Knowledge" in *Pursuit of Truth: A Journal of Christian Scholarship* http://www.cslewis.org/journal/lewiss-rejection-of-nihilism-the-tao-and-the-problem-of-moral-knowledge/ (September 28, 2007, downloaded June 4, 2020).

Russell, Bertrand, *A History of Western Philosophy* (New York, NY: Simon and Schuster, 1945)

Sapp, Henry F., "Whitehead, James, and the Ontology of Quantum Theory" 5(1) Mind and Matter (2007) downloaded at https://www-physics.lbl.gov/~stapp/WJQO.pdf (June 16, 2020)

Scott, Drucilla *Everyman Revisited: The Common Sense of Michael Polanyi* (Sussex, ENG: The Book Guild Limited, 1985)

Scruggs, G. Christopher, *Centered Living/Centered Leading: The Tao Te Ching Adapted for Christ-Followers* Rev. Ed. (Permisio Por Favor/ BookSurge, 2016)

_____, *Path of Life: The Way of Wisdom for Christ-Followers* (Eugene, OR: Wipf & Stock, 2014)

Settle, Jaime E., Christopher T. Dawes, James H. Fowler, "The Heritability of Partisan Attachment" 62 Political Research Quarterly 601 (September 2009) at https://web.archive.org/web/20100616133630/ http://jhfowler.ucsd.edu/heritability_of_partisan_attachment.pdf (downloaded April 10, 2023).

Shaviro, Steven, "Deleuze's Encounter With Whitehead" www.shaviro. com/Othertexts/DeleuzeWhitehead.pdf (Downloaded July 18, 2022)

Shottliff Mattingly, Susan, "Whitehead's Theory of Eternal Objects" A Dissertation Presented to the Faculty of the Graduate School of The University of Texas at Austin in Partial Fulfillment of the Requirements for the Degree Doctor of Philosophy.

Torrance, Thomas, *Transformation & Convergence in the Frame of Knowledge* (Grand Rapids, MI: William B. Eerdmans, 1984).

United States Constitution (US 1789)

Wheeler, Archibald, "Information, Physics, Quantum: The Search for Links" in Proc. 3rd Int. Symp. Foundations of Quantum Mechanics, (Tokyo, Japan: 1989)

Alfred North Whitehead, *Science and the Modern World* (New York, NY: Free Press, 1925, 1967)

_____, *Process and Reality* (New York, NY: Free Press, 1929)

_____, *Adventure of Ideas* (New York, NY: Free Press, 1933)

_____, *Modes of Thought* (New York, NY: Free Press, 1938, 1968)

_____, *Religion in the Making* (New York, NY: The McMillian Company, 1936)

Zizioulas, John D., *Communion and Otherness* Paul Martin, ed. (New York, NY: T&T Clark, 2006)

ENDNOTES

1   Gerhard Kittle & Gerhard Friedrich, eds. *Theological Dictionary of the New Testament* d. Geoffrey W. Bromley (Grand Rapids, MI: Eerdmans, 1985), 1262.

2   Id, 1056.

3   Plato, *Republic* tr. G. M.A. Grube rev. C.D.C Reeve (Indianapolis, IN: Hackett Publishing Company, 1992), 176ff. This translation is hereinafter referred to as "Republic."

4   Aristotle, *Ethics* tr. J.A.K. Thompson (Baltimore, MD: Penguin, 1955).

5   Charles S. Peirce, *Fixation of Belief*, in *The Essential Peirce: Selected Philosophical Writings* (1867–1893), Volume 1: Nathan Houser & Christian J. W. Klossel, eds. (Bloomington, ID: Indiana University Press, 1992), 132. Most citations to Peirce's work are from this edition, which will be cited as "Essay" TEP Vol., Page"

6   See Yael Levin Hungerford, *Charles S. Peirce's Conservative Progressivism*, PhD dissertation (Boston MA: Boston College, June 2016) found at https://core.ac.uk/download/pdf/151480189.pdf (downloaded April 27, 2023). Ms. Hungerford's excellent and important dissertation goes along different lines than the current paper.

7   Id.

8   Peirce was not particularly happy with how various philosophers (especially John Dewey and William James in America and F. C. S. Schiller in Germany) developed the principle along nominalist

lines. For Peirce, the reality of theoretical constructions must be preserved to ensure the progress of knowledge. As a result, he coined the term "pragmaticist" to describe his own theory.

9   See, *Republic*, previously cited. The forms exist as unchanging ultimate reality, as opposed to the flux of opinion that characterizes human history.

10   Id, 581c. Plato was familiar with Greek societies and those of the surrounding area. In these societies, there were six fundamental social groups: Rulers *(charches)*, Soldiers *(polymystes)*, Farmers *(perioikoi)*, Craftsmen *(tekton)*, Laborers *(helots)*, and Slaves *(douloi)*.

The first two groups are related, for the rulers generally came from an aristocracy *(aristoi)* with military training and ability. In the *Republic*, Plato reduces the various groups to three: rulers, warriors, and everyone else.

11   In this Aristotle adopts a view not far from the process philosopher, Alfred North Whitehead. In both, universals "exist" only as incarnated in actually existing entities.

12   Aristotle, *Ethics*, previously cited, 144–145.

13   St. Augustine, *City of God*, tr. Henry Bettenson (London, England: Penguin Books, 1984), at 72. See also Cicero, *On the Commonwealth*, tr. George Holland Sabine & Stanley Barney Library of the Liberal Arts, ed. (Indianapolis, IN: Bobbs-Merrill Company, Inc., 1929), 183. Augustine studied and appreciated Cicero.

14   *City of God*, previously cited, 139

15   "Shalom" is derived from the root word "shalam," which means "to be safe in mind, body, or estate." It refers to a condition of completeness, fullness, or wholeness. Although it can describe the absence of war or conflict, a majority of biblical references refer to an inner completeness and tranquility. It is this notion of shalom that unifies peace and justice. See https://firm.org.il/learn/the-meaning-of-shalom/ (downloaded October 9, 2020.

16   Thomas Aquinas, *On Law, Morality and Politics*, tr. Richard J. Regan, ed. William P. Baumgarth and Richard J. Regan, 2nd ed. (Indianapolis, IN: Hackett Publishing, 2002), 198. The quote is from the *Summa Theologica*: Q 47 Tenth Article.

17   Bertrand Russell, *A History of Western Philosophy* (New York, NY: Simon and Schuster, 1945), 472.

18   Hobbes, for example, was an absolute nominalist. Id, at 549. Locke was also nominalist, believing that general terms are merely names we give to groups of particulars. Id, at 611. Finally, Hume believes that all general ideas are nothing but particular ideas annexed to a term. Thus, there is nothing called "justice." There are only specific actions or decisions to which the general term is applied. This position leads directly to the emotivism and subjectivism of modern ethical and moral theory.

19   *Republic*, previously cited, 339.

20   Hobbes' life intersects with that of Isaac Newton (1642–1727) whose work laid the intellectual and mathematical foundations for modern science and which laid out a theory that undergirded the materialistic worldview of people like Hobbes. It is important to note that Newton was deeply religious and spent much of his life studying religious phenomenon. Newton was also a student of optics, as was Hobbes.

21   Thomas Hobbes, *Leviathan: Or the Matter, Form, and Power of a Commonwealth, Ecclesiastical and Civil*, ed. Michael Oakeshott (New York, NY: Collier-McMillan, 1971), 159. All references herein are to this edition of *Leviathan*. I have taken the liberty of rendering Hobbes' language into more contemporary English, since we do not use terms like "signifieth" in normal conversation.

22   Id.

23   Id.

24   Id, 160. This is not a theological essay, but it is fascinating how Hobbes and other early mechanists appear to be influence by an extreme predestinarian outlook on the world. One might say that a dark result of extreme Calvinism is the loss of freedom for both the individual and for creation as a whole.

25   Id.

26   Id, 161.

27   Id, 162. Notice again that sovereigns are free because they lack restraint. Thus, the kind of checks and balances that prevent democracy from degenerating into mob-rule, aristocracy from

degenerating into oligarchy, and kingship into tyranny is entirely lacking any foundation.

28   Id.

29   Oliver Wendell Holmes, for example, held that the law could and should only embody the will of the majority, which was entitled to enact such laws as they felt useful. This is not to say that he had no place for morality and abstract notions of justice, but his emphasis on power overshadowed this other side of his thought. Oliver Wendell Holmes, Jr., "The Path of the Law" 10 *Harvard Law Review* 457 (1897), reprinted in Milton R. Konvitz, ed, *The American Pragmatists* (Cleveland, OH, Meridian Books, 1970), 146, hereinafter, "American Pragmatists."

30   In the following, I have relied on George A. Morgan, *What Nietzsche Means* (New York, NY: Harper & Row1941) which is a sympathetic look at his thought and Friedrich Nietzsche, *Beyond Good and Evil* ed. Walter Kaufmann (New York, NY: Random House, 1966) and *Twilight of the Idols and Anti-Christ* tr. R. J. Hollingdale (New York, NY: Penguin Books, 1968). Professor Morgan would not agree with my conclusions.

31   Friedrich Nietzsche, *Beyond Good and Evil* tr. Marion Faber (London, Eng., Oxford World Classics, 2008), 153.

32   John Milbank, *Theology and Social Theory: Beyond Secular Reason* 2nd ed. (Oxford, UK.: Blackwell, 2006).

33   Id, xiii, and chapter 10, "Ontological Violence or the Postmodern Problematic" pp. 278-326

34   Alisdair MacIntyre, *After Virtue* 2nd ed. (Notre Dame, IN: University of Notre Dame Press, 1984), 17.

35   Charles S. Peirce, *The Essential Writings* Edward C. Moore, ed. (New York, NY: Harper & Row, 1972), hereinafter ECSP. For Peirce, the real is that which exists independently of our ideas of it, that is independently of our perceptions, theories, or capacities. Id, at 57. These are noetic realities that exist not in material form but in the human mind. Such general ideas are not infinitely manipulable but subject to the rules of logic and thought appropriate to the subject matter. Id, at 60.

36   Thomas F. Torrance, *Transformation & Convergence in the Frame of Knowledge: Explorations in the Interrelations of Scientific and Theological Enterprise* (Grand Rapids, MI: Wm. B. Eerdmans Publishing Co.), 134.

37   Peirce and the Swiss linguist Ferdinand de Saussure are credited with founding modern semiotics. There were several significant differences between their approaches, most importantly in Peirce's tripartite analysis of the relationship between an object, a sign, and an interpretant.

38   Peirce, Charles S., *Letter to Lady Welby*, found at Ben Chappel, "Folklore Semiotic: Charles Peirce and the Experience of Signs Folklore" *Forum* 30: 112 (1999) https://core.ac.uk/download/pdf/213810942.pdf (downloaded November 25, 2022).

39   Ludwig Wittgenstein famously rejected the notion that there could be a private language. For Wittgenstein, to speak a language was fundamentally a social activity, and to attempt a non-social language was a contradiction in terms. David Pole, *The Later Philosophy of Wittgenstein* (London, ENG: University of London Press (Athlone, 1958), 75.

40   Descartes, if you remember, claimed to doubt everything except his own ability to think. "I think, therefore, I am." His inquiry was not unmotivated; however, a factor of which Pearce takes note. His method of doubt was designed to defend the Catholic religion and the consensus of his day.

41   Rene Descartes, "On Method" in *The Great Books* (Chicago, IL: University of Chicago, 1952), 47.

42   Id, 51.

43   Id, 52.

44   Charles S. Peirce, "The Rules of Philosophy" (originally published in 1868) in *The American Pragmatists* (Cleveland OH & New York, NY: Meridian Books, 1970), 80-81. The "maxim" to which Peirce refers is "Cognito Ergo Sum," or "I think therefore I am."

45   Jurgen Habermas points out that Peirce sees doubt and knowledge as components of a discursive process by which human knowledge is extended through time. There is no "absolute or unshakeable

foundation for the kind of understanding humans achieve, there is a process of communal understanding at work throughout time. Jurgen Habermas, "Peirce's Logic of Inquiry" in *Knowledge and Human Interests* tr. Jeremy J. Shapiro (Boston, MA: Beacon Press, 1968, 1971), 97.

46 Werner Heisenberg, *Physics and Philosophy: The Revolution in Modern Science* (New York, NY: Harper Perennial, 1958)60-66.

47 Letter to Lady Welby, May 20, 1911.

48 C. S. Peirce, "Illustrations on the Logic of Science" in *The Essential Charles S. Peirce*, Edward C. Moore, ed (New York, NY: Harper & Row 1972), at 126. This work is hereinafter referred to as ECSP.

49 Plato, *The Sophist* 247e.

50 This particular notion was suggested to me by, among other persons, Daniel A. Dombrowski, *A Platonic Philosophy of Religion: A Process Perspective* (Albany, NY: State University of New York Press, 2005).

51 Id, at 95 ff.

52 "Review of the Works of George Berkley," *ECSP*, 54-55.

53 Id, 55.

54 Id, 57

55 Id, 57.

56 *Questions Concerning Certain Faculties, ECSP*, 115. The capitalization of Community is Peirce's.

57 Review of the Works of George Berkley" in *ECSP*, at 57.

58 Id, 60.

59 Id.

60 Id, 58.

61 *Fixation of Belief,* in TEP Volume 1, 114.

62 Id 115-119.

63 Id, 117

64 Id.

65 We have seen this regrettable aspect of contemporary campus life most recently in the banning of conservative thinkers from some campuses and in the rise of antisemitism on college campuses.

66 *How to Make our Ideas* Clear in *ECSP,* 132. Although I have quoted this before, it is of such importance that it is mentioned again here.

67   *Questions Concerning Certain Faculties*, in ECSP, 91.

68   See for example, Matt Loasch, "Conceptualizing Governance Decision Making: A Theoretical Model of Mental Processes Derived through Abduction" Old Dominion University Digital Commons (Summer 2019), Doctor of Philosophy (PhD), dissertation, School of Public Service, Old Dominion University, DOI:10.25777/xvpq-e948 https:// digitalcommons.odu.edu/publicservice_etds/41   (downloaded, March 28, 2022) and Eleonora Venneri, "Social Planning and Evaluation: The Abductive Logic" *International Journal of Applied Sociology*, 4(5):115-119 DOI: 10.5923/j.ijas.20140405.01 (2014).

69   Contemporary late-modern society is often characterized by a preference for "revolutionary change." The model of this kind of a revolutionary ideology of change is the French Revolution, where the entire structure of French society was destroyed and then rebuilt on Republican principles. As previously observed, the destruction of the existing order resulted in huge human suffering and ultimately the dictatorship of Napoleon and further suffering. See Karl Popper, *The Open Society and Its Enemies* (Princeton NJ: Princeton University Press, 1994)

70   "Karl Popper: Philosophy of Science: Methodology in the Social Sciences" in *The Internet Encyclopedia of Philosophy*, at https:// iep.utm.edu/pop-sci/#H4 (downloaded April 21, 2023).

71   Many Americans, including influential financial figures admire the "Chinese economic miracle" and might object to this comment. First, prior to the abandonment of communist economic policies, China was an economic disaster. Their form of privatization involved transferring public assets to the hands of government (communist) insiders and their children. The current form of Chinese economic organization is more national socialist than communist. Third, the economic growth of China has been heavily dependent upon United States and other nations moving their manufacturing to take advantage of cheap labor and on a real-estate bubble that has recently caused major losses to their banking system. In my view, the admiration for this kind of economy is misguided. Hitler engineered the same kind of economic marvel in Germany in the 1930's.

72   Karl Popper "Reason or Revolution" in *The Positivist Dispute in German Sociology: Adorno, Albert, Dhrendorf, Habermas, Pilot and Popper*, tr. Glyn Adey I. David Frisby (London, ENG: Heiemann 1969, 1977), 291.

73   Fallibilism sits under any "critical realistic" philosophical position. It is the view that all of our opinions are subject to critique and change but that the theories we develop are, nevertheless, insights into reality.

74   *Review of the Works of George Berkeley*, ECSP, 61.

75   *A Guess at the Riddle*, ECSP, 158-360.

76   Id, at 245. These three terms are derived from Greek terms meaning chance or fortune (τύχη), Greek (ἀνάγκη) necessity, and agape, or love (ηγαπ). Here is how Peirce describes these three modes of evolutionary development: "Three modes of evolution have thus been brought before us: evolution by fortuitous variation, evolution by mechanical necessity, and evolution by creative love. We may term them *tychastic* evolution, or *tychasm*, *anancastic* evolution, or *anancasm*, and *agapastic* evolution, or *agapasm*. The doctrines which represent these as severally of principal importance we may term *tychasticism*, *anancasticism*, and *agapasticism*. On the other hand, the mere propositions that absolute chance, mechanical necessity, and the law of love are severally operative in the cosmos may receive the names of *tychism*, *anancism*, and *agapism*."

77   Werner Heisenberg, *Physics and Philosophy*, 27.

78   Id, 116–117, 121–122. This is not the place to engage in a description of quantum physics, except to make the point that quantum physics is sympathetic to the Aristotelian notion of *potentia*.

79   At the moment of creation, this "first" was followed by a "second" in which a kind of mediated habit begins to be formed due to reaction to the first, this is followed then by a third, involves reflection, reaction, and the beginning of cause and effect which forms a habit, law, convention, or rule of action.

80   See "Evolutionary Love" in Nicholas Guardino, *Charles Pierce, and the Open Court, 1890-1893: Promoting an American Metaphysician* at https://scrcexhibits.omeka.net/exhibits/show/charles-s-peirce-open-court/-evolutionary-love- (downloaded April 11, 2022).

81   Empedocles (492-432 B.C.) was, like Pythagoras, a mixture of a philosopher, scientist, and poet. He was active in a democratic movement against tyranny and an orator of note. He developed the cosmogenic theory that the universe is made up of four classical elements: earth, air, fire, and water. Empedocles also saw the world as in a cosmic cycle of change, growth, and decay. His philosophy is similar to that of Heraclitus but with the difference that instead of strife being the fundamental principle of the universe, the cosmic cycle results from the interplay of Strife and Love or what we might see as a combination of blind material forces and attractive, relational and noetic forces.

82   See, John Polkinghorne, ed, *The Trinity and an Entangled World: Relationality in Physical Science and Theology* (Grand Rapids, MI: William B. Eerdmans, 2010). This volume, in which Polkinghorne is a contributor and editor, contains a variety of articles by scientists and others on the theme of relationality in the universe.

83   David Bohm, "The Enfolding Unfolding Universe and Consciousness" (1980) in Lee Nichol, ed., *The Essential David Bohm* (London, ENG: Routledge, 2003), 82-83, hereinafter EDB.

84   Argyris Nicolaidis, "Relational Nature" in *The Trinity and an Entangled world: Relationality in Physical Science and Theology*, in John Polkinghorne, ed, *The Trinity and an Entangled World* (Grand Rapids, MI: William B. Eerdmans), at 106.

85   Creativity is the feature of reality that A. N. Whitehead holds as the fundamental principle of his metaphysic. Alfred North Whitehead, *Process and Reality* (New York, NY: Free Press, 1929), 25. 'Creativity' is the universal of universals, characterizing ultimate matter of fact. It is that ultimate principle by which the many, which are the universe disjunctively, become the one actual occasion." Id.

86   *TEP*, Vol. 1, 364.

87   Id.

88   For an extended treatment of the role of transformation insight in personal growth, science, and religion, see James E. Loder, *The Transforming Moment* 2nd ed. (Colorado Springs, CO: Helmers & Howard, 1989).

89   *TEP*, at 357. See Charles Darwin, *Descent of Man* Ed, Mortimer J. Adler (New York, NY: Encyclopedia Britannica, Inc., 1952). In *Descent of Man*, Darwin noted how society interferes with the survival of the fittest, observations that were extended into political theory by the Social Darwinist movement. Peirce was appalled at the development of Social Darwinism, and his Evolutionary Love was an extended argument against Social Darwinism and the kind of logic that made it possible.

90   John D. Zizioulas, *Communion and Otherness* Paul Martin, ed. (New York, NY: T&T Clark, 2006), 54-55.

91   Josiah Royce, *Loyalty* (Long Island, NY: Sophia/Omni Press, 1908 [2017]), hereinafter "PL".

92   The convergence of Peirce and Royce and their respective "Absolute Idealism" and "Absolute Pragmatism" foreshadows the attempts by Whitehead, Bohm, and others to move beyond mind–body dualism. They wrote before modern relativity theory and quantum theory were well-known, the implications of which undermine such a distinction, as we shall see in the discussion of Bohm below. In all probability, if they were still alive, both would embrace some form of "dual-aspect monism."

93   *PL*, 127.

94   *The Super Implicate Order*, EDB 157."

95   Archibald Wheeler, "Information, Physics, Quantum: The Search for Links" in *Proc. 3rd Int. Symp. Foundations of Quantum Mechanics* (Tokyo, Japan: 1989), pp.354-368. "It from bit symbolizes the idea that every item of the physical world has at bottom—at a very deep bottom, in most instances—an immaterial source and explanation; that what we call reality arises in the last analysis from the posing of yes-no questions and the registering of equipment-evoked responses; in short, that all things physical are information-theoretic in origin and this is a participatory universe."

96   John Polkinghorne, *Quantum Physics and Theology: An Unexpected Kinship* (New Haven, CT: Yale University press, 2007), 8.

97   Josiah Royce, *Metaphysics* Richard Hocking & Frank Oppenheim eds (New York, NY: State University of New York Press,1998), 34

98   Id, 45.

99   PL, 86

100   Id, 46.

101   Id, 44.

102   Sophocles, *Antigone*, line 1350.

103   PL, at 85.

104   While I appreciate Royce's argument in *Loyalty*, I am personally persuaded that self-giving love (agape) and not loyalty is the fount of virtue. Love by its nature cannot tolerate injustice, unfairness, or violence against the other, and always whishes the best for the other. It seems to me that it is a much better ontological foundation for ethical reflection than loyalty.

105   Mario Puzo, *The Godfather* (New York, NY: Penguin, 1969).

106   PL, at 46.

107   Id, 18.

108   Id, 69.

109   Id, 143.

110   Id.

111   Id, 142.

112   Id, 23.

113   Josiah Royce, Josiah Royce, *The Problem of Christianity* (Washington, D.C.: Catholic University Press, 2001),109.

114   Id, 108.

115   Id.

116   The notion of moral inversion or moral reductionism will be discussed in detail below as a portion of the discussion of the thought of Michael Polanyi.

117   See, Revelation 21:1-4

118   PC ,112-113. In several passages, Royce speaks of the spiritual burden inherent in modern society which creates an intolerable stress on the conscience of the individual which burden grows; and the moral individual cannot bear it, unless his whole type of self-consciousness is transformed by a new spiritual power. Id, 113.

119   Peirce is a problematic thinker to locate on the political spectrum. Nevertheless, for an interesting take on his likely political thinking

(and a most revealing and important review of his thinking about education for political leadership), see Yael Levin Hungerford, *Charles S. Peirce's Conservative Progressivism*, Boston College Electronic Thesis or Dissertation, 2016http://hdl.handle.net/2345/bc-ir:107167 (downloaded May 19, 2022).

120 William James, "Letter to Mrs. Henry (Elizabeth) Whitman, June 7, 1899." *The Letters of William James,* ed. Henry James, vol. 2, p. 90 (1926).

121 William James, "Damn Great Empires! William James and the Politics of Pragmatism" reviewed in
Contemporary Political Theory (2018) 17, S6–S8. https://doi.org/10.1057/s41296-017- 0103-5; published online 7 March 2017 (downloaded April 21, 2022)

122 John Dewey, *Reconstruction of Philosophy* (New York, NY: Henry Holt & Company 1920), 187 https://www.gutenberg.org/files/40089/40089-h/40089-h.htm#CHAPTER_VIII (downloaded April 29, 2022), hereinafter referred to as "Reconstruction."

123 Id, at 188. The term "correlative" means "related," "reciprocal" or "corresponding" and is used to indicate that there is a relationship between individuals and community such that one cannot be found without the presence of the other.

124 Id, 200.

125 See, John Dewey, *Individualism Old and New* (New York, NY: Capricorn Books, 1930. This is one of Dewey's more popular books and sets out his political and social prejudices and beliefs more clearly than others.

126 PL, 32.

127 PC, 243.

128 This aspect of Royce's thought puts him at odds with certain other pragmatists, including his student, George Herbert Mead, who wrote of a perfected human community, "The human social ideal—the ideal or ultimate goal of human social progress—is the attainment of a universal human society in which all human individuals would possess a perfected social intelligence, such that all social meanings would each be similarly reflected in their respective social

consciousness…." George Herbert Mead, *On Social Psychology* rev. ed. (Chicago, Ill: University of Chicago Press, 1964), at 270-271.

129 Alfred North Whitehead, *Science and the Modern World* (New York, NY: Free Press, 1925, 1967), from now on "SMM."

130 Alfred North Whitehead, *Process and Reality* (New York, NY: Free Press, 1929, 1957), at 90. Hereinafter, "PR."

131 A. N. Whitehead, *Adventure of Ideas* (New York, NY: Free Press, 1933), hereinafter "AI".

132 A. N. Whitehead, *Modes of Thought* (New York, NY: Free Press, 1938, 1968).

133 SMM, 129-132.

134 Whitehead uses the terms "actual occasions" and "actual entities" almost interchangeably. For this reason, I think it might be best to consider a more general term.

135 PR, 90.

136 Steven Shaviro, "Deleuze's Encounter with Whitehead" http://www.shaviro.com/Othertexts/DeleuzeWhitehead.pdf (Downloaded July 18, 2022).

137 PR, 96-98.

138 SMM, 132-133.

139 PR, 40.

140 SMM, 118.

141 This is not the place for a discussion of these phenomena. For those who would like a deeper discussion, see John Polkinghorne, ed, *The Trinity and an Entangled World: Relationality in Physical Science and Theology* (Grand Rapids, MI: William B. Eerdmans, 2010). I have examined this phenomenon before in a blog entitled "Politics and the Order of the World" at www.gchristopherscruggs.com (July 8, 2020).

142 SM, 152.

143 AI, 230.

144 Id, 46.

145 Id, 41.

146 It should be obvious that the words "know," sense," or "feel" are used metaphorically. Subatomic particles do not have central nervous

systems or brains and are not capable of knowing, sensing, or feeling in human terms. Nevertheless, there exists something at the subatomic level that is best described by reference to the human experience.

147 AI, 230-233.

148 SMM, 69.

149 John Polkinghorne, *The Way the World Is: The Christian Perspective of a Scientist* (Louisville, KY: Westminster/John Knox Press, 1983), 22.

150 Thomas Torrance, *Transformation & Convergence in the Frame of Knowledge* (Grand Rapids, MI: William B. Eerdmans, 1984), 265.

151 This is a vast subject and there is much literature in the area. For a theological introduction, see John B. Cobb, Jr., *Process Theology as Political Theology* (Philadelphia, PA: Westminster Press, 1982), 111-134.

152 PR,128.

153 Whitehead makes a substantial contribution towards the development of "dual aspect monism," characteristic of more recent thought.

154 It is beyond the scope of this discussion, but the fundamental relatedness and meaningfulness of all reality has ecological as well as political implications.

155 PR 27, 90.

156 SMM, 132-133.

157 PR, 26

158 Id, 105

159 Susan Shottliff Mattingly, *Whitehead's Theory of Eternal Objects*, PhD dissertation, University of Texas at Austin. I am indebted to Mattingly for portions of this analysis.

160 It is beyond the scope of this analysis to exhaustively look at Whitehead's notion of God. He did view God as an essential element of his metaphysical system as the ground of the order and creative potential of the universe.

161 Alfred North Whitehead, *Religion in the Making* (New York, NY: The McMillian Company, 1936), 88.

162 In Whitehead's system all actual occasions have both a physical and a mental pole. Thus, intelligibility and the potential for the emergence of mind goes all the way down into the smallest actual entities in the universe.

163 AI, 166.

164 Id, 160.

165 Id, 161. It is beyond the scope of this discussion, but Whitehead believes that it is not the existence of dogmatics and religious theories that are the problem with religion, but the attitude of finality with which these opinions are voiced. In this, Whitehead echoes Peirce. The theories of theologians are evidence of the importance of reason to Christian faith, and reasonableness is one of the ways in which brute force is overcome.

166 Id, at 167. Plato had taught that the divine agency was persuasive, relying on reason not coercion to accomplish his goal.

167 Id, 17.

168 Id, 25.

169 Id, 83.

170 Id, 69.

171 Id, 70-84. This is a most interesting discussion in which Whitehead deals with Malthusian economics, and its limitations.

172 Id, 43.

173 Id, 44.

174 Id, 45.

175 Id, 45-7

176 Id, 51.

177 Id, 85-86.

178 Id, 261. In his chapter on beauty in AI, Whitehead speaks of harmony as the objective of the search for beauty. He also describes the way in which disharmony (destruction) and harmony are related. Disharmony requires the searcher for harmony to seek a higher and greater harmony, a new harmony. In the same way, each perception of harmony leads to a perception of its inadequacy, which leads to a greater harmony. This is the aesthetic ground of the progress of justice in society.

179 Id, 272

180 George Herbert Mead, *On Social Psychology* rev. ed. (Chicago, IL: University of Chicago Press, 1964).

181 Id, 251, footnote 2.

182 Id, 255.

183 Id, 262-262.

184 The failure of the League of Nations and the various corruptions of the United Nations and other international agencies reflect a continuing inability to find workable forms for institutionalizing this universalizing impulse, or perhaps it reflects the fact that no such "universal human institutions" of a governmental type are feasible at this time in history.

185 In the end, Socrates defends the view that justice is found in a well-ordered society. In such a society, there is social peace because people of different groups receive what they are due. Only in such a society can the traditional view of justice and a social view of justice be combined so that all people receive their due. A just society is, by analogy to the human person, a society in which the interests of each class can exist in harmony. Plato, *Republic*, tr. G. M.A. Grube rev. C.D.C Reeve (Indianapolis, IN: Hackett Publishing Company, 1992), at 581c.

186 "On the Social Contract" in *Jean-Jacque Rousseau: The Basic Writings* 2nd ed. Trans and Edited by Donald A. Cross (Indianapolis, IN: Hackett Press, 164.

187 Id.

188 Id.

189 Id.

190 Id, emphasis original.

191 Id, 201.

192 Id, 234-235.

193 Id, 21.

194 Id, 31.

195 *On Social Psychology*, at 256-257.

196 Id, 259.

197 Id, 259.

198 Id, 264-265.

199 Id, 265.

200 Id, 270-271.

201 At this point, the weakness of Mead's argument becomes evident. After 300 years of Enlightenment thinking, no evidence exists that such a situation can be peacefully obtained. The fact is that people have widely divergent notions of what is involved in social progress and what any "ideal universal society" should look like. Many of these notions are not only divergent but diametrically opposed. Abortion, transgender issues, the degree of economic freedom individuals should possess, and the degree of censorship the government should be able to employ: all these and more have vastly divergent proponents.

202 This is not to deny the enormous progress Western society has made in the past centuries in providing economic, political, and social access to minorities, women, and other socially disadvantaged groups. In fact, it is the progress made that provides hope that the current attempts to restrict speech will eventually diminish as an aberration in Western thought and action

203 *On Social Psychology*, 271.

204 Id, 282.

205 Id, 272.

206 Id, 272-273.

207 Id.

208 Id, 275-276.

209 Id, 328-341.

210 Scott London, "Organic Democracy: Political Philosophy of John Dewey" https://scott.london/reports/dewey.html (downloaded April 29, 2022).

211 See, John Dewey, *Individualism Old and New* (New York, NY: Capricorn Books, 1930. This is one of Dewey's more popular books and more clearly than others sets out his political and social prejudices and beliefs.

212 John Dewey, *Reconstruction of Philosophy* (New York, NY: Henry Holt & Company 1920), 187 https://www.gutenberg.org/

files/40089/40089-h/40089-h.htm#CHAPTER_VIII (downloaded April 29, 2022), hereinafter referred to as "Reconstruction."

213 Id, 188. The term "correlative" means "related," "reciprocal" or "corresponding" and is used to indicate that there is a relationship between individuals and community such that one cannot be found without the presence of the other.

214 Id, 200.

215 Stanford Encyclopedia of Philosophy, "Dewey's Political Philosophy" Wed Feb 9, 2005; substantive revision Thu Jul 26, 2018 at https://plato.stanford.edu/entries/dewey-political/ (downloaded April 29, 2022).

216 *Reconstruction*, at 202-203.

217 Id, 207.

218 Id.

219 John Dewey, *Democracy and Education*, transcribed by David Reed and David Widger (The Project Gutenberg EBook of Democracy and Education, by John Dewey https://www.gutenberg. org/files/852/852-h/852-h.htm (downloaded April 29, 2022), hereinafter, *Democracy and Education*.

220 Id.

221 Id.

222 Id.

223 John Dewey, *Logic: The Theory of Inquiry* (New York, NY: Henry Holt and Company, 1938), 42, hereinafter "TTI."

224 Id, 43.

225 Id, 44-45.

226 Id, 45.

227 Id, 50.

228 Id. Dewey would not necessarily agree with my insertion of the importance of spiritual and transcendental factors into the action of human decision-making. He is a determined materialist. The limitations of what he is saying here is precisely that rather than seeing the human person as a radical unity of all levels physical, mental, emotional, and spiritual, he ultimately reduces everything to the material level. With this, I disagree. The reductionist fallacy is one clue to the limits to the thought forms of the modern world.

229 John Dewey used this term to describe his version of pragmatism. In this sense, logic is an instrument for evaluating ideas and policy alternatives. This is to be distinguished from instrumentalism, which refers solely to the means and use of power.

230 TTI, 23-60.

231 Id, 14.

232 See *Stanford Encyclopedia of Philosophy*, "Quantum Logic and Probability Theory" (February 4, 2002, revised August 2021) at https://plato.stanford.edu/entries/qt-quantlog/ (downloaded May 17, 2024).

233 John C. Polkinghorne, *Science and Creation: The Search for Understanding* (Philadelphia, PA: Templeton Foundation Press, 2006), 30.

234 TTI, at 61.

235 Michael Polanyi, *The Tacit Dimension* (Gloucester, MA: Peter Smith, 1983).

236 TTI, at 64.

237 Id.

238 C. S. Lewis, *The Abolition of Man* (New York, Collier Books, a division of Macmillan, 1955): 28. For a Christian interpretation of the Chinese Tao, see G. Christopher Scruggs, *Centered Living/ Centered Leading: The Way of Light and Love* rev. ed. (Shiloh Publishing, 2016),

239 See Lit Charts, "The Abolition of Man by C. S. Lewis" athttps://www. litcharts.com/lit/the-abolition-of-man/terms/the-tao (downloaded May 7, 2024).

240 *Abolition of Man*, 28.

241 Litcharts, footnote 30 above.

242 TTI, at 498.

243 Id, 10.

244 Id, 497. A generalization in the form of a hypothesis is a prerequisite condition of selection and ordering of material as facts. Id, at 498.

245 Id. "The notion that evaluation is concerned only with ends and that, with the ruling out of moral ends, evaluative judgments are ruled out rests, then, upon a profound misconception of the nature

of the logical conditions and constituents of all scientific inquiry. All competent and authentic inquiry demands that out of the complex welter of existential and potentially observable and recordable material, certain material be selected and weighed as data or the 'facts of the case.'"

246   Id, at 506.

247   Bertrand Russell, *History of Western Philosophy* (New York, NY: Simon and Schuster, 1945), 827.

248   TTI, 161.

249   *Michael Polanyi and Tacit Knowledge* at https://infed.org/mobi/michael-polanyi-and-tacit-knowledge/ (downloaded May 27, 2020). For those wanting the best introduction to his thinking, see Drucilla Scott, *Everyman Revisited: The Common Sense of Michael Polanyi* (Sussex, ENG: The Book Guild Limited, 1985). His major work is *Personal Knowledge: Towards a Post-Critical Philosophy* (Chicago, IL: University of Chicago Press, 1958), hereinafter "PK".

250   Michael Polanyi, *Science Faith and Society: A Searching Examination of the Meaning and Nature of Scientific Inquiry* (Chicago, IL: University of Chicago Press, 1946), hereinafter "SFS".

251   PK, 237-239. One sees an emerging danger of this in today's West.

252   Id. It is impossible to overestimate the moral and intellectual damage Marxism does to a society. I traveled to Russia in 1995 and saw personally the moral, political and economic devastation that seventy years of socialism wreaked on Russian society. One reason for the current regime is the moral and political consequences of this period and the lack of the moral, spiritual, intellectual, and political foundations for democracy.

253   See Karl Popper, *The Open Society and its Enemies*, at 62.

254   PK, 15-17.

255   SFS, 17, PK, 203-204.

256   Thus, Polanyi subscribes to the Platonic and Aristotelian notion that the real is that which has power. Goodness, truth, beauty, and other immaterial values have an unseen reality in that they fruitfully guide action and continue to reveal themselves to those who seek them.

257   PK, 53-54

258 Id, 53ff.

259 See, Michael Polanyi, *The Logic of Liberty* (Indianapolis Indiana, Liberty Fund, 1998). In this book, Polanyi outlined his views on the requirements and characteristics of a free social order.

260 SFS, 71.

261 Id, 17, 71-73.

262 PK, 212.

263 PK, vii.

264 SFS, 17.

265 Id, 81.

266 PK, 227-233. This is not the place to outline the long line of moral reductionism that ends in a Marxist denial of morality. Nor is it the place to discuss the movement of the Enlightenment towards nihilism, first fully exposed by Nietzsche and his concept of the Will to Power. It suffices for present purposes to observe that modern Western society, lacking a transcendent faith in the reality of moral values, has entered a period of moral nihilism that can impact even those who deny that they accept it. The power orientation of our culture is a part of its plausibility structure. Lesslie Newbigin, *Truth to Tell: The Gospel as Public Truth* (Grand Rapids, MI: William B. Eerdmans, 1991)

267 Michael Polanyi, *The Logic of Liberty* (Indianapolis Indiana, Liberty Fund, 1998), 131.

268 PK, 230-233.

269 *Everyman Revisited*, 99.

270 While Polanyi was primarily interested in Western society, it may be observed that the phenomenon of moral inversion can be present in other cultures as well. For example, Mao encouraged the criticism of Confucianism because it had formed the basis of the historic order of China.

271 The Christian author C. S. Lewis speaks of this tendency for contemporary people to discount the vast interlocking web of morality, which he sometimes calls the Tao, to exalt one moral principle to the detriment of ethical thinking. This has led to a preference for public morality and, on the right, a preference for

private morality. See David Rozema, "Lewis's Rejection of Nihilism: The *Tao* and the Problem of Moral Knowledge" in *Pursuit of Truth | A Journal of Christian Scholarship* http://www.cslewis.org/journal/lewiss-rejection-of-nihilism-the-tao-and-the-problem-of-moral-knowledge/ (September 28, 2007, downloaded June 4, 2020).

272 I do not by this want to be seen as not believing that moral protest against racism is wrong. It is not. I also do not minimize the activities of political opportunists and terror groups that may have contributed to the problems we are currently experiencing. These groups use the moral inversion of others for purely selfish purposes.

273 Quotations are taken from *Edmund Burke: Selected Writings and Speeches*, Peter J. Stanis, ed. (Washington, DC: Regency Publications, 1963).

274 Id, at 522.

275 This might serve as a warning to our leaders. There is no doubt that the spending habits of the US government have resulted in an enormous debt burden that constitutes a failure of the government to keep faith with its people.

276 *Selected Writings and Speeches,* 527. I have added the date in parentheses for readers unfamiliar with Burke.

277 David Pratt, "David Bohm and the Implicate Order" at https://www.theosophy-nw.org/theosnw/science/prat-boh.htm (downloaded April 12, 2023).

278 Id.

279 David Bohm and F. David Peat, *Science, Order & Creativity* (New York, NY: Bantam Books, 1987), 88.

280 David Bohm, "The Enfolding Unfolding Universe and Consciousness" (1980) in Lee Nichol, ed, *The Essential David Bohm* (London, ENG: Routledge, 2003), 82-83.

281 Id, 81.

282 There are significant points of connection between the work of Bohm and the process views of Whitehead. Bohm, like others, distinguishes his work from that of Whitehead but uses some of Whitehead's ideas.

283 Id, 82-83.

284 Id, 172.

285 See, David Peat, "David Bohm and the Implicate Order," cited above. This section draws extensively on Peat's analysis.

286 David Bohm, *Wholeness and the Implicate Order* (London ENG: Routledge, 1980), at 48, hereinafter WIO.

287 "Soma-Significance and the Activity of Meaning" (1980) in *The Essential David Bohm*, 160.

288 Id, 161.

289 WIO, at 11.

290 *EDB* 164. In this sense, Bohm's theories are a form of "dual aspect monism."

291 Id, 163.

292 WIO, 1-2.

293 "Soma-Significance and the Activity of Meaning" (1980) in *The Essential David Bohm*, 165.

294 Id, 165.

295 Id.

296 Id, 166.

297 WIO, at 15.

298 Id, 16.

299 Id.

300 In this, Bohm's thinking is similar to that of Habermas, with his ideas of the role of social discourse in moral and political life. Much like Bohm's idea of "dialogue," Habermas calls social speech explicitly oriented towards reaching rationally motivated consensus discourse.

301 David Bohm, *On Dialogue* (New York, NY: Routledge, 1996, 2004), 7. *On Dialogue* was published posthumously and is based on his writings and speeches.

302 Id, 4-5.

303 Id.

304 Id.

305 WIO, at 151.

306 Id, 157.

307 Jeroen van Dongen, "On the Role of the Michelson–Morely Experiment: Einstein in Chicago" athttps://arxiv.org/pdf/0908.1545.

pdf (downloaded December 5, 2022). Einstein was unclear about the exact role of the experiment in his formulation of relativity theory, though it is fairly certain he knew something of it.

308 C. S. Peirce, "The Rules of Philosophy" in *American Pragmatists*, at 81.

309 C.S. Peirce, "Questions Concerning Certain Faculties Claimed for Man," *Journal of Speculative Philosophy*,1868, as reprinted in *Essential Writings*, 87.

310 Id, 118.

311 PR, 242-243. Whitehead refers to this as the transition from existent (actual occasion) to existent (actual occasion) which takes place in the process of concrescence, i.e. the process by which a new actual occasion emerges from the prior state of process. Id.

312 AI, 194.

313 For the way in which scientific paradigms emerge and are superseded, see Thomas S. Kuhn, *The Structure of Scientific Revolutions* 2nd enlarged ed. (Chicago, IL: University of Chicago Press, 1963, 1970).

314 Declaration of Independence (US 1776).

315 United States Constitution (US 1789).

316 Peirce put it this way, "[T]he catholic (universal) consent that constitutes the truth is by no means limited to men in this earthly life or to the entire human race, but extends to the whole communion of minds to which we belong, including some whose senses are very different than ours...." *The Essential Writings*, 60. See also, G. Christopher Scruggs, *Path of Life: The Way of Wisdom for Christ-Followers* (Eugene, OR: Wipf & Stock, 2014), 69.

317 Peirce, Charles S., *Collected Papers of Charles Sanders Peirce* Vols. 1 and 2. Charles Hartshorne and Paul Weiss eds. (Cambridge, MA: Harvard University Press, 1965), at 6.610. (Private letter to Paul Carus) I am indebted for this quote to Librizzi, Jacob, *The Haunted Animal: Peirce's Community of Inquiry and the Formation of the Self* (2017). Dissertation, USM, Maine. 317. https://digitalcommons.usm.maine.edu/etd

318 See Jacob Librizzi, above, at 51.

319 See St. Augustine, "On Christian Doctrine" in *A Select Library of Nicene and Post-Nicene Fathers of the Christian Church*. Edited by

Philip Schaff and Henry Wace. 28 First Series, Volume 2. 1886–1889. (Peabody MA: Hendrickson Publishers), 528-534.

320 *PL* , 27.

321 Peirce discusses what he calls "the Gospel of Greed in Evolutionary Love," which was first published in *The Monist* and introduces his theory of agapism, the cosmic principle of love. This love is cherishing because it recognizes that which is lovely in another being and sympathetically supports its existence. Peirce contrasts his "agapism" with evolutionary theories based on a selfish form of love, which resulted in social Darwinism and "the Gospel of Greed." Agapism includes helping one's neighbors and is consistent with Christian social ethics. See "Evolutionary Love" at https://scrcexhibits.omeka.net/exhibits/show/charles-s-peirce-open-court/-evolutionary-love-(Downloaded August 3, 2020).

322 *PL*, 23.

323 PC, 107.

324 Id, 108.

325 Id, 123.

326 SFS, at 47ff. The subject of self-governance is very broad. A host of policing measures exist in any discipline. The competition for academic posts is normally intense; and, in every institution, faculty look for the best possible candidate for openings. Academic societies are prevalent, and entrance at the highest level is not automatic. Journals have boards to advise them on which articles should be published. Of course, all of these safeguards are subject to failure and even corruption, which is why some disciplines can go into long periods of decline.

327 Of course, the fact that many minds have examined a problem before singular acts of insight indicates the importance of the community to the success of even the most seemingly singular genius.

328 OD, 7. This analysis is not intended to eliminate the importance of debate in developing human knowledge and making decisions. Debate and dialogue both have their place in politics and law. My point is only that conversation and debate are not the sole or necessarily best method.

329 David Bohm, "Meaning and Information" in *The Search for Meaning: The New Spirit in Science and Philosophy* (London, ENG: Crucible Press, 1989) found at www.implicity.org/Downloads/Bohm_meaning+information.pdf (downloaded April 14, 2023), 17.

330 This is an important difference between what is being said here and what some proponents of dialogue urge. For example, David Bohm believes that a dialogue requires that we suspend our own opinions and beliefs. When Bohm urges suspension of beliefs, he means creating a situation where we neither believe nor disbelieve. It is doubtful that this is even possible or desirable as to our most deeply held beliefs, or those of others.

331 *Questions Concerning Certain Faculties*, ECSP, 88.

332 Charles Sanders. Unpublished manuscripts. Copies from Peirce Edition Project of Indiana University—Purdue University, Indianapolis. MS 298:6 found at Oliver Labs, "Dialogue in Peirce, Lotman, and Bakhtin: A Comparative Study." https://www.researchgate.net/publication/312509433_Dialogue_in_Peirce_Lotman_and_Bakhtin_A_comparative_study (downloaded December 8, 2022).

333 "Fixation of Belief" in *The American Pragmatists*, at 87.

334 Id, at 88.

335 Peirce, as a scientist, does not believe that this state of ease necessarily results in action, though it might. *Illustrations from the Logic of Science,* ECSP, at 126.

336 Id, 126.

337 PC, at 333.

338 Id, 242-245.

339 Id, 248,

340 Id.

341 Id, 333.

342 OD, at 8-9.

343 Id, 10-11.

344 Id, 16-17.

345 Id, 22.

'46 The classic statement of the philosophy of the immoralist is found in Plato's *Republic* in the debate between Socrates and Thrasmachus where Thrasmachus makes the point that justice is nothing but the advantage of the stronger. *Republic*, Book 1, at 343c.

347 SFS, 18.

348 This is not to say that premodern societies where without their flaws or that the Enlightenment was somehow mistaken and societies need to regress to a premodern state. Such a view would be contrary to the process and evolutionary focus of this study. Nevertheless, the focus on power that modernity embraced and the increasing nihilism of elites is a danger in the future of human freedom and development into societies where all human beings can flourish.

349 SFS, 17.

350 Henry F. Sapp, "Whitehead, James, and the Ontology of Quantum Theory" 5(1) *Mind and Matter* (2007) downloaded at https://www-physics.lbl.gov/~stapp/WJQO.pdf (June 16, 2020), 85. In this quote, Sapp is not speaking of the exact phenomena that I am concerned with here—the tendency to view all reality as a machine—but his quote is equally applicable to what I am saying in this essay. Sapp is concerned with the assumption of materialistic theory that our experience of human freedom and the efficacy of human thought is an illusion.

351 *PR*, 27.

352 SFS, 10.

353 See, *Wholeness and Implicate* Order, 63. Although Bohm is not talking about politics, he notes that the embodiment of any particular notion of totality is part of a process of the movement of thought, with an ever-changing foreman content. In other words, as applied to justice, our ideas of justice are a constantly evolving movement of human thought and action characteristic of a society. The mistake made by ideologist left and right is to believe that a particular form or notion accepted at any point in time is final. As has been mentioned before, there is no final achievement of justice inside of human history. Id

354 SFS, at 56.

355 Id.

356 It is the fundamental insight of quantum physics that it is impossible to disengage the observer from the examined event, as was the model of investigation dominant in the modern world under the influence

of the Newtonian view of science. This insight, first discovered at the subatomic level of physical reality, has implications in other areas and is a part of the emerging postmodern view of science. Peirce foresaw this insight in his relational theory of signs when he spoke of the relationship between reality (an object under observation), an interpreter (observer), and the sign used to understand the reality observed. "Questions Concerning Certain Faculties" in *The Essential Charles S. Peirce*, 1972.

357   *Fixation of Belief,* TEP Vol 1, at 121-122.

358   Peirce uses the term "habit" to refer to a rule of action or mode of action that can be repeatedly embraced to lead to successful behavior. *How to Make Our Ideas Clear,* TEP Vol. 1, at 129.

359   Id. at 132. See also, "Issues of Pragmatism" in *The American Pragmatists*, at 119.

360   *How to Make Our Ideas Clear,* TEP Vol. 1, at 129. Thus, Peirce considers any idea as a moment in the symphony of our intellectual life in which doubt has been put to rest but also a starting place for new thought. Id.

361   *Evolutionary Love,* TEP, Vol. 1, 352-353; "Guess at the Riddle" in *Essential Writings*, 249-250.

362   See, G. Christopher Scruggs, *Centered Living/Centered Leading: The Tao Te Ching Adapted for Christ-Followers* Rev. Ed. (Permisio Por Favor/BookSurge, 2016).

363   John Polkinghorne, *One World: The Interaction of Science and Theology* (Philadelphia, PA: Templeton Foundation, 2007), 102 and *Exploring Reality: The Intertwining of Science and Religion* (London, ENG: SPCK, 2005).

364   Roman Krznaric, "The Ancient Greeks' Six Words for Love (And Why Knowing Them Can Change Your Life)" in *Solutions Journalism* (December 28, 2013), at www.yesmagazine.org/health-happiness/2013/12/28/the-ancient-greeks-6-words-for-love-and-why-knowing-them-can-change-your-life/ (downloaded June 19, 2020).

365   Id.

66   *Centered Living/Centered Leading: The Tao Te Ching Adapted for Christ-Followers*), 136.

367   Reinhold Niebuhr, *The Nature and Destiny of Man* Vol. 2 (Louisville, KY: Westminster John Knox Press, 1986), at 246.

368   Id.

369   Id.

370   Id, 248.

371   Id, 249.

372   See Jaime E. Settle, Christopher T. Dawes, James H. Fowler, "The Heritability of Partisan Attachment" 62 Political Research Quarterly 601 (September 2009) at https://web.archive.org/web/20100616133630/http://jhfowler.ucsd.edu/heritability_of_partisan_attachment.pdf (downloaded April 10, 2023).